Ascension Activation Meditations of the Spiritual Hierarchy: A Compilation

Ascension Activation Meditations of the Spiritual Hierarchy: A Compilation

Dr. Joshua David Stone
Janna Shelley Parker

Writers Club Press
San Jose New York Lincoln Shanghai

Ascension Activation Meditations of the Spiritual Hierarchy:
A Compilation

All Rights Reserved © 2001 by Dr. Joshua David Stone

No part of this book may be reproduced or transmitted in any form or by any means, graphic, electronic, or mechanical, including photocopying, recording, taping, or by any information storage retrieval system, without the permission in writing from the publisher.

Writers Club Press
an imprint of iUniverse.com, Inc.

For information address:
iUniverse.com, Inc.
5220 S 16th, Ste. 200
Lincoln, NE 68512
www.iuniverse.com

ISBN: 0-595-17760-3

Printed in the United States of America

Dedication

This book is dedicated to all the Masters, male and female, of the Cosmic and Planetary Hierarchy. This includes all the Archangels and Angels, the Elohim and elemental line of evolution, and all the Christed Extraterrestrials such as the Ashtar Command and the beloved Arcturians, to name a few. This book has been a co-creative effort, and it is my great honor at this time to give these wonderful Masters their appropriate acknowledgement and recognition. Co-creation between the lightworkers of Earth and these wonderful and glorious beings is one of the key principles and touchstones to the unfolding of the New Millennium and the Seventh Golden Age.

Dr. Joshua David Stone

Contents

Introduction ix
1 Developing A Full Spectrum Relationship with GOD 1
2 Isis & The Great Pyramid & Sphinx Ascension
   Activation Meditation 8
3 Cosmic Ascension Activations in the Temple of GOD 14
4 GOD and the Mahatma Ascension Activation Meditation 20
5 GOD and Metatron's Cosmic
   Tree of Life Ascension Activation Meditation 30
6 GOD and the Elohim
   Ascension Activation Meditation 39
7 GOD and the Divine Father Ascension Activation Meditation ..52
8 The Earth Mother, Pan, Archangel Sandalphon and
   the Material Face of GOD Ascension Activation Meditation 64
9 Sacred Flames Ascension Activation Meditation 76
10 GOD and the Archangels Ascension Activation Meditation 88
11 GOD, Christ, and the Holy Spirit Ascension
   Activation Meditation 100
12 GOD and the Godforce Golden Chamber of
   Melchizedek Ascension Activation Meditation 112
13 GOD and the Actual Wesak Ceremony Meditation 120

14 GOD and the Construction of your Light Body, Love Body and Power Body Ascension Activation Meditation 128
15 Mt. Shasta 50 Point Cosmic Cleansing Meditation 155
16 Ultimate Cosmic Ray Ascension Activation Meditation 160
17 GOD Ascension Seat Meditation 165
18 Divine Mother & Lady Masters Ascension Activation Meditation 169
19 Ascension Activation Meditation and Treatment 176
20 Specialized Ascension Activation from the Spiritual Hierarchy ..185
21 Cosmic Ascension Activations from the Planetary and Cosmic Hierarchy 189
22 Planetary World Service Meditations 197
23 The Cosmic and Planetary Hierarchy Protection Meditation 225
24 The Lord of Arcturus and Arcturian Ascension Activation Meditation 233
25 GOD and the Cosmic and Planetary Hierarchy "Higher Light Body" Ascension Activation Meditation 235
26 Revelation of GOD Ascension Activation Meditation 240
27 My Spiritual Mission and Purpose by Dr. Joshua David Stone 254
About the Author 271

Introduction

My Beloved Readers, this book is a most wonderful compilation of my best meditations from all my books. It is designed so you can have these meditations all in one book instead of spread out over 40 volumes. I have also added 12 new meditations, plus a chapter on developing a full spectrum relationship to God! It is my great joy and pleasure to bring you this, the 26th volume of my Ascension Book Series and Easy to Read Encyclopedia of the Spiritual Path! This book is guaranteed to accelerate your Ascension and Initiation Process a thousandfold. I also offer 15 of these Ascension Activation Meditations in audiotape form, which are all available from the Academy for those who are interested! I personally like to call working with the inner plane Ascended Masters "The Rocketship to God"! You will get a direct experience of this in reading and working with this book! On this note, I officially introduce my book *Ascension Activation Meditations of the Spiritual Hierarchy*!

1

Developing A Full Spectrum Relationship with GOD

In beginning this chapter, I want to let you know that there is no subject more meaningful and exciting for me to write about. I have been looking forward to writing this chapter for two weeks. Developing a relationship to GOD is a multifaceted subject. We must begin by defining our terms here, for the experience of God to every person is quite different. Let me explain here, my beloved readers, what I mean by this.

One's first relationship to GOD is really their relationship to their own higher self. In different spiritual schools of thought the higher self can also be termed the soul, the oversoul, the higher mind, higher mental body, or superconscious mind. This is every person's inner teacher until they reach the fourth initiation. After the fourth initiation, the disciple or student has fully integrated the vibration and consciousness of the higher self and then is provided a new teacher by GOD, which is the Mighty I Am Presence, or Monad. The Mighty I Am Presence is the individualized presence of GOD within each person. Ascension is the full merging and embodiment of the Mighty I Am Presence, or Monad, on earth in all its glory.

Now, some people experience GOD by not focusing consciously on their higher self or Mighty I Am Presence, but rather on an inner or outer plane spiritual teacher. Examples are Jesus, Buddha, Mohammed, Moses, Krishna, Rama, Mother Mary, Quan Yin, Isis, or Sai Baba. The effects of this form of worship of GOD are similar, but with a slightly different unique vibration.

A slight variation of the above theme of GOD worship would be having a guru in either physical or non-physical form. In this capacity, there is the complete surrender to one embodiment of GOD. The true guru, however, such as Sai Baba, is always the first to point out that his devotees are embodiments of GOD as well. The true guru is always focused on empowering his students, not trying to retain power over them. This form of worship of GOD is 100% appropriate and legitimate, as long as negative ego aspects have not contaminated the guru. Students must be spiritually discerning if this is the form of worship that they resonate with.

The next form of developing a relationship with GOD has to do with understanding the Trinity of GOD. By this, of course, I mean GOD, Christ, and the Holy Spirit. Everyone is connected to the Holy Spirit, also sometimes termed the Holy Ghost or Shekinah. It is the very breath and voice of GOD throughout creation. The Holy Spirit is kind of like the higher self, except it is the cosmic version, not just the personal version, for each individual. The Holy Spirit speaks for the atonement or the at-one-ment. The Holy Spirit is the Voice of GOD throughout Creation, and is the answer to all problems and challenges.

There are only two voices in the infinite universe if you take everything back to its bare essence. There is the voice of spirit (Holy Spirit) and the voice of negative ego (glamour, maya, and illusion). Unfortunately, most people do not take advantage of the tremendous powers and wisdom of the Holy Spirit. This is true regardless of what religion or spiritual path one is connected to. The Holy Spirit's specialty is the "undoing" of the negative ego and its effects mentally, emotionally, physically, environmentally and socially.

The Christ principle is embodied by Jesus/Sananda, Lord Maitreya the Planetary Christ, Kuthumi who is preparing to take over this position and already has to a certain extent, and Sai Baba, who is the Cosmic Christ for this planet. The Christ principle, however, exists behind and through all Sons and Daughters of God. The Christ principle, or essence, lives on a planetary, solar, galactic, universal, multiuniversal and cosmic level. The path of ascension is learning to embody this Christ principle or essence at continually higher and/or more expansive levels. So, for example, we on Earth are striving to become fully realized planetary, solar, and beginning galactic Christs. Sananda, Lord Maitreya, and Kuthumi are "fully realized" galactic Christs. Sai Baba is striving to become a fully realized multiuniversal Christ. Melchizedek is now in the process of becoming a fully realized Cosmic Christ at the 352nd level of the Godhead.

Now, this brings us to developing a relationship to GOD or the Godhead. GOD, in the fullest sense of the term, is the "First Cause" and Ultimate Creator. We are all soul extensions or Sons and Daughters of this One, Infinite, Eternal, Loving, Limitless, Divine Being.

When a person calls to GOD they must realize that it is their own higher self, Mighty I Am Presence, Holy Spirit, Guardian Angel, Spirit Guide, spiritual teacher, and inner plane Ascended Masters who respond as intermediaries for GOD.

GOD, or the Godhead, is both an impersonal and personal being. GOD lives in everything, including physical matter, yet is also the consciousness that exists even beyond the 352nd level of Divinity. On Earth, we are focusing on, for the most part, initiations 1–12. GOD is beyond initiation 352. Even Jesus/Sananda, Kuthumi, Lord Maitreya, and all the planetary Ascended Masters who we work with are only two inches up a ten-inch ruler, in terms of their full and complete realization of GOD in the ultimate sense of the term. So when people in the New Age Movement or religion claim to have realized GOD, what they are really claiming is that they have realized their soul (Third Initiation) or planetary ascension (Initiations Six through Ten). This is something to be humbly proud of, but realistically, be aware that there are still 345 initiations to go to achieve what I am going to call here "Cosmic Ascension."

So, definitely pray to GOD and develop a personal relationship with GOD; however, fully understand that the full realization of GOD takes place in stages. First beginning on a planetary level, then a solar level, then a galactic level, then a universal level, then a multiuniversal level. For more information on cosmic ascension, I would encourage you to read my book entitled *Cosmic Ascension*. Before cosmic ascension can be begin, we must first complete our planetary ascension.

Now, other people on this planet may worship GOD through the Trinity and lens of Brahma, Vishnu, and Shiva. In English terms: the Creator, Preserver, and Destroyer. They also worship the physical embodiments of these Beings in the form of Rama, Krishna, Sai Baba, and others.

In Buddhism, it is very interesting that such a beautiful religion does not believe in GOD or the Godhead. They do believe in the Buddha and becoming "a Buddha," which is like a Christ. I asked the Masters about this lack of belief in GOD, and they told me that this was a misunderstanding of Buddhism, yet Buddhism holds great purity and truth in much of its teachings. So, Buddhism is GOD-infused, but the prime cause was left out.

Christianity sees Jesus as the "exclusive" Son of GOD. This is, of course, true, but the missing point here is that we are all exclusive Sons and Daughters of GOD, and this is, in truth, what the Master Jesus taught.

So, this brings us to another aspect of developing a relationship to GOD, which is that a great many people involved in traditional religion worship GOD in the form of their negative ego. They have not cleared their own negative ego from their mental emotional vehicles and subconscious mind, so their negative ego has created a false understanding of what GOD is. This can be seen in Old Testament Judaism, Fundamentalist Christianity, Buddhism, the Islamic faith, and even Hinduism. I speak here of the wrathful, punishing, fearful, guilt producing GOD; and the self-righteousness, wars, caste systems and various erroneous beliefs contaminating all religions and ministers of these faiths. This is not a judgment, just an insight into how some people develop a relationship to GOD. They are actually, to a certain extent, living under the tyranny of their own negative ego and calling this GOD.

Now other people, especially women, may experience GOD through the Divine Mother or Goddess energy. This may also be embodied in the form of Mother Mary, Quan Yin, and Isis. I am currently in the process of writing a book called *Empowerment and Integration Through the Goddess*, which is both for women and men alike, which speaks to this form of worship and relationship to divinity.

Other people worship and relate to GOD through a lens of one of the Seven Rays. By this I mean, some people worship and relate to GOD in themselves and the world in the form of power and politics, which is the First Ray. Others worship and relate to GOD in the form of an unconditional love and wisdom focus as a spiritual teacher, which is the Second Ray. Others still, do this on the Third Ray of active intelligence or GOD action on the physical plane, and may focus primarily in business acumen. Others worship and experience God on the Fourth Ray in the form of being a musician, artist, poet, dancer, and relate to GOD through this lens exclusively. Michelangelo comes to mind. Others still, worship GOD through the Fifth Ray lens of science or mathematics, and may see the world exclusively through a scientific paradigm. Often people do not think of being a scientist as a form of GOD worship; however, in truth, it is if approached from a spiritual rather than a negative ego perspective. Still others worship GOD and his embodiments in a more devotional sense, which is the Sixth Ray. Lastly, others worship and relate to GOD on the Seventh Ray through ceremonial order and magic. This would be a soul involved in many forms of spiritual rituals: the spiritual magician, alchemist, and metaphysician.

Lastly, we see others still developing a relationship with GOD through nature and the Earth Mother. Most people do not realize that there are four faces of GOD. These are the spiritual, mental, emotional and physical faces. Most New Age lightworkers gravitate to the celestial realms. One of the things the Mahatma is here to teach us is that GOD lives as much in the material universe as he does in the spiritual universe.

True realization of your ascension is not leaving this world or dematerializing, it is fully grounding your Oneness and merger with your Mighty I Am Presence, or Monad, on earth. Each person's true mission in developing a relationship to GOD is to not ascend, but to descend GOD to earth, and to find their true puzzle piece in the Divine Plan and manifest it fully "on the earth plane." The material universe is one of the seven heavens of GOD, and the Divine Plan is to make the physical universe be a perfect reflection and mirror of the spiritual universe. As His Holiness the Lord Sai Baba has said, "Hands that help are holier than lips that pray." It is time now for all lightworkers to honor, worship, and relate to the material face of GOD; and ground their ascension and their service work onto this plane. Also experience and enjoy GOD in the beauty and glory of nature.

Lastly, my beloved readers, to sum up this chapter on developing a relationship to GOD, it can be seen that there are many lenses, levels and stages to experiencing GOD. I have humbly endeavored to elucidate and clarify a few of these. As my dear friend Lord Melchizedek has so beautifully stated, "The experience of GOD is like a many faceted cosmic prism with many lenses to this prism." In this chapter, I have attempted to synthesize many of the lenses of this prism through which people on earth develop a relationship to GOD. By understanding these different lenses of GOD worship, we can expand our own relationship to GOD and be more compassionate and understanding to other people's form of GOD worship.

In conclusion, it is my suggestion, if this feels comfortable to each of you my beloved readers, to approach your relationship to GOD from the lens of synthesis. Melchizedek, the Mahatma, and Metatron have taught me to attempt to see and experience my divinity through as many lenses of the cosmic prism as possible. This is what I am recommending to you, my beloved readers. I have found approaching my relationship to GOD in this manner to be a revelatory experience. This is why I have written the

"Easy to Read Encyclopedia of the Spiritual Path," and created the global synthesis event at Mt. Shasta for 1200–3000 disciples, initiates, and ascended beings of all spiritual paths and religions.

In approaching GOD in this manner, we get the opportunity to experience the infinite nature of GOD through thousands and even millions of lenses, not just a small number. There is no judgment if a person wishes to follow a singular form of worship, for this is beautiful. Opening, however, to all aspects of divinity in all its various lenses, forms, aspects, levels and stages, provides a richness and fullness which I know all of you reading this can understand. In this fashion, you can enjoy the experience of all the forms of GOD I have mentioned in this chapter and many more that I have not mentioned. This, my beloved readers, I call "becoming a fully realized Integrated Ascended Master who is on the path of synthesis." Although you open your consciousness to the path of synthesis, you may still vibrate and attune to certain spiritual teachers, and this is not only good, but also totally appropriate. Framing it in this way, however, allows the door to be open to work with all the aspects of GOD, faces of GOD, and all the inner and outer plane teachers of the Planetary and Cosmic Hierarchy. My beloved readers, is not the worship of GOD in all His glory and diversity a wonderful experience!

Namaste!

2

Isis & The Great Pyramid & Sphinx Ascension Activation Meditation

---

To begin this meditation, close your eyes.

We now call forth the Cosmic and Planetary Hierarchy to help in this meditation.

We also call forth Isis, Osirus, Thoth, Horus, Master Serapis Bey, and the Melchizedeks of the Ancient Order of Melchizedek.

We also call forth Ra, the Sun God of ancient Egypt.

Isis steps forward in splendid glory; shimmering in a sea of golden white light!

Isis lifts up her spiritual veils and embraces the entire group in a giant Merkabah in the form of a 12-pointed star.

Isis now carries us to Egypt, where we land at the foot of the Sphinx.

Let us take careful note of the form of the Sphinx, and see the perfect blend of the Divine Feminine and Divine Masculine.

We see the strong masculine lion's head flow into the soft feminine curvature of the lion's body.

In a similar fashion, Isis blends with Osirus.

Allow the masculine and feminine energies of each one of you to also now find the perfect balance within yourself.

As this preparatory process is completed, we begin traveling through the subterranean levels of the Sphinx into the Great Pyramid of Giza itself.

We feel the intensity of the energies of antiquity as they stimulate, and reawaken the ancient knowledge that abides within each and every one of us.

We notice a lake of midnight blue waters, and several streams that run through this level.

We see that the water bears the reflection of an underground moon; shimmering platinum/silver and gold upon the waters.

We are inwardly aware that these energies radiate the qualities of the Divine Mother Herself.

* * *

While meditating in the stillness of the energies of the Divine Mother, Thoth now appears, in radiant splendor.

He lovingly takes you by the hand and guides you into a chamber within the Great Pyramid known as The Well of Life.

There Thoth asks you to gently lay down on a soft white mattress.

He covers you with a golden white blanket, as you lay your head upon a silk pillow.

Thoth then gently takes you in your soul body up the shaft of The Well of Life to the Chamber of New Birth, also known as the Queen's Chamber.

There you are greeted by Isis and Osirus.

Isis blesses you with a complete downpouring of Goddess' love, gentleness, purity, tenderness, nurturing, compassion, and mercy.

Osirus then steps forward and blesses you with Divine strength, decisiveness, courage, and spiritual discernment.

Isis and Osirus now lead you in your soul body to the King's Chamber of Initiation.

You are now asked to lay down again, on a platinum mattress of light, with a platinum pillow and blanket.

As you look up you see the top of the pyramid, with a gigantic capstone crystal shining Divine Light into the chamber.

Surrounding you are Isis, Osirus, Thoth, Serapis Bey, and Horus.

They collectively chant the OM mantra.

You are telepathically told that you will be going through the seven levels of initiation testing, through a series of seven questions.

A "yes" response to each question on the inner plane will allow you to pass this initiation and go to the next one.

Initiation and Question #1:
Do you choose to be the Master of your physical body and lower appetites?

Initiation and Question #2:
Do you choose to be the Master of your emotions, astral body, and desire body?

Initiation and Question #3:
Do you choose to be the Master of your mind and negative ego?

Initiation and Question #4:
Do you choose to let go of all your attachments to people, places, and things, and only have preferences?

Initiation and Question #5:
Do you choose to fully merge with your Monad, or Mighty I AM Presence, and to be freed from all spiritual blindness?

Initiation and Question #6:
Do you choose to take on the responsibility and spiritual leadership that goes along with passing this ascension initiation?

Initiation and Question #7:

Do you choose to live on Earth, as the Mighty I AM Presence, in a totally integrated and egoless manner in service of all sentient beings?

As these seven initiations are passed, Thoth steps forward and performs a blessing over your head, and intones the following statement:

"Thou art crowned in the Hall of Renunciation, that hereafter thou mayest wear a Crown of Life that fadeth not away."

Isis now steps forward and takes you by the hand, in your soul body, to the star Sirius, also known as the Great White Lodge.

There you see a temple carved of crystal and diamond.

You are asked by whose name you seek admission.

Isis replies, *"In the name of the Mighty Ones, the Sons and Daughters of Melchizedek the Just, the Grand Carpenters of the Universe of Worlds, of Male and Female, by whom all things are made."*

You now walk with Isis up seven sacred steps, to stand in the midst of the pure, radiant white light.

As you stand in the pure white light, Master Serapis steps forward with the Ascension Flame from Luxor.

He now sends a purifying current into your entire 12-body system.

Osirus now steps forward, and with the wave of his hand, fully anchors into the core of your being your anointed Christ Overself Body and your Zohar Body of Light.

He also anchors into your 12-body system your 36 chakras, and your 99% Planetary Light and Love Quotient.

Thoth, also known as Hermes, now places wings on your feet and guides you to Horus.

There you find yourself within his sacred left eye.

Here the right side of the brain is totally activated.

These higher emotional and intuitive faculties are now cleansed of any last blockages.

Feel your intuition and Divine feminine faculties being activated to their highest potential.

You now find yourself within the right eye of Horus.

Here all the logistical and masculine faculties are cleansed, and purified.

You now drink in the essence of Divine logic, the understanding of sacred geometries, and the wisdom within the language of light.

Melchizedek, the Universal Logos, now steps forward out of the brilliant light, with his Rod of Power.

He touches you on your third eye, and you are officially crowned a Melchizedek, and full-fledged Ascended Master.

You now find yourself in a large courtyard, surrounded by the Egyptian contingent of Masters, fellow Melchizedek priests and priestesses, and the entire Planetary and Cosmic Hierarchy.

Lord Buddha steps forth, and with His Rod of Initiation, anoints you on your crown chakra and welcomes you into the ranks of the Spiritual Hierarchy.

Lord Maitreya steps forward and places an Ankh necklace made of gold, with a radiant crystal in the center, around your neck.

Sananda steps forward and places around your shoulders a white robe, symbolic of the purity of spirit you have now attained.

Horus steps forward and places a sacred Scarab in the palm of your hand, symbolic of Divine protection.

The Lord and Lady Masters of Sirius now step forward and place upon your head the Hierophant's hat.

This hat is symbolic of your status as priest or priestess of the Great White Lodge, and of the sacred Order of Melchizedek.

As this final gift is given, your ascension and resurrection as the fully integrated Mighty I AM Presence on earth is complete!

The congregation of Masters rejoice, as another fully realized Ascended Master of the Great White Lodge, and fellow Melchizedek, has joined their ranks.

All the Masters gathered, now bow to the Mighty I AM Presence and the Integrated Christ you have become.

Take a moment now to fully enjoy the profundity and spiritual magnitude, of what you have received and have been blessed with in this meditation!

Know that this meditative experience has opened the gateway to enormous acceleration of your ascension path.

On this note, Isis steps forward and once again embraces and enfolds you in her Divine Merkabah.

As a group now, we find ourselves gliding back from Sirius to the Great Pyramid in Egypt.

Your soul now re-enters your etheric body in the Great Pyramid, and then continues its journey back into your physical body.

You now completely hold within yourself all that you have just received.

When you are ready, you may open your eyes.

3

Cosmic Ascension Activations in the Temple of GOD

To begin this meditation, close your eyes.

Take a deep breath.

Exhale.

We call forth all the Masters of the Planetary & Cosmic Hierarchy to help in this meditation.

We call forward Melchizedek, the Mahatma, Metatron, and Archangel Michael to bring forth a Platinum Net to remove any and all imbalanced energies.

We now call forth our inner plane Spiritual Hosts, to bring forth a gigantic interdimensional crystalline Merkabah.

This Merkabah is in the form of a dome-shaped mothership, with windows covering the entire top of the dome.

Let us see ourselves entering this domed Merkabah, with everyone in attendance, both on the inner and outer planes.

As everyone finds their seat, the gigantic domed Merkabah begins to rise, as all look out the windows.

As we begin to rise, we find ourselves moving through a sea of interdimensional color.

We first rise through the red dimensional frequency.
Then up through the orange color frequencies.
Now the yellow frequencies.
The emerald-green frequencies.
Now the blue frequencies.
The indigo spectrum.
Now moving up into the violet frequencies, as we lift higher and higher.
And now into the ultraviolet.

We move up higher still into the frequencies of White Light, as we begin to leave the planetary dimensions of reality.

Rising higher still, now into the solar dimensions of Helios & Vesta.

We are immersed in the color spectrum of copper-gold.

Rising higher, now into the galactic regions of Melchior, which are golden in color.

We continue to rise into the universal realms of Melchizedek, composed of the most rarefied and refined golden hues.

Rising even higher through the multiuniversal levels of platinum space.

Rising higher and higher, we now enter into the very Heart of Father/Mother GOD, at the 352nd level of Divinity.

The Merkabah now lands within the pure colorless Light of the GODHEAD.

We immediately find the Merkabah disappearing.

We find we are now in the most glorious spiritual cathedral that the mind and heart could possibly imagine.

We have entered, as a special dispensation of GOD and the Cosmic & Planetary Hierarchy, the Temple of GOD.

This temple is also known on the inner realms as the Temple of I AM THAT I AM!

See, feel, and visualize with all your inner senses this most sanctified place we find ourselves in.

His Holiness Lord Melchizedek, the Universal Logos, now steps forward in a radiance of splendorous golden-white light.

With his sacred Rod of Initiation in hand, he brings it forward, touching each person's Crown Chakra.

This immediately awakens and reactivates the key codes, fire letters, and sacred geometries of the ancient Order of Melchizedek within each person.

The Mahatma, also known as the Avatar of Synthesis, steps forward in a magnificent auric field of rainbow colored white light.

He now reaches into the very core of each person's cellular being and installs the Crystal of Synthesis, that has never been anchored and activated on earth before.

This will activate an aura and stabilization of harmony and unity within each person.

This will also bring you into Divine resonance with the All That Is.

Archangel Metatron steps forward, wearing a robe of electric platinum light.

He places within each person the GOD Electron into the etheric heart center.

This electronic crystal stimulates the removal within each person, of the veils hiding the Hidden Chambers of Light.

Feel a new awakening to truth arising within you.

Now stepping forward are the Cosmic Trinity of Melchizedek, the Mahatma, and Metatron, in unified magnificence.

They collectively bring forth their combined Universal Rod of Light, to increase ascension potential a thousandfold.

Fully receive this blessing now.

Archangel Michael now steps forward with his Blue Flame Sword.

He materializes an exact etheric duplicate in each person's right hand.

This is a gift and symbol of his eternal protection and connection with you.

His Holiness the Lord Sai Baba, the Cosmic Christ, now steps forward in his flaming orange robe.

He places within each person's heart a rose quartz crystal filled with his eternal energy and love.

This sacred gift serves as a symbol of Sai Baba's eternal love connection with you.

His Holiness the Lord of Sirius, from the Great White Lodge, steps forward in flowing robes of white light.

He now presents to each person a Golden Key.

This key holds the matrix which unlocks the secret chambers residing in Shamballa, and the Great White Lodge.

Allow this key to open the secret chambers now.

Now stepping forward is Vywamus, in a brilliant aura of yellow-gold light.

He offers forth the gift of expansion of each person's spiritual and psychic inner senses, for the purpose of planetary world service.

Receive this blessing and activation now.

Now stepping forward in a blaze of copper-gold, are Helios & Vesta, our Solar Logos.

They collectively ignite the Solar Essence within each person.

This gift and activation forms a deep integration on a permanent basis with the Great Central Sun!

Now stepping forward is the Ascended Master Djwhal Khul, in a radiant field of electric blue light.

He brings forth the gift and blessing this evening of brain illumination.

This profound gift is serving to fully activate the 72 areas of the mind.

Receive this gift and activation now.

Stepping forward now is the beloved Lord Maitreya, the Planetary Christ.

He comes clad in a robe of golden-white light, within an aura of pink radiating from his Heart Center.

He offers forth first a gift of an archetypal imprinting of his Universal Love, into each person's chakra system.

He seals this sanctified blessing into each person's auric field with a wave of his hand.

Now to close this ascension activation meditation, the Seven Chohans of the Seven Rays step forward one by one to give their personal blessings and activations.

El Morya steps forward with the gift and activation of greater personal power for each person in their daily lives.

Receive this blessing now.

Beloved Master Kuthumi steps forward with the gift and activation of greater heart/mind integration.

Receive this activation now.

Master Serapis Bey steps forward with the gift and activation of the quickening of the ascension process.

Receive this acceleration now.

He also offers a personal invitation to come to his ascension retreat in Luxor on the inner plane.

Paul the Venetian now steps forward with the gift and activation of perceiving the Divine artistry and beauty of the Cosmos.

He also harmonically attunes each person's consciousness to inwardly hear or sense the Music of the Spheres.

Receive this blessing and attunement now.

Master Hilarion steps forward with the gift and activation of a greater understanding of the science involved in the manifestation of the New Age.

Receive this expansion of consciousness now.

Beloved Sananda steps forward with the gift and activation of greater devotion and commitment to the higher spiritual principles and ideals for which you stand.

He also installs in this moment, a special encodement to activate the devotion to compassion.

Receive this special activation now.

St. Germain steps forward with the gift and activation of a greater power, faith, and strength in your daily life in the utilization of the Violet Flame.

Receive this gift and blessing now from Master St. Germain.

Take a moment silently to inwardly thank GOD and the Cosmic and Planetary Masters for the gifts and blessings that have been bestowed this evening.

We find ourselves magically sitting back in the dome-shaped crystalline Merkabah.

Feel the Merkabah begin to descend.

First descending downwards through the platinum fields, then the golden dimensions, copper-gold, and white light.

Descending further down now, through the ultraviolet, violet, indigo, blue, green, yellow, orange, and red color spectrum.

Finally now, let us feel ourselves coming back into our physical bodies. Carrying now, fully within yourselves, all the gifts, love, activations, and light just received.

While still keeping your eyes closed in a state of meditation, experience now, as a final benediction and completion of this meditation, His Holiness the Lord Sai Baba, stepping forward again in etheric form.

For his final benediction and blessing, he showers everyone with his sacred Verbuthi ash.

This sacred ash carries in its essence the purest Unconditional Love!

Breathe and drink in this love.

Allow this Cosmic and Universal love to fill every cell, molecule, atom, and electron of your being.

Send this love now to all of your brothers and sisters around the globe, and to all sentient beings.

Take one last moment now to experience the light and love pouring in from His Holiness the Lord Sai Baba, and the Planetary and Cosmic Masters.

4

GOD and the Mahatma Ascension Activation Meditation

To begin this meditation, close your eyes.

We now call forth the Mahatma to overlight and infuse us with his Divine Presence of Synthesis, Love, and Light.

Let us now take a deep "Breath of Oneness," as we prepare now to be carried up the 352 levels of Existence, to the Throne of Creation.

The Throne of Creation I speak of here, is at the level of the Godhead Itself.

To begin this meditation, the Mahatma now etherically manifests a "Mahatma Merkabah" composed of an aspect of all 352 levels of his being.

Magically find yourself now within this Group Merkabah, and become aware of your physical body.

Feel yourself in touch with Mother Earth, as you sit and feel your feet upon her.

Now also feel the embrace of the wings of Archangel Sandalphon, who helps to anchor the Mahatma at this third-dimensional level.

Feel the incredible "Love Infusion," from both the Mahatma and Archangel Sandalphon, and know at this moment that the Essence of

GOD interpenetrates and blesses your physical embodiment totally and completely.

Feel the profundity of this union as the Mahatma installs and fully activates and actualizes the Matrix of Synthesis of his very self, within every cell, atom, electron, and subatomic particle, of your physical vehicle.

As you drink in this joy of unity, let yourselves now begin to be carried upwards within the 352 levels of the Mahatma.

Feel the equanimity of grace and love as you move smoothly and calmly up through the Seven Subplanes of the Emotional Dimension of Reality.

It is here now that the Mahatma, Quan Yin, and Mother Mary connect the "Spark of the Heart of GOD" directly with each individual person's heart.

Feel now the bliss and joy, as unconditional love and compassion fill your entire being.

Feel, see, and visualize beloved Archangel Michael encircle you in a ring of blue fire, with his all-powerful Blue Flame Sword of Protection.

Archangel Michael comes forth, creating a "Platinum Gold-Blue Bubble of Light" at the request of the Mahatma, in order that you feel 100% empowered and protected throughout this meditation.

The Mahatma wishes you to know in this moment that each and every level of Existence is the manifestation of the Godhead.

In the reality of the Mahatma, also known as the Avatar of Synthesis, all 352 levels of his group consciousness are equally valued, honored, and sanctified.

Feel now, through your GOD and GODDESS selves, the feeling of love and unity which is truly what you are.

Feel the magnificent radiance of "Pink Love," expand and enlarge, as you are now drawn upward, to embody all Seven Subplanes of the Mental Realm.

In a burst of "Cosmic Fire," comes forth Lord Maitreya, who is the essence and embodiment of love and wisdom.

Lord Maitreya and the Mahatma now fill your entire mental sphere with Divine love and brain illumination.

The Mahatma now comes forward and connects the "Spark of the Mind of GOD" directly with the mind of each of you.

Bask in this radiant glow of synthesis, as the Mind of GOD and your mind merge as never before.

Receive this blessing of the Mahatma, that from this moment forward, your thoughts shall be blessed by the intent of the Universal Mind of the Mahatma.

We now move upwards into the Buddhic, or Causal Plane.

Here Lord Buddha and the Mahatma download into your higher mind, the encoded wisdom of all the causes that have set your individual lifestream in motion.

Know this wisdom is now being installed into the causal, or higher mind of each one of you, along with the encodements that will activate you to fulfill your Divine blueprint and destiny.

Feel yourselves moving now into the Atmic Plane.

Know it is the Mahatma who is now carrying you up the many levels of his being.

Feel yourself now expanding into your Monad, or Mighty I Am Presence, as you move through the Monadic Plane and into the Logoic Dimension of Reality.

The Mahatma now takes you into full integration and oneness consciousness with your Solar selves.

In a blaze of copper-gold, Helios and Vesta, and the Mahatma merge your body with theirs.

They permanently install within the Heart and Crown Chakras of each and every one of you, a portion of the "Flame that Burns but Does Not Consume."

By the grace of the Mahatma, you are now merged 100% with the Solar Logos, and are now being gifted with an aspect of Solar Fire that shall ever radiate within you, by Helios and Vesta, and the Mahatma.

As the warmth, unity, love and light of this fire glows within, Lord Melchior surrounds you with his Galactic embrace.

The Mahatma and Melchior move you now further within the vastness of the 352 levels of the Mahatma, into the deepest expanse of the Galactic Core, over which Melchior presides as the Galactic Logos.

Beyond what the mind can possibly conceive at this level, you are now suddenly aware that an incredible downloading of Galactic light and information is pouring into your Crown Chakra and 12-Body System.

This downloading is a spiritual current that moves from the Galactic spheres down into and through your 12-Body System, and through your first 150 chakras.

This includes grounding into your seven primary third-dimensional chakras.

Both the Mahatma and Lord Melchior now state that this Galactic downloading manifests as a great increase of love and light upon the Physical Plane in your physical/etheric vehicle.

His Holiness Lord Melchizedek, our Universal Logos, now stands before you.

His body is composed of the very essence of this entire universe.

His expanse carries you far up the 352 levels of Divinity.

Lord Melchizedek now takes on "Robes of Gossamer Golden White Light" and the form of the Higher Adam Kadmon Body.

He does this in order to personally connect with you at this high point upon the spiraling ladder within the Mahatma's vastness.

He touches each and every one of you with the essence of his light, and caresses each of you with the essence of his love.

He now places a "Crystal of his Universal Golden Light" into each of your 200 chakras.

This light permeates your being from the Universal Level through all the intermediary levels, including the physical vehicle.

He now awakens at each of these levels, the most sacred Universal Fire Letters, Key Codes, and Sacred Geometries, into the core of your being.

As a special blessing and grace, the Mahatma and Melchizedek now install to each person's highest potential, their Zohar Body of Light and Anointed Christ Overself Body.

As a second special universal blessing, the seven lady Archangels: Faith, Christine, Charity, Hope, Mother Mary, Aurora, and Amethyst, now step forward and anchor and activate the "Universal Archetypal Imprint" of perfect God/Goddess balance within each person, both male and female.

This activation of the universal God/Goddess within each of you will in turn allow you to activate the God/Goddess ideal within all whom you meet and interact with.

Now see, feel, or visualize the "Platinum Light of Archangel Metatron" carrying you upward ever so gently towards the Throne of Creation.

To the left of Archangel Metatron, Archangel Michael appears.

To his right, Archangel Gabriel sounds forth his trumpet.

As the luminous tones and colors of Gabriel's trumpet move through the universe and your being, you begin to hear and/or feel the "Music of the Spheres" bathing you in exquisite tones and colors of Cosmic spheres.

Even as this is occurring, feel now the full totality of the Mahatma.

Know that he is about to bring you into the very heart of the Godhead.

Before this is done, he does what is called simply, the "Mahatma Activation of Synthesis."

This he now does by placing his "Cosmic Hand" over your Highest Body, or Vehicle of Light, which is the Lord's Mystical Body, which he now fully activates within each of you.

He now moves his hand down through all 352 levels of your being and activates all of your 352 bodies.

He simultaneously integrates an aspect of his infinite Cosmic Body into all 352 levels of each person.

Any illusion of separation between the Godhead and your third-dimensional existence are now healed by the mighty hand of the Avatar of Synthesis itself.

From within this place of absolute oneness, we now call forth the Holy Spirit for a "Cosmic Baptism of Light and Love."

The Holy Spirit also brings forth a second baptism for all now.

This second baptism activates and cleanses the four elements that make up the "Manifested Worlds."

The Holy Spirit now baptizes, activates, and cleanses all now through Fire, Air, Water, and Earth.

In doing so, the Holy Spirit is now "undoing" all remnants of negative ego, separative consciousness, imbalanced consciousness, and physical lack of health, in each person's 12-Body System.

We ask that this great blessing of the Holy Spirit now continue unceasingly until this process is complete within each person here, for all who would like to receive this.

We now call forth all the male and female Archangels connected with earth's evolution.

We now ask for a Divine dispensation for the anchoring and activation for each son and daughter of God here, of all 330 chakras back to the Godhead.

Be still, and receive this enormous Cosmic blessing now.

We now call forth the Mighty Elohim and all Elohim Councils connected with earth's evolution.

We now call forth for a second Divine dispensation for the highest potential anchoring and activation of our Elohistic Lord's Body, our Higher Adam Kadmon Body, our Electromagnetic Body, our Paradise Son's Body, our Overself Body, our Order of Sonship Body, our Gematrian Body, our Epikenetic Body, our Aka Body, our Monadic Blueprint Body, and our Mayavarupa Body, as described in the book *The Keys of Enoch*.

We ask for these things in the name of the Melchizedek, the Christ, and the Buddha, so we may be of greater service.

We now find ourselves ascending even higher by the grace of the Mahatma, and find ourselves in the presence of the Divine Mother at the left side of the Throne of Creation.

The Divine Mother lovingly and sweetly brings forth her "Cosmic Hand," and gently touches each person on the Third Eye.

As she does so, she activates and actualizes the "Twelve Strand of DNA/RNA God Matrix," both on the Etheric and Physical level, as her special gift and blessing.

Receive the full impact and spiritual penetration of this gift and blessing now.

As this activation is complete, the Mahatma magically transfers the entire group to the right side of the Throne of God, to be in the presence of the Divine Father.

The light here is so brilliant, as was the case with the Divine Mother, that it takes a few moments for our spiritual eyes to adjust.

The Divine Father is very pleased to welcome us in this fashion.

The Divine Father also has a very special gift and blessing for this sanctified group, which is a special dispensation of unimaginable magnitude.

The Divine Father now brings forth his luminous right hand and touches each person on the Crown Chakra, which causes an instantaneous merger and integration at each person's highest potential with the 48 dimensions of reality that compose the 352 levels of Divinity.

My beloved brothers and sisters, be still and receive this sublime and profoundly gracious gift of the Divine Father now.

As this activation is complete, the beloved Mahatma now brings us directly in front of the Throne of Creation itself!

There, standing before the Throne of Creation is the Cosmic Council of Twelve, also known as the Twelve Cosmic Logoi.

Seated behind them in a semicircle, are the Twenty-Four Cosmic Elders of Light, who surround the Throne of Grace.

It is by the grace of the Mahatma, as his special gift to this group, that we are graced with this experience.

The Cosmic Council of Twelve and the Twenty-Four Elders that surround the Throne of Grace, are very joyous and pleased to receive this gathering of lightworkers and servants of GOD.

They too wish to now join in the festivities and blessings that are being given forth.

The Twenty-Four Elders and the Cosmic Council of Twelve all raise their right hands with an open palm and send forth a beam of unfathomable Cosmic light.

This collective Cosmic beam of light and love now causes an anchoring and activation for the first time in earth's history of the Cosmic Monad at each person's highest potential, and for the beloved Earth Mother herself.

My beloved brothers and sisters, the Cosmic Monad I speak of here is not the individualized Monad merged with to achieve Planetary Ascension, but rather the Cosmic equivalent at the 352nd level of the Godhead to achieve full Cosmic Ascension.

The profundity and significance of this activation is beyond words and comprehension.

My beloved brothers and sisters, be still and receive the full impact and spiritual penetration of this enormous gift of the Cosmic Council of Twelve and the Twenty-Four Elders now.

As this activation concludes, the Cosmic Council of Twelve and the Twenty-Four Elders disappear, and by the grace of the Mahatma we stand before the Throne of God!

The light is so brilliant that it is almost blinding.

The love and peace so profound that even a word such as "bliss" does not come close to describing the feeling.

We stand in the presence of "Sat Chit Ananda."

"Pure Existence, Consciousness, and Bliss"!

Out of this unfathomable Cosmic light, love, and power, GOD steps forward with a final gift and blessing, on this momentous occasion in earth's history and evolution!

Appearing now, out of this glorious light, emerges the "Cosmic Burning Bush."

GOD now takes an "Infinitesimal Spark of His Burning Bush," and places it as GOD's special gift into each person's Heart Chakra.

This Spark of GOD serves as a "Light of Remembrance" that each of the 352 levels in GOD's Body is sanctified and holy ground.

It is GOD's wish that each person receiving this gift of gifts, take it back to the earth and share it through the "Vehicle of Loving all your Brothers and Sisters."

Also sharing it with all animals, plants, minerals, sentient beings, the very earth, and the Material Universe itself.

GOD now asks each person, under complete Divine protection of GOD and the Mahatma, to now consider stepping forward as an individual and as a group, and bathe yourself in the "Burning Bush" that "Burns But Does Not Consume."

This unbelievably profound blessing, gift, and grace of GOD will serve to completely purify and cleanse any last remnant of thought, word, or deed that is not completely in harmony with the will of GOD, or perceive anything as separate or outside of GOD.

GOD now invites you, with your free choice and free will, to fully step forward, individually and as a group, and receive this blessing of all blessings; and in so doing, dedicate your life to serving the GOD in all.

If you choose in this moment to receive this gift of all gifts and make this your intent, then be still in your consciousness and step forward in your Light Body and receive this purification and anointing of "The Burning Bush of GOD."

We will now take a minute of silence to fully receive this gift of gifts and blessing of blessings now.

Now fully bathed and purified in GOD's "Burning Bush," find yourself conscious now of being in the loving, cool embrace, of the Mahatma's Merkabah.

Feel the Mahatma's Merkabah begin to move the group out of the area of the "Burning Bush," and prepare for descent back to earth.

Take one last moment to face GOD and to give thanks for this profound blessing and the grace we all enjoy in our daily lives from this blessing and under GOD's care.

Feel the Mahatma's Merkabah begin to descend now, first moving down through the Cosmic Logoic Plane.

Now descending down through the Cosmic Monadic Plane.

Descending down through the Cosmic Atmic Plane.

Descending down through the Cosmic Buddhic Plane.

Descending further now, through the Cosmic Mental Plane.

Descending further still, through the Cosmic Emotional Plane.

Now entering the Cosmic Physical Plane.

Feel yourselves moving now down through the Seven Subplanes of the Cosmic Physical Plane.

Feel yourselves now seeing and enjoying the panoramic view of the earth.

Finally now, feel yourselves entering the room and now slowly and comfortably anchor yourself fully into your physical body; bringing all that you have just experienced fully back with you into your physical vehicle and this present moment.

Take one last moment to inwardly thank the Mahatma for the grace he has bestowed upon each and every one of us, to allow us to travel through the 352 levels of his sublime, infinite body.

When you are ready, open your eyes and see the manifestation of GOD and the Mahatma all around you; in the beloved hearts, minds, and souls of your beloved brothers and sisters.

5

GOD and Metatron's Cosmic Tree of Life Ascension Activation Meditation

---

To begin this meditation, close your eyes.

We now call forth beloved Archangel Metatron and the entire Planetary and Cosmic Hierarchy to help in this meditation.

We ask for a balancing of the energies.

We call forth a Platinum Net from Metatron, the Mahatma, and Melchizedek to cleanse any and all unwanted energies.

We call forth to Archangel Michael for a "Sapphire Blue Cosmic Dome of Protection" throughout this entire meditation and experience.

We officially begin this meditation by calling to each person's 144 Soul Extensions from their Monad, to join us for this meditation, if it is their free choice to do so.

We call forth now the full anchoring of the Garment of Shaddai, also known as the Light Body of Metatron, to serve as our Merkabah for this meditation; both individually and collectively.

We now call forth from Metatron, the Mahatma, and Melchizedek, the full anchoring and activation into each person here, and for the entire group, the Cosmic Tree of Life.

We begin this Cosmic Tree of Life ascension activation by calling forth a "Cosmic Ascension Column" and "Pillar of Light," back to Source.

Within this "Cosmic Pillar of Light," we request from Archangel Metatron, the Mahatma, and Melchizedek, the establishment of each person's Antakarana, back to the Godhead.

We call forth from beloved Ascended Master Djwhal Khul, the full anchoring and activation of each person's Mighty I AM Presence, or Monad, at the 100% Light and Love Quotient level.

We call forth for the anchoring and activation from El Morya, Kuthumi, Serapis Bey, Paul the Venetian, Hilarion, Sananda, and St. Germain of each person's 12 higher bodies.

We request from Lord Buddha, Lord Maitreya, and Allah Gobi for the anchoring and activation of each person's Zohar Body of Light and each person's Anointed Christ Oversoul Body.

We call forth from Metatron, the Mahatma, Melchizedek, and Archangel Michael for the anchoring and activation of each person's 330 chakras.

We call forth from the Divine Mother and the Divine Father for the full anchoring and activation of each person's 48 Dimensional Bodies, providing complete connection and attunement back to the Godhead.

We call forth to His Holiness the Lord Sai Baba for the highest potential cleansing of karma that is permitted by Divine Grace for each person here.

We call to Metatron for the permanent anchoring and activation of the GOD Electron into each person here.

We call to the Divine Mother and all the Lady Masters for a Cosmic downpouring and Divine increase of each person's Love Quotient.

We call to Sanat Kumara, Vywamus, and Lenduce for the integration and cleansing of each person's one million Soul Extensions in their Higher Monadic Group Body.

We call to Melchizedek to now anchor and activate all the Fire Letters, Key Codes, and Sacred Geometries to fully ignite the Cosmic Tree of Life and Seven Sacred Seals.

We call to the Elohim Councils for the full anchoring and activation of each person's Elohistic Lord's Body, Paradise Son's Body, and Order of Sonship Body.

My beloved brothers and sisters, now that we are officially warmed up and cosmically activated, we are now ready to begin our climb up the Cosmic Tree of Life back to Source.

We call forth Archangel Metatron and Archangel Sandalphon to officially ignite, anchor and activate the First Sephiroth of the Cosmic Tree of Life; known as "Malkuth, or the Kingdom."

As this Sephiroth is ignited, we are given from Sandalphon, a Divine vision and experience of the "Infinite Physical Omniverse."

We now call forth Archangel Gabriel to officially ignite, anchor, and activate the Second Sephiroth of "Yesod, or Foundation."

As Archangel Gabriel ignites this Sephiroth, we collectively experience a "Vision of the Subconscious Mind of GOD."

We now call forth Archangel Raphael to fully ignite, anchor, and activate the Third Sephiroth, known as "Hod, or Splendor."

As Raphael ignites this Sephiroth, we fully receive the experience of the "Splendor of the Divine Mind of GOD."

We now call forth Archangel Auriel to fully ignite, anchor, and activate the Sephiroth known as "Netzach, or Victory."

As Archangel Auriel does this now, we receive the vision and experience, of the "Perfect Divine Feeling of GOD throughout the Cosmos."

We call forth Archangel Michael to fully ignite, anchor, and activate the Sephiroth known as "Tiphareth, or Beauty."

As Archangel Michael does this now, we receive the vision and experience of the "Perfect Harmony of GOD throughout Creation."

We now call forth Archangel Khamael to fully ignite, anchor, and activate the Sephiroth known as "Gebrurah, or Severity."

As Archangel Khamael does this we now receive the vision and experience of the "Power of GOD throughout Creation."

We now call forth Archangel Zadkiel to fully ignite, anchor, and activate the Sephiroth known as "Chesed, or Mercy."

As Archangel Zadkiel does this, we receive the vision and experience of the Divine Cosmic Mother, "Face to Face."

We now call forth Archangel Ratziel to ignite, anchor, and activate the Sephiroth known as "Chokmah, or Wisdom."

As Archangel Ratziel does this, we receive the vision and experience of the Divine Cosmic Father, "Face to Face."

We call forth Archangel Metatron to ignite, anchor, and activate the Sephiroth at the top of the Tree of Life, known as "Kether, or the Crown."

As Archangel Metatron does this, we receive the vision and experience of "Union with the Cosmic Light of GOD."

We now call forth His Holiness Lord Melchizedek to fully ignite, anchor, and activate the "Cosmic Hidden Sephiroth of Daath, or Hidden Wisdom."

As beloved Melchizedek does this, we receive the vision and experience of the "Wisdom of the Universe Unfold Before Us."

We now call forth the Mahatma to ignite, anchor, and activate the never before revealed Twelfth Sephiroth in the Cosmic Tree of Life, known as "Synthesis"!

As the Mahatma does this, we receive the vision and experience of all Twelve Sephiroth working together in perfect integration, balance, synergy, and synthesis.

Be still and receive this blessing and activation now if you would like to receive this.

We now call forth Metatron, the Mahatma, and Melchizedek to fully anchor and activate the Three Pillars of the Cosmic Tree of Life known as the "Pillar of Severity," the "Pillar of Equilibrium," and the "Pillar of Mercy."

As Metatron, the Mahatma, and Melchizedek do this, feel the incredible sense of balance now within yourself of firmness and compassion, as these pillars are installed.

We now call forth all the Archangels of the Cosmic Hierarchy to fully anchor and activate into the Cosmic Tree of Life for each person the Twelve Signs of the Zodiac, in perfect balance and integration.

We now call forth the Elohim Councils to fully anchor and activate the Major Archetypes of the Tarot Deck into the Cosmic Tree of Life, in perfect balance and integration, for each person here, as GOD would have it be.

We now call forth the Holy Spirit, who appears as the "sap" breathing through the entire Cosmic Tree of Life.

The Holy Spirit now requests that we deeply feel and experience it's energies as we breathe the holy breath of the Holy Spirit together through the entire Cosmic Tree of Life that is now installed within us.

We now continue climbing into even higher dimensions of reality by the grace of His Holiness Archangel Metatron and his Light Body Merkabah.

We now move from the Crown, or top of the Cosmic Tree of Life, into the sphere above the Cosmic Tree, known as the "Ain Soph Or, or Limitless Universal Light."

Here the light is so bright, one can hardly see.

Metatron now continues to take us even higher still, into the "Ain Soph, or Undifferentiated Source."

Here the light is so refined that it has become colorless, and can only be described as the "Clear Light of GOD."

Archangel Metatron takes us even higher still, into the region of GOD's Kingdom known as "Ain, or Utter and Complete GOD Essence."

The peace and love at this 352nd level of Divinity is a grace beyond words and description.

It is here we find ourselves standing before the 12 Cosmic Logoi, and the "24 Elders that Surround the Throne of Grace."

The 12 Cosmic Logoi, also known as the 12 Cosmic Ray Masters, lift up their individual Light Rods and one by one ignite within each person here, the 12 Cosmic Rays that are the foundation and source of GOD's infinite Creation.

Be aware that this activation is not of the 12 Planetary Rays we are all familiar with, but rather an activation of their 12 Cosmic equivalents at the 352nd level of the Godhead.

Receive this extraordinary blessing now, as a gift of the Creator and of the Cosmic Ray Masters.

We also ask at this time that this gift be given to the Earth Mother herself, to accelerate her spiritual and material evolution as well.

Let us all receive this blessing and gift as well now, from each of the individual Cosmic Ray Masters.

The "24 Elders of Light that Surround the Throne of Grace" now step forward.

Through a process that can only be described as the "Language of Light," the 24 Elders now transfer telepathically to each person here, a "Light Revelation" into each person's Crown Chakra.

The 24 Elders give the gift of the "Cosmic Wisdom of the Ages," which will unfold as an acorn grows into an oak tree, throughout each lightworker's cosmic journey back to Source.

Be still and receive this tremendous blessing now.

As this enormous blessing is fully received, we find ourselves raised even higher by Metatron and the 24 Elders, and we find ourselves in the Ashram of GOD, at the Throne of Creation.

We have moved beyond the beyond, by the grace of Metatron.

Here GOD now steps forward with His Light Rod, and as a special dispensation He brings forth His Light Rod upon each person's Crown Chakra.

GOD does this for the specific purpose of "Bestowing Full Sonship and Daughtership at the Highest Possible Level," for all here.

Be still and receive this blessing of all blessings and activation of all activations now, if you would like to receive it

As this is complete, GOD now bestows a second blessing of "Unfathomable Magnitude."

GOD now brings forth what is esoterically known as the "Waterfall of GOD," from the Throne of Creation.

Experience this Cosmic cleansing and purification of this "Waterfall of GOD" now.

Adding and joining the experience now is the entire Cosmic and Planetary Hierarchy and over one million Masters that are in attendance.

Let yourself now experience the "Light and Love Shower of all Light and Love Showers," from GOD and the entire Godforce.

We humbly now request that this shower be given to the Earth Mother and all sentient beings on earth.

Now, as a final Cosmic gift and blessing from GOD, GOD requests that we collectively focus our attention on "GOD's Cosmic Inbreath and Outbreath."

GOD requests now that we listen to His "Cosmic Pulse," or even more exactly, to the "Stillpoint between His Cosmic Inbreath and Outbreath."

It is in this stillpoint between the inbreath and outbreath of GOD, that GOD can truly be experienced.

Let us be silent now and experience this "Final Revelation of GOD."

As we conclude this process, take a moment to thank GOD for this experience and to also thank Him for all the blessings you have received now and in your daily life.

As you conclude this process, you find yourself floating before the Throne of Creation in Metatron's Light Body Merkabah, with all your brothers and sisters.

Metatron's Group Merkabah begins to descend back down through the Cosmic Dimensions of Reality, to the Multiuniversal level.

Find yourself now sitting upon the top of the Tree of Life, at the Multiuniversal level."

Feel Metatron's Merkabah descending the Cosmic Antakaranah, like an elevator, to the Universal level.

Here again you find yourself sitting on top of the Cosmic Tree of Life of Melchizedek, at the Universal level.

As Metatron's Group Merkabah continues to descend, we find ourselves now sitting on top of the Cosmic Tree of Life at the Galactic level, with Melchior, our Galactic Logos.

Descending further still, we find ourselves now at the top of the Cosmic Tree of Life at the Solar level, with Helios and Vesta.

Descending again within Metatron's Merkabah, we find ourselves sitting at the top of the Cosmic Tree of Life at the Planetary level, with Lord Buddha in Shamballa.

Lord Buddha gives us a special blessing and ascension activation, as we begin to travel downwards through his Planetary Cosmic Tree of Life, to ground ourselves once again to planet earth.

As we begin grounding ourselves now, and back into our physical bodies, simultaneously feel and know that all of the Cosmic Trees at all the different levels of Divinity of life, remain connected within you through the Cosmic Antakaranah, which is now fully established between yourself and the Godhead.

Now feel yourself fully connecting with your physical body and the Earth Mother, with the help of Archangel Sandalphon, Pan, and the Earth Mother herself.

It is only by the grace of Archangel Metatron's Protective Light Body and Merkabah, that we have been allowed to make this sojourn to GOD, as a special gift and blessing from Him.

Take one last moment now to thank beloved Archangel Metatron for his "supreme grace" in allowing each and every one of us to make this journey to Source and back again.

When your are ready, you may open your eyes, feeling the entire Cosmic Tree of Life fully anchored and activated within you by the Grace of GOD and the Godforce!

As your eyes fully open now, share this profound new sense of love, wisdom, and power, in perfect balance with your brothers and sisters, in a moment of heart expanding love for them.

6

GOD and the Elohim Ascension Activation Meditation

To begin this meditation, close your eyes.

We invoke the Platinum Light of Archangel Metatron to bathe this room and all of us with his holy purifying light.

We now request from Archangel Metatron, Lord Melchizedek, and the Mahatma for a full sweeping of their combined Platinum Nets through each of our entire 12-body systems.

We ask that this triple layered Platinum Net be run through the entire room, to further cleanse, clear and purify all unwanted energies.

We request now that the Holy Spirit undo any and all negative programming and negative energy patterns, frequencies, vibrations or cellular memory that has lodged within any of our 12-body systems.

We feel the gentle cleansing wind of the Holy Spirit as she moves through each of us; clearing away any last remnants of negative memory that we may have unknowingly carried within us.

We now reaffirm our connection to the Earth Mother as we send energies of radiant love from our hearts directly into her heart.

We feel the tremendous love of the Earth Mother as she sends us her Love in return.

We call forth now to beloved Archangel Michael to anchor us within his Golden Dome of Protection.

Archangel Michael does this now, and also seals us within the light radiance of his blue flame Sword of Protection.

We look up together now and see a translucent and luminous winged Merkabah in the shape of a spiral.

The spiral contains seven tiers, each tier representing a pair of the seven great Elohim, who are the Creator Gods.

Each of us enters the Merkabah now, intuitively taking a seat on the tier that we feel most in harmony with.

As each pair of Elohim are on one of the seven Major Rays, we are drawn to the tier that holds the ray energy that is most dominant in each of our lives.

The Merkabah begins to slowly rise now, moving through the various dimensions of time and space.

We are carried upward through the various levels of our Planetary system.

Our Merkabah now pauses in Shamballa, where we are greeted by beloved Lord Buddha, our Planetary Logos.

He raises a golden-colored staff and gently taps our Merkabah, making contact with only the first tier of the spiral.

We watch now as a golden-green light flows from Buddha's staff and swirls like a million twinkling lights around each tier and curve of our spiral Merkabah.

As the golden-green light moves around the sphere that we are seated in, we feel a wondrous current move through us now, awakening and enlivening every cell of our beings.

We feel our Crown Chakras become extremely open as each one of the thousand-petal lotuses is stimulated by the golden touch of the staff of Lord Buddha.

We also feel a very definite aliveness stimulating the chakras within our feet.

We notice now a faint reddish-magenta glow emanating from within the foot area.

Lord Buddha smiles as he turns to make his way back to his meditation chamber.

Our Merkabah once again makes its spiraling ascent upwards.

We move now through the various dimensions of our solar system.

The Merkabah pauses again, within the core ashram of Helios and Vesta, our Solar Logos.

These resplendent beings of light walk toward our Merkabah now, each holding a staff similar to that of Lord Buddha.

Helios and Vesta approach our Merkabah, each of them positioned at opposite ends of the spiral.

Helios taps the second tier of the spiral Merkabah with his golden staff, while Vesta taps the first sphere standing at the opposite end of the Merkabah.

Yellow, gold, and blue rays—like soft but intense sunlight and electricity—spiral around and around the Merkabah.

This yellow, golden, and blue light also spirals around each one of us blessing and stimulating our entire 12-body system.

We are filled with a feeling of incredible love, as Helios and Vesta whose Solar Body we live and move and have our beings within, begins to vibrate at a higher and higher frequency.

Infused with this Solar "love light," we continue to journey upward into a greater dimensional expanse of beingness.

Our Merkabah lands now at the foot of the Temple of Melchior, our Galactic Logos.

Melchior moves toward us, holding an orange staff in his right hand.

He taps the third tier of our Merkabah, and a beautifully resplendent shimmer of yellow light begins to spiral around the Merkabah and within each one of us.

We feel now an intensity of energy within each of our own hands, as if we ourselves hold the power of Creation within our own hands.

This yellow light moves to the seat of intelligence within our Crown Chakras, awakening our level of understanding and clarity to new expanses.

Once again our Merkabah moves upward through interdimensional space.

We are now at the sanctuary of His Holiness Lord Melchizedek, our Universal Logos.

Lord Melchizedek has been awaiting our arrival.

He holds a golden-orange rod in one hand and a golden-green rod in his other hand.

He now taps both the fourth and fifth tiers of our spiral Merkabah simultaneously.

Golden-orange light flickers like the light of ten thousand suns, as it spirals around the entire Merkabah.

Simultaneously, green lights of every imaginable shade and hue spirals around the Merkabah, intersecting and blending with the golden-yellow Light.

The lights from these combined Light Rods of Melchizedek move into and through the very core of our being.

We now have the most profound sense of healing that we have ever experienced.

We also feel filled with the Divine Light of Courage, as we now know that we are blessed, graced, and love-empowered members within the ancient Order of Melchizedek.

Our Merkabah once again begins to climb, landing now at the summit of the Multiuniversal level.

The light at this level is so brilliant that we are at once immersed within the essence of pure Light itself.

Our Merkabah lands now upon a platinum-indigo surface.

We sense and feel the presence of the Multiuniversal Logos as he approaches us in a form of Light.

Raising up his platinum-indigo staff, he touches our Merkabah at the sixth tier.

We are each immediately filled with the deepest, most sincere, and all-powerful sense of pure devotion imaginable.

Our hearts instantaneously embrace the entire Cosmos with unconditional love and light, and we now know that there is nothing we would ever hold back on any level in order to be of service to all Creation.

As our Merkabah once again begins to climb upward, we feel our hearts continuing to expand in ever greater devotion to the pure Will of God and to Creation upon all 352 levels of existence.

We feel a sense of utter joy as our Merkabah begins to climb higher and higher within the expanse of GOD.

Finally, our spiral Merkabah comes to rest on a crystal mountain.

The brilliance of the light here is unfathomable.

We perceive it to be almost colorless, yet radiating the faintest and most refined hues of platinum, gold, violet, and pink.

We sense the presence of the Divine Mother and the Divine Father.

The Divine Father holds a platinum-gold rod.

The Divine Mother holds a violet-pink rod.

As they come closer and closer to our Merkabah, we feel completely infused with the purest and most perfect blend of pure Divine Will, Love, and Light.

As the Divine Mother and the Divine Father now simultaneously tap our Merkabah at the seventh tier, we become immersed in a brilliant light; flickering the most refined platinum, gold, violet, and pink colors.

These colored Lights spiral throughout our entire 12-body systems and into and throughout every cell of our beings on all dimensions.

As we bathe in the complete and total Bliss of Light, Love, and the Will of God, we feel our Merkabah once again begin to climb higher still.

Our Merkabah now lands upon region of pure, colorless light.

We now sit at the top of the 352nd level of Creation, within the Temple of the GODHEAD Itself.

We notice within the grace of this pure Light Essence, that 14 beings of indescribable beauty walk toward us.

We bask now, with a sense of power and grace that we have never felt before.

Unable to stand, we realize that rainbow colored cushioned seats have manifested directly beside each one of us.

As we take our seats and relax comfortably with the soft cloud-like feel of the cushions, we notice that the 14 figures are in pairs and have encircled our entire group.

Through their all-creative power, these blessed beings now give us vision that extends 360° in every direction.

In one voice they tell us that they are the Elohim, the Creator Gods, and that it is through their power, in combination with our free choice, that they have facilitated our journey to their sacred retreat within the Temple of the GODHEAD.

We now feel even a greater increase of light, love, and vibrational energy as they begin to introduce themselves.

By the power of a super-telepathic link, we hear the voice of the Elohim of the First Ray resonate within the very core of each of our beings.

Speaking as one, we hear the words, "We are Hercules and Amazonia, the Elohim who overlight the First Ray of Creation."

We hear the words, "We are Apollo and Lumina, the Elohim of the Second Ray of Creation."

Now the telepathic words, "We are Heros and Amora, the Elohim of the Third Ray of Creation."

We hear the telepathic words, "We are Purity and Astrea, the Elohim of the Fourth Ray of Creation."

Now the words, "We are Cyclopia and Virginia, the Elohim of the Fifth Ray of Creation."

And the telepathic words, "We are Peace and Aloha, the Elohim of the Sixth Ray of Creation."

Now the last pair telepathically speak the words, "We are Arcturus and Victoria, the Elohim of the Seventh Ray of Creation."

They ask to please prepare to journey with them and share with them the vision, purpose, and some of the Cosmic Secrets of Creation Itself.

We now enter into even a deeper telepathic rapport with all 14 Elohim.

The first thing we become aware of is their perfect link with the mind of the Godhead.

We feel their incredible will, power, and purpose.

We also feel their Cosmic Love, as it embraces all of Creation as various aspects of themselves.

They tell us now that it is through the very essence of their own beings that all of the manifested worlds are brought into being.

By the power of the alchemy of the most high Godhead, we see the Elohim merge into the seven primary Rays that govern all Creation.

We now watch in amazement as the Light Essence of each of these Cosmic Rays, which are in actuality the Mighty Elohim, move through all 352 levels of Divinity, actually *creating* these levels by putting forth their own essences.

We see now with utter clarity how it is by their Essence of Light as it moves downward from the Throne of Creation to build and source, level by level, all that has form and substance.

Magically we seem to have our vision move to the physical body of planet earth.

We watch the Elementals building the outer forms of all kingdoms.

We watch in amazement as the overlighting Deva of each plant, flower, mountain, tree, blade of grass, droplet of water, and great ocean are revealed to be sourcing and creating all these myriad aspects of Creation from their own essence.

They who source and overlight all of Creation, in a similar way do the great Devas source and overlight the manifestation of specific aspects of Creation.

The Elohim tell us that this is true, even as the tiniest Elementals work in group formation in order to create a single blade of grass or the smallest grain of sand.

We now find ourselves face to face with a most magnificent being who is 14 feet tall and whose greenish aura seems to radiate a hundred feet in all directions, forming a most luminescent, pearlescent glow.

He tells us that he is the overlighting Deva of the beautiful field in which we now find ourselves.

He magically reveals to us how it is from his aura or his light substance that all the lesser evolved Devas and Elementals draw on to do their creative work.

He tells us that just as we who are the sons and daughters of God follow a certain lineage and line of evolution, it is the same for those who are Devas and Elementals.

Even the tiniest of Devas will one day evolve to be an overlighting Deva such as himself.

He shows us now, to our amazed inner vision, how he too is evolving and will some day be the overlighting Deva of an entire planet.

He tells us that should one of us choose the path that leads us onward to hold the position of a Planetary Logos, that we would possibly be working within him.

Before we can respond to this incredible statement, the Great Elohim now turn our vision to the Fairy Kingdom.

They tell us that Fairies are on the line of evolution of Angels.

The Fairies work closely with the Elementals in a similar way that the Archangels work in conjunction with the Mighty Elohim.

They once again tell us that all in the Cosmos is on a path of evolution and expansion.

They mystically and magically show us how an aspect of our Monad in eons past inhabited the mineral form.

For the brightest of an instant now, each one of us re-experiences the most rudimentary consciousness that inhabits a mineral.

We feel ourselves, ever so briefly inhabiting the body of a planet.

We now experience being within the form of a wild animal.

Now a beloved animal held in the embrace of a human heart.

We now are once again, returned to our expanded consciousness as the Great Elohim continue to teach and reveal the process of creation to us.

We see with great clarity, how the Deva overlighting a group of shrubs gives his light to the little Elementals who then build the form of the shrubs out of their own essence.

We become aware that there is an overlighting Deva of each shrub who acts as intermediary between the overlighting Deva of the groups of shrubs and the tiny Elementals doing the building.

We see how each aspect of Creation sources every other aspect of Creation and that the seemingly overused phrase "All is One," is, in truth, a statement of pure fact.

Suddenly now, our consciousness begins to expand upward and outward into the Cosmos.

We see before our inner vision the creation of worlds.

We see how the Mighty Elohim are the source of the substance of all Creation.

We see by their side the Mighty Archangels, who serve through love and help to create through their contributions and gifts that are similar yet uniquely their own.

We see now how lightworkers evolving through the graded ranks along our own line of evolution, contribute to the creation of worlds.

We envision countless universes, galaxies, and star systems appearing and disappearing before our inner eyes.

Once again, we become slowly aware that we are seated on our cushions within the sanctuary of the Elohim.

Our vision remains at 360° and we now see the 14 Elohim standing in circular fashion around us.

Telepathically they tell us that, in truth, we have been within their hallowed sanctuary in the Temple of the GODHEAD.

They go on to tell us that we needed to experience creation in order to understand even an aspect of that which, in truth, comprised "The Order of the Elohim."

They telepathically assure us that they are ever available to us, and all we need do is to call upon them.

They tell us that they can be of service to us the greatest in matters dealing with creation and manifestation, and ask us to never hesitate to call them.

We understand that they wish to be more actively called upon, much as we call upon the Archangels and the Angels.

They tell us that the very purpose of our journey to their sanctuary was to inspire us to attune to them more frequently.

The Elementals, which are miniature Elohims, advise us to speak to them mentally and remind us to notice that even the name "elemental" contains the word mental within it.

They ask us now to please realize that these beings are open to commune with and co-create with, even as are the Elohim.

They also advise us to keep calling upon the Angelic Kingdom, from the tiniest Flower Fairy all the way to the Mightiest Archangel.

We tell them that, of course we will, and thank them from the depths of our beings for the gift of the Wisdom Light of Creation that they have imparted to us.

They now in turn thank us, and remind us again that the Order of the Elohim is available to assist us in all manner of creation.

They smile in unison now, as they tell us that when we want or need to create a home, car, a painting, or a job, they are as qualified, willing, and able to assist as are the Archangels or any of the Cosmic or Planetary Masters.

We intuitively know that it is time for us to etherically journey back to earth.

They acknowledge this, and as they turn to take their leave, we each hear within ourselves their choir of telepathic voices saying, "In truth, there is nowhere in the cosmos you can go where we are not."

Magically our spiral Merkabah appears in front of us.

We now enter our Merkabah.

We find our seats and now settle comfortably within them.

We are aware that it is from the light, love, and creative power of the Elohim that this Merkabah was manifested.

Feeling now blessed with a deeper and intimate connection with these creative Gods, the beloved Elohim, we feel our spiral shaped Merkabah lift up from the sanctuary of the Elohim within the Temple of the GOD-HEAD and begin its descent back to earth.

As we travel down through the various realms and levels of Creation, we no longer have the sense of up or down in the same manner as we did at the start of our journey.

Instead we feel the circular aspect of the Cosmos, the sphere and the spiral that, although it is filled with a multitude of levels and various grades of evolution, is truly one whole, all GOD, all eternally bonded and connected.

We pass again through the Multiuniversal level where our Merkabah and ourselves are bathed, cleansed, and shaped in the color tone frequencies of platinum-indigo.

Descending further still, we reach again the Universal level.

Here we are now bathed within the golden-orange and golden-green of beloved Lord Melchizedek.

Lord Melchizedek tells us that we indeed have the courage of a Master Priest or Priestess of the Order of Melchizedek.

He also tells us that we will more easily be able to transmit these qualities and color tone frequencies to others.

Lord Melchizedek assures us that he will ever be with us, and invites us to call upon him whenever we so desire.

He tells us now that we can even use his name as a mantra to invoke Courage, Healing, Light, Love, and Power.

He tells us that we should do the same with the names of each of the Elohim and with the combined tonal frequency of chanting simply "Elohim."

Our Merkabah now moves through the Galactic sphere, where we are immersed again in the golden-yellow frequencies.

Again, our Merkabah begins to descend in further.

We find ourselves once more in the radiance of our Solar Logos, Helios and Vesta.

Copper-gold sunlight softly permeates our Merkabah and fills us with the intense love and light that is the every core essence of our Solar sphere.

With joy, love, light, and a feeling of an extreme grace in our hearts and souls, we descend into the radius of earth.

We are filled with the golden-green light of the earth's Fourth Ray frequency.

We are also filled with the gift of greater attunement to Lord Buddha.

As we descend toward earth, our Merkabah pauses within the ashram of beloved Master Djwhal Khul.

He comes to greet us all and raises forth a Rainbow Staff.

Now entering our field of vision the Mahatma stands to the right of Djwhal Khul, stretching forth a pearlescent Rod faintly ordained with luminous rainbow colors.

Together they telepathically speak the words "In the name of Synthesis we now bless thee."

We are now the recipients of the most resplendent Rainbow Light Shower that we have ever seen or imagined.

We feel the deepest sense and oneness with all of life at every level of Creation than we have ever felt before.

Our Merkabah begins to descend once more.

As our spiral Merkabah lands in the room where we first sat to meditate, one by one we silently exit the Merkabah.

As we do so now, the Merkabah magically disappears.

Slowly filled with grace, love, and illumination, we enter our physical bodies.

We give thanks to the Mighty Elohim, who play such a vital role in creating the form of all Creation, including our physical vehicle.

We now feel ourselves fully grounded inside our bodies.

We send our grounding cord to our beloved Earth Mother, channeling deep love and gratitude for the part that she holds in the creation and maintenance of our earth.

We now send her healing love and healing light.

Having done this, we move our attention fully back into our bodies, becoming aware of our feet touching the floor of the room in which we are sitting.

When you are ready, you may open your eyes.

7

GOD and the Divine Father Ascension Activation Meditation

To begin this meditation, close your eyes.

We call upon the combined energies of Lord Melchizedek, the Mahatma, and Archangel Metatron to sweep a Platinum Net through the room in which we are gathered.

We now request that they also sweep their Platinum Net through each one of us and through our entire 12-body system, clearing away any unwanted energies.

We call upon the entire group of Planetary and Cosmic Masters to overlight us in our meditation.

We call upon the blessing of the Divine Father, as we now prepare to journey together to His most blessed sanctuary.

Before us we see the most splendorous 12-starred Merkabah, anchored within a perfect sphere, descend before us.

The Merkabah glows with a luminous white light, as one by one we find our seats.

We feel a great exhilaration as the Merkabah now begins to rotate.

The Divine Father I speak of here is the counterpart of the Divine Mother.

The throne of the Divine Father is located on the right side of the Godhead Itself.

We travel in our Merkabah through the various levels of Solar Creation.

Expanding into higher and more inclusive realms, we travel through the dimensions and levels of Galactic Creation.

Higher and vaster in scope, our Merkabah now ascends through the various dimensions and realms of the Universal level of Creation.

Ascending further still through the incredible expanse and vastness of the Multiuniversal levels of Creation.

Moving now through the incredible realms where dwell the 12 Cosmic Logoi and Cosmic Monads, the "24 Elders that surround the Throne of Grace," the Supreme Council of 12, and the Hyos Ha Koidesh.

Our 12-pointed star Merkabah circles its way first through the sanctuary of the Archangels and now through the sanctuary of the Elohim.

We feel our Merkabah begin to slow down and come to rest within the throne room of the Divine Father at the 352nd level of the Godhead.

As the Merkabah now comes to a full stop, we step out into a realm that is comprised of the essence of pure Light itself.

We see what can only be described as colorless light of various shapes and density.

We now walk within the hallowed sphere of the Divine Father, as slowly and with great reverence, love, and respect we walk to the very throne where the Divine Father sits.

We hear the very sound of Creation, like a deep soft OM.

This sound penetrates the very core of each of our beings, filling us now with a sense of immense harmony.

We feel now, as the sound continues to permeate every cell, atom, and electron of our 12-body system, that by the grace of this Cosmic OM, which vibrates almost like a hum, we are each wheels within wheels of the all-embracing movement of all Creation.

Synchronistically, the Divine Father opens His arms in embrace.

We each walk into this embrace, feeling the exquisite joy of love that overflows from the Heart of the Divine Father into our own hearts.

As we walk toward the cushions that surround the Throne of the Divine Father, we note that He has connected two extremely thin tubes of light from Him to each of us.

We first notice that there is an etheric line of light running directly from the Heart of the Divine Father into our own Heart Chakras.

We notice now that a liquid-like shimmering substance flows through this tube of light, filling each of our hearts with the combined energies of absolute love and absolute strength.

Intuitively, we each realize that this is the perfected Love of the Divine Father.

The Divine Father telepathically tells us that we are correct in our intuition, and that this "tube of love" will eternally remain connected from Him to each of us.

We notice now the second tube of light.

This tube extends from the Crown Chakra of the Divine Father to the center of each of our own Crown Chakras.

The Divine Father tells us that He has permanently anchored what He calls the "Gridline of God Wisdom."

Through this tubing, the Divine Father tells us that we are now and eternally connected with the Source of God's Wisdom and Light.

We feel a great expanse of light fill every petal of our thousand-petaled lotus, as we sit upon our cushions of light.

Walking toward us is Archangel Metatron, wearing robes of liquid platinum light.

We realize that this is the first color that we have seen since our arrival, and it is magnificent.

Archangel Metatron reveals a light rod composed of pure platinum.

Archangel Metatron walks over to each of us and touches us one by one upon the left shoulder with his light rod.

Upon the touch of Archangel Metatron's platinum rod, an etheric duplicate of his rod is anchored within the left shoulder area of each of us.

As the rod begins to expand until it runs across the back from the left shoulder to the right, Archangel Metatron tells us that he has installed within us the Light Rod of Strength.

Metatron continues to say that by gifting each of us with this rod, we will be able to draw upon Light Itself as a source of immense strength.

This rod, Metatron now states, will support us in our mission and in our lives, acting as an unbreakable support of strength and binding our strength eternally to the Light.

Now coming toward us is His Holiness Lord Melchizedek, wearing robes of a fiery gold essence.

Melchizedek reveals a cup that contains a golden Liquid.

He tells us that encoded within this liquid is the very essence of the Language of Light.

Lord Melchizedek passes the cup to us, and invites us each to sip from this sanctified and blessed liquid.

As we each take a sip and pass it on, one by one we begin to take on a golden hue.

Melchizedek tells us that this liquid light is moving through our entire 12-body system and encoding every level of our being with the ability to decipher, comprehend, and communicate in the Language of Light.

We feel the essence of Divine Wisdom and Grace as we each give our thanks to Lord Melchizedek.

Walking toward us is the Mahatma, in shimmering robes that are luminous with every color in all Creation.

The beloved Avatar of Synthesis, the Mahatma reveals to us that he carries with him a very small replica of his garment in the shape of a headband.

Walking over to each of us, he now gently places the soft rainbow-colored fabric around our head, in a manner that covers our eyes.

We see with our inner vision into the Core Heart of Synthesis, Unity, and Integration.

As these headbands are integrated within each of us, the Mahatma tells us that he has permanently installed the "Rainbow Band of Synthesis" within each of our third eyes.

The Mahatma tells us that we will view both the inner and outer world through the "eyes of synthesis," if it is our slightest desire to do so.

We each now know, feel, sense, and see the reality of the synthesis of all life.

In a blaze of yellow-gold lightening, Vywamus appears.

He extends his hand to reveal a tiny yellow-green seed.

As he walks over to us and anchors a seed within each of our etheric Heart Chakras, Vywamus tells us that the "Seed of all Creation" must grow and blossom first within the heart.

We feel the immense love contained both within the seed and within the touch of Vywamus' hand.

As we sit immersed in the splendor of the love from which Creation flows, Vywamus promises us that we each hold within our own hearts the capacity to express the fullness of this love in all that we venture forth to do.

Now walking toward us is Lord Lanto, in robes of turquoise-blue light.

Lord Lanto holds within the palm of his hand several tiny aqua-colored rods of light.

As Lanto installs one of the rods into each of our thymus centers, he tells us that this rod will put us in perfect timing with the rhythm of all Creation.

Lord Lanto says that from this moment forward, no matter what plane or dimension we will be serving on, all we need to do to be in perfect rhythm with the Divine timing of that specific realm is to tune into the aqua-colored rod that he now installs.

Lord Lanto tells us that we might want to give three gentle taps to the thymus area, whenever we feel we are not in perfect rhythm with the Universe.

We see the majestic figure of Allah Gobi as he suddenly stands among us.

Allah Gobi is adorned in a three-layered robe.

The outer color is a rich blue, the middle color an exquisite magenta, and the inner color the red of a setting sun.

Allah Gobi holds a luminous sphere that radiates the same colors of his robe.

The sphere is aproximately the size of a basketball.

Allah Gobi releases the sphere, which hovers in mid-air and begins to encircle each one of us in a perfect figure-eight.

As we each receive the blessing of the sphere of light, Allah Gobi tells us that we are each being infused with the combined essence of Light, Love, and Will as it exists at the level of the Godhead.

He goes on to say that unless Will is perfectly integrated with Love and Light, it is the "will" of the separative self and not that of the Christed Self.

As the sphere encircles the last person, Allah Gobi tells us that we have been permanently infused with the Divine Will of God, and that it is now ours to bring forth into manifestation whenever we will it to be so.

Before us stands the beatific and resplendent figure of beloved Lord Maitreya, our Planetary Christ.

As he begins to move among us, his pure white robes begin to shimmer with a billion flickers of spiritually charged light.

As he walks by us, one by one we see a faint pink essence interweave with the white light.

He asks that we each touch the hem of his luminous spiritual garment and asks us to gather into our hands a portion of the radiant light.

As we do this, he invites us to place these shimmering lights upon our heads, and to etherically wrap the light from our Crown Chakra around each of our entire bodies.

As we do this, we notice that the small piece of his garment of light keeps expanding and expanding as we drape our entire etheric forms in his luminous robes of purity and love.

A deep and abiding sense of eternal and unconditional love and purity fills us to the core of our being.

Lord Maitreya tells us that from this moment forward we will always be graced by this light essence of pure and total love and purity.

As he now magically fades from our field of vision, we notice another being of light begin to take shape and form before our eyes.

Standing before us is beloved Master St. Germain whose expanded duties recently moved him into the position of the Mahachohan.

St. Germain stands before us in robes of the most exquisite violets and purples.

Above his head is a violet cone-shaped aura, which immediately brings to mind the part St. Germain had to play as Merlin the magician and alchemist during the times of ancient Camelot.

St. Germain takes the cone-shaped aura from his head and places it upon the heads of each one of us.

We notice that while doing this, the aura around St. Germain's head does not diminish one iota, but seems to increase in power and radiance each time he removes it from himself and gives it to one of us.

St. Germain, reading our thoughts, tells us that what we are seeing demonstrated is the "Divine Alchemy of increased abundance through the Law of Giving."

He also tells us that the cone-shaped violet "aura hat" that we all wear will not only serve to transmute and protect us from any negative ego energies that come from outside of ourselves, but that it will likewise help to transmute negative ego energies that emerge from within ourselves.

St. Germain advises us that as soon as there is even the slightest hint of a negative ego thought, emotion, or feeling within us, to instantaneously throw it upward into each of our cones of transmutation.

In doing this, he says, the negative ego energy will be immediately disempowered, transmuted, and purified.

We sit for a moment in the radiance of the Violet Light, enjoying the profound sense of purity, clarity, alchemy, and unity with beloved Master St. Germain that it brings.

Walking toward us now are beloved Lord Buddha and beloved Sanat Kumara.

Buddha and Sanat Kumara magically split into several aspected parts of themselves so that we each have an aspect of Lord Buddha standing at our right side and an aspect of Sanat Kumara standing at each one of our left sides.

Both Masters now reveal to each one of us that they hold in each of their right hands magnificent, golden scepters of light.

Beloved Sanat Kumara touches each one of us upon the Crown Chakra with his scepter, while beloved Lord Buddha simultaneously touches each one of us upon the Throat Chakra with his scepter.

As they do this, we feel a tingling sensation as they each install a small replica of their scepters respectively within each of our Crown and Throat Chakras.

We both feel and know that we have been given a secret initiation into a higher frequency of Divine Wisdom and Divine Creative Abilities.

Lord Buddha and beloved Sanat Kumara confirm this as they confer upon each one of us the Power of Creation in the Name and Wisdom of the Divine Father.

We feel the potency of this incredible blessing, as we observe a moment of silence and gratitude.

We sense the presence of the seven masculine Elohim.

We feel the very aura of Creation envelope and infuse Itself within the very core essence of each of our beings as the Elohim: Hercules, Apollo, Heros, Purity, Cyclopia, Peace, and Arcturus individually bless each and every one of us with the power of the Divine creative masculine energies.

The Elohim tell us that the creative Divine Masculine are energies that are not to be understood through the concrete mind, but are rather to be experienced through the intuitive higher mind.

We sit and receive the enormity of grace and blessings that these beloved Elohim confer upon each one of us.

The Elohim now disappear as mysteriously and magically as they appeared, leaving each one of us with the glorious, wondrous, and powerful sense of positive creativity.

We feel the grace and blessing of the seven masculine Archangels.

One by one each of the Archangels brush us gently with their wings.

As they do this, we are each infused with an aspect of their energy.

First we feel the blessed winged touch of Archangel Michael.

Now the winged touch of Archangel Jophiel.

And the touch of Chamuel.

Now the blessed winged touch of Archangel Gabriel.

The touch of beloved Archangel Raphael.

The winged touch of Archangel Uriel.

And now the touch of Zadkiel.

With each touch of these most blessed Archangels, the feeling of Divine Love, Grace, and Gratitude expands ever greater.

We feel and hear the wings of the Archangels fly off into the colorless light as we take a moment to bathe in their resplendent light and love.

Now, walking toward us is the High Priest of Shamballa.

We each are now filled with a great sense of honor as he moves toward us in luminous robes of light.

We all simultaneously realize that we are being greeted by one whom we are at once exceedingly familiar with and yet somehow unfamiliar with.

The High Priest of Shamballa tells us that what we sense is true, and that it is time to be further acquainted with him on a much deeper level than heretofore experienced.

As we walk in his Divine radiance, the High Priest of Shamballa takes a golden-white circular key from a secret pocket inside his robe, and hands a key to each one of us.

He asks us to place this key between both hands, holding our hands in prayer position.

He asks us to first hold our hands about 3 inches from the Heart Chakra, and about 3 inches above the Third Eye Chakra.

As we do this, he tells us that he has given to each one of us the golden-white key that allows us to freely come and go in the Courts of Shamballa.

We feel the utter profundity of this gift and blessing, as we see the High Priest of Shamballa walk slowly away and merge once again into the pure colorless Light of the Godhead.

One by one, the Chohans of the Seven Rays walk toward us.

As they do, they each simultaneously touch us on the Crown and Heart Chakras, before moving on to the person seated at our left.

First we receive this blessing from beloved Master El Morya.

Now from beloved Master Kuthumi.

Now from beloved Master Serapis Bey.

We now feel the sacred touch and blessing of Paul the Venetian.

Now from Master Hilarion.

We now receive this blessing from Lord Jesus/Sananda.

Now from St. Germain, who is assisted by a Master who we are not completely familiar with yet, whose blessed touch feels like the touch of grace itself.

Finally, beloved ascended Master Djwhal Khul bestows this blessing upon each of us.

As the last among us are touched, we sit in the heightened frequency of all seven major Rays; feeling more fully blessed with "ray integration" than we ever have before.

As we enjoy these incredible blessings, we watch these most beloved Masters magically fade into the colorless light that vibrates here at the level of the Throne of Creation.

The Divine Father once more extends His arms in embrace.

His face is filled with Radiance and Love, as He magnetically calls each one of us toward Him.

We each slowly and reverently rise from our cushions and begin to walk to our most beloved Divine Father.

Divine Father, now, Himself, rises off the throne He is seated upon and walks toward us.

Feeling the profound sense of absolute Love, Wisdom, and Power, the Divine Father embraces us within His very self, and enfolds us with His very being.

We feel a sense of Peace, Protection, and Trust, the likes of which we have never known before.

Let us each take a moment to fully feel the Profundity, Peace, Grace, Wisdom, Protection, Light and Love of He who is the very Will and Power of the Godhead, our most beloved Divine Father.

We take a moment to feel these profound energies.

Filled now with the Energies and Grace of the Divine Father, and with boundless gratitude, we see the sphere encasing our 12-starred Merkabah arising in our midst.

One by one, we very silently and reverently walk onto the Merkabah, and each now take our seats.

Feeling filled with the Essence and Blessings of the Divine Father and each of the Masters who graced our meditation, we feel our Merkabah now begin to move from the Throne of Creation of the 352nd level of the Godhead, and begin its descent back to earth.

We pass through the blessed sanctuary of the Archangels and Elohim.

Descending, our Merkabah carries us through the many realms and dimensions that exist within the Multiuniversal level of Creation.

We descend now, through the various dimensions and realms of the Universal levels of Creation.

And through the dimensions of the Galactic level of Creation.

Descending still further, we move through the realms of our solar system.

And through the various realms of our planetary system.

Slowly we become aware that we are descending through the various vibrational frequencies of our etheric level of reality.

With the full Grace of the Divine Father, we feel ourselves magically departing from our 12-pointed star Merkabah and the sphere that encased it.

We feel our breath become deeper and more grounded as we slowly anchor back into our physical bodies.

We feel that we are fully anchored and grounded within our physical bodies from head to toe.

We now extend our grounding cord into the Heart Core of the Earth Mother.

Each of us sends the gift of Eternal Love from the Divine Father directly into the Heart of the Earth Mother.

We feel a great sense of loving warmth, as in return the Earth Mother sends her great ove up to each one of us, through our individual and collective grounding cords.

Allow yourself to be 100% fully anchored into your physical bodies now.

When you are ready, you may open your eyes

8

The Earth Mother, Pan, Archangel Sandalphon and the Material Face of GOD Ascension Activation Meditation

---

To begin this meditation, close your eyes.

We call forth Lord Melchizedek, the Mahatma, and Archangel Metatron to sweep through us with the Platinum Net, and to clear away any imbalanced energies.

We now ask Archangel Sandalphon and Pan to assist us in this meditation with the Earth Mother and the Material Face of GOD.

We also call forth Archangel Michael to surround us with a Golden Dome of Protection and his Sapphire Blue Light.

We ask Pan and Archangel Sandalphon to attune us to the Devic, Elemental, and Angelic Kingdoms.

Archangel Sandalphon and Pan together now create a crystalline, organic sphere-shaped Merkabah and invites us all inside.

As we enter, we notice that although the Merkabah is translucent, enabling us to see outside, we immediately feel as though we have stepped within a self-contained greenhouse.

The Merkabah seems to have a sky all of its own, with a warm and comforting yellow sun at the center.

We seem to be walking on a pure earth road, with luxurious grassy knolls, flower gardens, and trees.

There are also several streams running throughout the Merkabah.

Each of us finds a seat of our choosing with some of us on very comfortable rocks, others on patches of the soft velveteen grass, still others on driftwood floating in the streams, while some of us find white cottony clouds on which to take our journey.

Now as we are all appropriately seated, the Merkabah begins to rise and we prepare to journey interdimensionally within the loving winged embrace of Archangel Sandalphon.

As the Merkabah begins to move, we hear the sweet, melodic tones of Pan as he begins to play his pipes.

We find that we are traveling down the inner corridors of the earth.

Within our Merkabah we interdimensionally move through the crust of the earth, traveling through rock.

We pass through streams of water and pockets of minerals.

Moving deeper still, we pass through the subterranean cities.

The Merkabah begins to move ever more slowly.

We each feel a great warmth and a deep and penetrating sense of the most phenomenal embrace of love that we have ever felt.

We notice that our Merkabah now sits upon a golden-pink heart, and that it is from this heart that the sublime, all-encompassing love and warmth is emanating.

We step out of the Merkabah and onto the most healing, warm, gentle and yet powerful surfaces that we have ever stood upon.

A love so deep rises from this surface, which is, in truth, the Heart Core of Earth Mother, that we can barely stand.

We now find that the golden-pink Heart of the Earth Mother has enfolded each one of us in her Divine embrace and holds us to her heart, cradling us in her Divine essence.

As we surrender to the embrace of the Earth Mother, we begin to be aware of the beating of our own hearts.

We feel that she is fully synchronizing the beating of each of our hearts with her own.

As the beating of the heart of the Earth Mother and our own become now fully aligned, we feel the deepest sense of love for all life on planet earth that we have ever felt before.

This love now reaches out to every single aspect of life on earth; all kingdoms, all evolutions, all elements.

This love also extends to ourselves and each other, as it flows in perfect rhythm from us to the Earth Mother and back again.

We find that we are once again standing upon the very heart of the Earth Mother.

Filled with overflowing love, we now once again, enter our group Merkabah.

As we begin moving upward through the various levels of the inner Earth, oceans and oceans of blessings flow from our heart into each rock, mineral, stream, piece of soil, and particle of Creation that we move through.

We feel now the potency of our group blessings moving through the inner structure of the earth and healing potential fault lines, rearranging and realigning the very core structure of the earth to one of balance and harmony.

We come now to one of the subterranean cities, and this time Archangel Sandalphon is allowing our Merkabah to land.

He telepathically tells us that we had to experience the full love and blessings of the Heart of the Earth Mother and carry them within our own hearts, before we would be allowed to interact with the beings that populate the inner cities.

We step forth from our Merkabah, radiating the love that the Earth Mother has graced us with.

We begin to walk through beautiful crystalline passageways.

Small aqua inlets form healing baths, as seafoam-green streams flow down violet, golden, and platinum crystal rock formations.

There is an incredible warmth which we inwardly know is coming from a subterranean sun.

The vegetation is lush and beautiful, although much of it is unfamiliar.

Coming to greet us now are a group of inhabitants from this wondrous inner city.

They are dressed in gossamer-type robes, that are at once simple yet indicative of great status.

They tell us that they are ancient priests and priestesses of a very ancient order.

We intuitively know that they are speaking of the ancient and sacred Order of Melchizedek!

We follow them now into the heart of their city.

Their city is built of crystals and is dispersed among their woodlands, glades, and rivers.

They tell us that they live here with no separation between the various kingdoms and species.

A few of them walk us over to a beautiful grassy area filled with bushes, trees, and much flora.

From behind one of the bushes steps forward what we would call a Gnome.

Instantaneously he is joined by Fairies, Elementals, and Devas of various sizes and functions.

The priests and priestesses introduce us and then proceed to have a short conversation with them in an unfamiliar tongue.

They all bow to each other, and the Devas, Fairies, and Elementals disappear into the woods and streams.

The Head Priestess invites us to feel free to come again, but that for now the Divine purpose of unveiling their subterranean city of oneness has been fulfilled.

The entire group of priests and priestesses escort us back to our Merkabah.

Before entering, we bow to them and they bow now to us.

A visible, pink "light of love" flashes between our two groups and our hearts are once again filled to overflowing.

We now once again find our seats within the Merkabah as we begin our journey upwards onto the surface of the earth.

Our Merkabah moves through the final layers of rock and soil and emerges onto the surface of a beautiful field.

Each of us now steps out of the Merkabah, which has the effect of helping us to renew our respect and reverence for the earth upon which we stand.

Pan once again begins to play his pipes.

The music is soft, sweet, and melodious, yet within it we each hear the thunderous voice of Father/Mother GOD saying, "Take off thy shoes for thou art on Holy Ground!"

We know now that it is upon the beloved Earth Mother that we stand and that she is at One with the Godhead.

We understand that we are also at One with the Godhead and share with the Earth Mother, the Goddess, and all of manifested Creation on all planes and levels of existence the "Material Face of GOD."

We feel our hearts beating in complete unison with the Heart of the Earth Mother, as we reverently remove our shoes.

We stand barefoot now and feel the warm grass tickle and caress our feet.

We rejoice in how good, right, and perfect it is to feel the grass and soil beneath our feet.

As we walk through this field, we notice a particularly beautiful patch of flowers.

We very gently touch the stems of the most magnificent magenta roses we have ever seen, as we each bend over to smell the equally magnificent perfume.

As we gaze deep within the roses, each of us now notices that each of the flowers holds within its center a tiny human-like winged figure.

The little ones begin to talk to each of us, telling us how they are the Fairies of the flower, and humbly yet joyfully admit that the exquisite beauty of the flower is a co-creation between themselves, the flower, Pan, the Earth Mother, and GOD.

We now hold out our fingers and the flower Fairies perch upon it much like a bird.

They tell us that they don't normally reveal themselves to humans, but because we come filled with the love of the Goddess and blessed by the Divine Heart of the Earth Mother, they are unafraid.

They tell us now that the more love humanity can give, the more love the many faces and forms of GOD can give back.

They thank us for our love, and disappear once more into the field of magenta roses.

We find ourselves standing by a beautiful stream of water.

Gazing into the water, we see schools of multicolored fish swim by.

Each of us focuses upon our own reflection as the movement of the stream slows down to a placid, peaceful flow.

Looking at ourselves within the water we now become aware on an even deeper level how each of us is, in truth, one of the Physical Faces of GOD.

The feeling of love that this deeper knowingness brings forth is soft, gentle, and motherly.

This love now overflows into the stream, which magically turns into a river and then an ocean.

Gazing into this ocean, we see yet another face of GOD.

We see Mermaids and Mermen, we see schools of Dolphins and Porpoises splashing like children in the water.

We see groups of Whales come now to join the Dolphins, as together they burst forth in their otherworldly song.

We watch the Undines move through the currents of the great ocean.

Turning our gaze upward, we see the Sylphs riding the currents of the air.

From the Heart of the Sun above us, we suddenly become aware that Helios and Vesta, our Solar Logos, are looking down upon us smiling invitingly.

We now step into our Merkabah and take our seats.

As we move through space and a time towards the Sun, Archangel Sandalphon reminds us that there is a Material Face of GOD at every level.

He reminds us that beloved Helios and Vesta are another aspect of the Material Face of GOD!

Our Merkabah lands deep within the Core of the Sun.

We are reminded of the story of Moses and the Burning Bush of GOD upon Mt. Sinai.

We understand completely what is meant by the words, "the bush burns but is not consumed."

For this reason the Core Fire of Helios and Vesta within the Heart of the Sun is safe for us, for by the grace of Sandalphon we visit there now in our own bodies of Fire and Light, to fully experience our blessed unity with the Solar Logos.

As Light and Love are ultimately one as well, we feel the pure essence of Love from the hearts of Helios and Vesta, enter our own hearts.

Filled with more Light and Love than we thought we would ever experience, we once again step back into the Merkabah.

We move higher still within the Material Face of God, until we land now at the Galactic Core.

Here we come face to face with our Galactic Logos, Melchior, to feel the Divine embrace of Galactic Love and Light.

The power at this height is incredible, yet we are able to contain it for it is the power of the Will of GOD perfectly blended and integrated with the Light and Love of God/Goddess.

We magically find ourselves now within our Merkabah, being carried upward to the Universal Core and to the Golden Chamber of Melchizedek, our Universal Logos.

We step out of our Merkabah and move about this chamber of pristine gold.

We are filled with the deepest love we have yet experienced, coupled with the greatest Light and Will of GOD that this journey has taken us on so far.

There is something familiar in these feelings.

Standing before Lord Melchizedek and receiving his sanctified blessing, we suddenly become aware of the source of these feelings of familiarity.

We recall now the priests and priestesses living in the subterranean cities, and the type of love that they radiated and words that they spoke about the ancient Order of Melchizedek.

We become aware now of just how interconnected all of life truly is, and marvel at the bond of love that exists between the Universal Core within the vastness of the Cosmos and the subterranean city which we visited within the Earth's Core.

Melchizedek smiles and says the simple phrase, "All is One," and we know this to be so within every cell, atom, electron, and particle of our entire being.

Our Merkabah carries us now to the Multiuniversal level.

Visions of vast universes dance before our inner eye.

The sound of all Creation, Evolution, and Ascension becomes the music of all the spheres and the symphony of the Material Face of God.

Upward we now travel, until we land at the 352nd level of the Godhead.

Here we are greeted by the Mahatma, as we step out of our Merkabah and into Source.

Standing at the top of Creation, we realize now that there are an infinite number of gridlines, bylines, and interdimensional portals that reach from these vast heights into the very depths of Creation.

We see, feel, and know that all Creation, from the 352nd level through and into the first level and dimension, is one.

We also see, feel, and know now that the formless Face of GOD is completely at one with the form of GOD, on the Material Face of GOD!

The Ain Soph Or is one with Malkuth.

The Divine Father is one with the Divine Mother.

Yin is one with Yang.

Undifferentiated Source is one with that which appears so separate, isolated, and alone on earth.

All is unity.

The being that embraces this unity, whose function it is to incorporate, integrate, and synthesize all of this, is the Mahatma.

As we stand before the Mahatma now, we know Him, Her, Them, to be everywhere and everything.

We also know this of ourselves.

In Divine reverence and gratitude we bow before the Mahatma, who in turn bows to us.

We once again enter our Merkabah to begin our descent back to earth.

As we take our seats within our Merkabah, we feel a unity and connection with pure undifferentiated Source and with the vast and infinite multiplicity of forms within all Creation.

In this place of blissful oneness, we move now through the 352 levels of Divinity back to earth.

We descend through the Multiuniversal level and know that we are ever connected to this glorious realm.

We descend into and through the Universal level, feeling a new and glorious attunement to our Universal Logos, Lord Melchizedek.

Descending further still, we move through the Galactic level, and feel the incredible love of Melchior penetrate every cell of our being.

Now we descend further still, through the Solar level.

We feel the fiery love of Helios and Vesta, our Solar Logos, touch our hearts now with the Hand of Grace.

We move now through the Planetary level, where we receive a special blessing, as Lord Buddha, our Planetary Logos, touches each one of us upon the Crown Chakra.

Our Merkabah keeps descending, until it finally lands on the physical plane dimension of earth.

As we exit now from our Merkabah, we thank beloved Archangel Sandalphon, and Pan, for the magnificent journey of many blessings that they have taken us on.

We slowly reintegrate with our physical vehicles now, as the Earth Mother says she has one more gift for each of us.

She asks us to feel ourselves within our own physical bodies and to attune to her love for each one of us.

As we do this now, we suddenly are aware of how precious and sacred our physical vehicles are in the Divine design and structure and plan of the Cosmos.

The Earth Mother asks us to become fully aware of our grounding cords and to anchor them from our heart eternally into her Core Heart at the center of the earth.

As we do this, we are aware of the most magnificent feeling of gratitude and reverence for each aspect of our physical bodies.

We feel love for our physical hearts, as well as for our Heart Chakras.

The bliss of this love is so great that we can hardly contain it.

Sitting within the intense pink radiance of golden-pink love, we see and feel now the Mahatma extending a golden cord from the 352nd level of Divinity into each of our Crown Chakras.

The Mahatma tells us that this cord is permanently being anchored within each of our 12-body systems so that we will never again loose the realization that Source or the formless Face of God are eternally interconnected.

We again become aware of our physical form.

With great appreciation we look at our hands and feet and know that they are the Hands and Feet of GOD.

We feel the Love/Light of GOD and all the Goddesses pouring through our eyes and blessing all creations.

The Earth Mother now magically holds up a full-length mirror to each of us.

She asks us to fully bless and honor the wondrous, exquisite, and glorious materialization of GOD in the outpicturing of our own individualized form.

We do this now and experience the pure love and acceptance of our physical bodies that the Earth Mother has for us.

We know fully what unconditional love and self-acceptance, for this particular incarnation we are in, truly feels like.

The Divine reverence and love is so great, that we know we are blessed as never before, for we accept and rejoice in the Material Face of GOD, or the Goddess.

We now send this immense unconditional love and reverence through the cord connecting each of our Heart Chakras with the Heart of the Earth Mother.

We feel Her acceptance of this love.

We also feel the perfect rhythmic attunement with her heart and our own.

We focus on the breath of the Earth Mother, the Wind of GOD, and our own breath now.

We know this breath to be one and the same.

We allow our breathing to become deeper and to help us ground fully into our physical forms.

We begin now to wiggle our fingers and toes.

We allow our bodies to arch and stretch.

When you are ready, open your eyes.

Allow yourself to look around the room and make contact with those who shared this sacred meditation with you.

Allow yourself to smile at one another, as you freely, joyfully and fully now, acknowledge them as the Material Face of GOD.

Give yourself a great big hug, as you fully and completely revere your own physical incarnation and existence as the Expression of GOD on earth.

9

Sacred Flames Ascension Activation Meditation

To begin this meditation, close your eyes.

We call forth a Platinum Net from beloved Archangel Metatron, to sweep over the entire group and to clear away any unwanted energies.

We call forth the Cosmic Masters: His Holiness Melchizedek, the Mahatma, Archangels Metatron, Michael and Faith, Raphael and Mary, beloved Quan Yin and Lord Buddha.

We call forth beloved El Morya, Kuthumi, Serapis Bey, Paul the Venetian, Hilarion, Sananda, and St. Germain, along with Lanto, Djwhal Khul and Lady Portia.

We also call forth the Masters and Angels of Color and Sound, and ask for their assistance in helping us fully attune to the frequency of the color and tones that each of the Sacred Flames radiate.

As we feel the blessings of these beloved Masters, we become aware that a flame-shaped crystalline Merkabah surrounds us.

We feel the radiant touch of Light Essence itself, as Archangel Metatron enfolds us within his Merkabah of the most refined platinum light.

As we begin to rise, we notice that there is a translucent quality to this Merkabah that makes its platinum light essence almost colorless.

Within the Divine embrace of Lord Metatron, we begin our journey to the temples of the Sacred Flames.

We travel first to the Sacred Flame of El Morya, the Chohan of the First Ray.

We feel the presence of this most beloved Master El Morya, and the strength of his all-pervading will and discipline, as we glide within the radiance of his ashram into the sanctified temple of his Sacred Flame.

As our Merkabah approaches this holy fire, we see, feel, and/or visualize beloved Archangel Michael guarding this most hallowed altar.

We notice Archangel Michael wielding his Blue Flame Sword of Protection, touching each one of us upon the Crown Chakra with his sword, as though he was bestowing knighthood upon us.

With the touch of his sword we can see even deeper, and we notice that the Sacred Red Burning Flame of the First Ray is also radiating the most rarefied of blue light.

As our Merkabah lands, we each walk up to this Sacred Flame and feel the most incredible sense of Divine willpower and protection that we have ever experienced.

We realize that we are being given the vision and blessing of the esoteric Flame of Will, which burns both red and blue, enabling us to be fully empowered with the Will of God and yet blessed by the Love/Wisdom of God.

This will ensure that, even as we bathe in the frequency of Divine power, will, strength, fortitude, and courage, we will yet know at the core level of our beings that this energy must always be used only in support of the Love/Wisdom of God.

Take a moment now to drink in the frequency of this First Ray Sacred Flame until it is infused within every level of your being.

We once again enter the Merkabah of Metatron.

We are taken now within the hallowed ashram of the Second Ray, where Master Kuthumi, Djwhal Khul, and Lord Maitreya preside.

We feel the energies of pure love/wisdom as we are taken within our Merkabah to the sacred altar that houses the Sacred Flame of the Second Ray.

This flame burns a most intense blue, which is at once soothing, cooling, loving, and inspiring.

We each walk toward this glorious flame and form a circle around this flame that burns in the center of a crystal room.

As we bathe within the emanations of the blue flame, we feel filled with a sense of the most all embracing love coupled with the most profound wisdom we have ever felt.

We know that every cell and atom of our beings are being attuned to these glorious frequencies in a manner never before experienced.

We sense and know that we are being encoded with the secrets of antiquity, as well as with the ability to gradually unfold these ancient truths and bring them forth into our conscious remembrance.

We are also being harmonized with the secret truth and wisdom which governs our solar system, and therefore ourselves.

We know that these truths will slowly reveal themselves to our conscious minds as well.

The frequency of love is so great that it is unfathomable.

We are able to hold it fully within ourselves, as we are each made in the image and likeness of this most profound intense love.

We rejoice, as we are once again reawakened to the beings of love we truly are.

For a brief moment we see beloved Lord Maitreya in his incarnation as Krishna, and notice the blue coloring of his skin.

Before once again entering our Merkabah, we glance at our own etheric bodies as well as each other's and notice that they are also blue in color, the same as Krishna's!

We enter the Merkabah of Metatron and move through the ashram of Serapis Bey and into the golden dome which houses the golden-yellow Ascension Flame.

As we leave our Merkabah to stand around the Ascension Flame, we each feel an immediate acceleration to the very core of our beings.

We are flooded with the burning knowledge that our ascension process is being accelerated a thousandfold just by the grace of being within the presence of this flame.

Our heads begin to tingle as we feel the intelligence of the Universe being activated inside of ourselves.

Soon we feel the same tingling sensation over our entire etheric body and know that each of our 12 bodies are being stimulated with the principle of intelligence, as the hologram of both ascension and intelligence become fully active on every level of our existence.

As we bathe in this most exquisite golden-yellow Ascension Flame, we know beyond the shadow of a doubt that we are the principle of active intelligence itself!

We now are carried in our Merkabah and into the ashram of Paul the Venetian, to the altar that houses the green Flame of Healing and Harmony.

Once again we form a circle around this flame that burns with the most exquisite and subtle variety of hues of green that we can imagine.

If we were to picture a forest at noon being lighted with direct sunlight, each leaf, bush, hedge and blade of grass capturing a different nuance of light and radiating a different glow of green, we could have the merest semblance of the greens that burn upon the Sacred Altar of the Fourth Ray.

As we gaze into this most magnificent sight, we are immediately aware why this is the Sacred Flame and Ray that governs art.

We can even hear within our inner ear the sound of this multitude symphony of green light.

Never before have we felt such profound tranquillity, such complete and total harmony within every cell, atom, electron and particle of our entire 12-body system.

We stand in silent reverence, breathing in this harmony, this healing and this oneness into every aspect of our being.

We feel a special frequency move into our heart centers, and know that in the higher realms love and abundance are one.

We allow this particular facet of love and abundance to permeate us as well.

Feeling a brand new, never before experienced sense of harmony, love and healing, we enter our Merkabah and are carried to the ashram governed by the Chohan Hilarion.

We stand in our circle, this time around the Sacred Orange Flame that governs the Fifth Ray.

Bathing within this orange fire, we feel ourselves awakening to the science that overlights and directs all of Creation.

We feel the essence of the sacred science of all things being encoded, activated and awakened within every cell of our beings.

As we stand in this radiance of this fire, drinking these frequencies within, we become aware of the presence of Master Hilarion.

He telepathically tells each of us that we have been brought to this Sacred Flame, in order to more fully awaken to the "science" of the New Age.

He tells us that we each have a specific role, puzzle piece and mission in order to manifest the New Millennium according to the Will of God, and that the energies from his Sacred Flame will impart to us the "science" of each of our missions.

Master Hilarion departs and we stand in silent reverence, each of us accessing from the Orange Flame of Science that which will assist us in manifesting our mission upon the earth.

Once again we are carried in our Merkabah to the altar of a Sacred Flame.

This time we form a circle around the indigo Flame of Devotion, governed by beloved Master Jesus/Sananda.

Our hearts are immediately filled to overflowing with a feeling of the deepest and most sincere "devotion" we have ever felt.

This devotion is all embracing and flows through our hearts to touch the very pinnacle of the Godhead Itself, as well as to the very depths of the Earth Mother herself.

Our devotion is totally complete and unconditional, embracing all Creation.

We feel a special heart flow of devotion, both to and from beloved Sananda.

We feel equally, the most profound and connected devotion that we have ever felt toward our particular puzzle piece and to the fulfillment of each of our particular ascension missions.

We bathe within this resplendent indigo flame, and drink in the essence of devotion so deeply that we know that no force in the cosmos can ever divert us from fully manifesting our particular mission.

We are one with the essence of pure unconditional, balanced devotion as we enter our Merkabah.

We are now carried to the Heart of the Great Central Sun where the Temple of the Violet Fire is located.

Standing in our usual circular fashion around the Violet Flame, we notice that we each have the actual sensation of taking a bath or shower.

Beloved Master Saint Germain telepathically tells us that this is 100% accurate!

The purpose of the Violet Flame is to transmute all unwanted or less than God perfect energies into energies that are 100% in perfect attunement with God.

The Violet Flame does this by one of two ways.

First, we can offer all our impurities into the Violet Flame.

This method frees us from negative ego emotions, thought forms, negative implants, negative elementals, and negative patterns of any and every kind upon our offering them to the Violet Flame.

The Violet Flame then transmutes and transforms these energies' structures into cleansed and purified streams of energy, which can be reclaimed and used for higher and purer purposes.

St. Germain tells us that by virtue of our coming to this sacred altar, this is now occurring.

The second way that the Violet Flame works in transmutation is by entering the cellular structure within our 12-body system and transmuting negative energy patterns within.

As we now stand gathered around the Violet Flame, this is also occurring.

We are being cleansed, healed and purified both within and without as we bathe in this brilliant and beautiful alchemy.

A feeling of lightness, purity, wholeness, and joy fills each of our entire 12-body systems as we telepathically thank St. Germain.

We enter our Merkabah again and by the grace of Archangel Metatron, we are taken to the altar of the Eighth Ray.

This flame burns the color of seafoam-green, and despite the fact that it is a flame, it has a most cooling effect.

As we bathe within its radiance, we are further cleansed of any and all impurities.

Our Merkabah now carries us to the altar of the Ninth Ray, whose flame burns a beautiful blue-green.

Forming a circle around this flame, we find that we are filled with the most wondrous and joyous feeling.

We smile as we bathe within the radiance of this Sacred Flame as our hearts expand into greater and greater joy.

Now our Merkabah carries us to the altar of the Tenth Ray, whose fire is a most resplendent pearlessence.

As we gather around this Sacred Flame, we feel connected and anchored to our Light Bodies in a deeper and more profound way than ever before.

The glorious light of the pearlescent flame penetrates each of us in a way that creates total infusion with our Light Bodies and allows us each to feel and become an anchor for our bodies of light.

Fully integrated with our Light Bodies, we enter our Merkabah and are carried to the Eleventh Ray altar where the Sacred Pink-Orange Flame burns.

Standing in circular fashion around the Sacred Flame, we each know to the very core of our being that like the flame that burns before us, we ourselves are the bridge to the New Age.

We stand and bathe in this knowingness, as the frequencies of this flame instills within each one of us a strong and active resolve to complete our service mission, as well as specialized encodements on how to accomplish our individual tasks.

Filled with these blessings, we step into our Merkabah.

Archangel Metatron now carries us to the Twelfth Ray, where we see the Planetary Christ, beloved Lord Maitreya, face to face.

We are touched with the deepest and most glorious sense of love yet, as we move into the temple where burns the Twelfth Ray Flame of golden-white light.

Standing around this most magnificent flame, each of us feels our oneness with humanity and all sentient beings in a way never before experienced.

As we continue to bathe within the radiance of this most magnificent light, we feel ourselves completely merged with Lord Maitreya and his love, wisdom and purpose.

Filled with this attunement, we are asked to once again step into our Merkabah to continue our journey.

Having given our thanks and gratitude to beloved Lord Maitreya, we take our leave of this most wondrous golden-white Sacred Flame, secure in the knowledge that we now carry the flame's essence within us.

Lord Metatron now carries us to the Cosmic Flame of Quan Yin.

This flame emits the softest, yet most intense pink light one can imagine.

As we gather around this flame, we are filled with a sense of unconditional mercy and compassion.

We bathe within this soft yet powerful glow until we ourselves are the embodiment of compassion.

We are now carried in our group Merkabah to the inner plane ashram of the Cosmic Christ, His Holiness the Lord Sai Baba.

Our Merkabah lands within the sacred Temple of Cosmic Love, where a flame of the most brilliant golden-pink burns.

This flame is thousands of feet in diameter and its fire extends far above our field of vision.

Within the radiance of this hallowed light we know that the expression "GOD is Love" is 100% literal fact.

We merge within the radiance of this flame of Cosmic Love until we reach the total embodiment of Love itself.

As we again enter our Merkabah, Lord Metatron tells us that we are now ready to go with him to his Sacred Flame at the top of the Tree of Life.

Within his Merkabah we find ourselves in the Kether, or Crown of the Tree of Life.

Archangel Metatron asks us to follow him to the Altar within the Crown where burns his Platinum Flame of Light.

We stand awestruck around this most magnificent of flames, as we realize that the light of this fire extends upward and into the Godhead, the Void, the Ain Soph Or and also throughout the entire Tree of Life.

We feel the blessing of this most wondrous and sacred gift from our host, who has been carrying us within the sanctity of his Merkabah.

Words cannot describe the purity of the Platinum Flame that we bathe in, and we stand in sacred silence.

Lord Metatron asks us to enter his Merkabah once again.

We follow his bidding and realize that he is now taking us to the Flame of Synthesis at the 352nd level of the Godhead.

We find ourselves standing now before the Rainbow Flame of the Mahatma.

The rainbow colors of this flame are infinite, with millions of the most magnificent colors that we have ever seen or imagined.

As we stand around this Sacred Rainbow Flame, we feel a unity with all Creation, both manifest and unmanifest.

We know our oneness with the Divine Mother and Divine Father.

We know *we* are the Goddess and also in complete unity with GOD.

Standing here at the 352nd level of Divinity where all flames merge as one, we find that we kneel in gratitude to the entire Cosmos, both within and without.

We bathe in the exquisite multidimensional rainbow colors until Archangel Metatron signals us to once again enter his Merkabah.

As we do, he tells us that there is one last major flame yet to visit.

Metatron, the Mahatma, Melchizedek, the Divine Mother, and Archangel Michael now appear and take us in our combined Merkabah to the Temple of the Sacred Flame of GOD.

We find ourselves inside the most beautiful temple you could possibly imagine.

In front of us stands the Sacred Flame of GOD, which ignites and sustains all Creation.

This Sacred Flame is so immense and brilliant in radiance that it is hard for the eyes to adjust to even see it.

It is of such a high vibration that it is beyond color.

The beloved presence of GOD now calls us forward one by one, to walk up seven steps onto the altar of the Most High GOD and walk directly into the Sacred Flame and be purified and completely resurrected!

Metatron, the Mahatma, Melchizedek, the Divine Mother, and Archangel Michael now reappear and have you enter their Merkabah as you step out of the Sacred Flame of GOD.

On our return journey home we make one last series of stops for the purposes of reintegration and grounding.

We stop at the ashram, altar and flame of our Universal Logos, His Holiness Melchizedek.

Gathering around this Flame of Multicolored Gold Tones, we all synchronistically remember that we are indeed members of the Sacred Order of Melchizedek.

We bathe in the most glorious golden frequencies as we rejoice in humility and gratitude that we are indeed the earthly, as well as spiritual hands and feet of His Holiness Lord Melchizedek.

Lord Melchizedek promises us that as we stand within the magnificent radiance of his Golden Fire, all fire letters, key codes and sacred geometries that have been dormant within our soul's remembrance shall now be brought forth into full waking consciousness.

He tells us this will not be instantaneous except in some cases, but will unfold petal by sacred petal until clarity is achieved.

We stand in reverence and gratitude until Archangel Metatron signals us to enter his Merkabah again.

We are now brought to the Sacred Flame of Melchior, our Galactic Logos.

As we bathe in the radiance of this Sacred Flame we realize the profound effect that each of these Sacred Flames has and will continue to have upon us.

As we continue to move down the "Ladder of Creation," we stop at the Sacred Flame of Helios and Vesta.

Here we bathe in the copper-gold Sacred Flame.

It is here that all impurities are removed.

Upon completion we continue to move downward to the Planetary level.

Entering again our Merkabah, we find ourselves at Shamballa and the altar of Lord Buddha.

We now find ourselves gathering around the Flame of the Planetary Logos, which is also overlighted by Sanat Kumara.

Here we find ourselves in the pure white light of this flame as well.

While standing around this Sacred Flame, we each vow, if we so choose, to live a life of service, to anchor onto and into the physical and etheric, astral and mental levels of the earth all of the blessings of the Sacred Flames that we have received.

As we bathe within these frequencies, Lord Buddha, Sanat Kumara, and Vywamus give us their combined and solemn vow to help us manifest Heaven upon earth.

Our hearts are dancing with love, joy, light, and commitment as we enter our Merkabah one final time.

We feel the blessings of the Mahatma and Djwhal Khul as they collectively work with each of us in the full integration of all of the Sacred Rays we have experienced.

We take deeper and deeper breaths of integration and synthesis and our Merkabah travels downward to anchor back on earth.

With the assistance of beloved Archangel Sandalphon and the Earth Mother, we now emerge from our Merkabah blessedly transformed by the Sacred Flames.

More resolute than ever in our will to serve, we slowly anchor back into the room in which we are sitting.

We anchor further still into our physical bodies, filled with the Love, Wisdom, and Power of GOD!

When you are ready, you may open your eyes.

10

GOD and the Archangels Ascension Activation Meditation

To begin this meditation, close your eyes.

We call forth all the Mighty Archangels and Elohim and ask for a balancing of the collective energies of this group.

We ask for the balancing of all the energy centers within us.

We call forth the entire Planetary and Cosmic Hierarchy to assist us in the personal balancing of all chakra centers, energy grids and yin/yang energies of each one of us gathered here.

We call forth His Holiness Lord Melchizedek, the Mahatma, and Archangel Metatron.

We ask now for you to sweep your Platinum Nets through the entire room.

We request that you sweep your Platinum Nets through each one of us here; cleansing and clearing any and all imbalanced or unwanted energy from our entire 12-body system.

We ask beloved Archangel Michael to surround us all with his Blue Flame Sword of Protection.

We ask Archangel Sandalphon to keep us anchored and grounded to the Earth Mother in full love and unity, as we prepare to journey interdimensionally.

We also ask for the purposes of further cleansing and purification for beloved Master St. Germain to directly connect us with the Temple of the Violet Flame, which burns in the Great Central Sun.

We request that any remnants of negative or unwanted energies be taken directly into the Violet Flame, where it may be alchemized into the purest energy of love possible, by the power of Divine Transmutation.

We call forth an axiatonal alignment for ourselves and for anyone connecting their hearts with our meditation.

We also request an axiatonal alignment for the entire earth.

From the crown at the top of the Tree of Life, Archangel Metatron sends forth a gigantic diamond-shaped Merkabah.

This special Merkabah which Metatron sends to us has been manifested by him with the assistance of all of the Archangels.

It is not only in the shape of a diamond, but is actually made of the highest quality of pure diamond.

We now enter this magical Merkabah and find that the seats each have the most refined sapphire-blue hue.

As we take our seats we are amazed at how soft and velvety they feel and how we each melt into them, as though each seat was specifically molded with each of us in mind.

As the Merkabah begins to rise, we are aware that we hear a sound very much like the beating of wings.

We sense an incredible depth of love and know that we are, in truth, being guided through this journey by the grace of several Angels.

We are now moving through interdimensional space.

We pass through the seven subplanes of the Cosmic Physical Plane.

Climbing higher still in our diamond Merkabah, we are carried now through the seven subplanes of the Cosmic Astral Plane.

Our journey continues and we move through the Cosmic Mental Plane.

Now, up through the Cosmic Buddhic Plane, we feel a beautiful sense of serenity filling our entire 12-body systems.

We continue to climb higher still, as our diamond Merkabah carries us up into and through the Cosmic Atmic Plane.

We feel an increasing sense of serenity, love, and joy.

Our magical Merkabah does not stop but continues journeying upward into the Cosmic Monadic Plane.

Here we feel an increase of the sense of Divine unity, as though within this realm the core of our true spirit family embraces us in total love.

Climbing higher still we move into the Cosmic Monadic Plane.

Here we feel an all-encompassing resonance and love.

Archangel Metatron tells us that we are moving past the top of the Tree of Life.

He tells us that by special dispensation, he, along with the assistance of the other Mighty Archangels as well as that of the Council of Twelve, the Hyos Ha Koidesh, the Mighty Elohim, the Paradise Sons and a vast host of Angelic Beings, is bringing us to the cathedral of the Mighty Archangels.

We are filled now with a sense of profound love and gratitude, as our Merkabah moves into an enormous outdoor crystalline cathedral.

As the Merkabah lands, we see through the diamond windows the soft glow of a rainbow.

As we step slowly outside, we look up to see that the sky is itself a rainbow of the most subtle, yet luminous colors imaginable.

We also notice that the cathedral is made of crystal unlike any that we have ever seen before.

Each crystal radiates its own color and tone and a sweet musical note quietly vibrates from each individual crystal.

We listen a little closer now, and are suddenly aware that we can hear all the notes simultaneously.

The sound is beyond description or any earthly imagination and we realize now that we are standing within the cathedral of the "Music of the Spheres."

Archangel Metatron is first to greet us.

He subdivides himself in order to individually stand before each one of us in attendance.

He opens the palm of his right hand to reveal a small platinum-gold crystal in the shape of a crown.

He now tells us each individually, that this crystal is symbolic of the Sephiroth of Kether, the Crown of the Tree of Life, and that the crown of the Tree of Life is much like our own Crown Chakra as it is the place that holds the greatest light.

It is also the crown, he says, that is the ultimate link between all other sephiroth, as well as being the link and directing light of all worlds.

He now individually places the platinum-gold crystal within each of our individual etheric Crown Chakras.

As Archangel Metatron does this, he tells us this will permanently establish a gridline of light directly from Kether into each one of us.

The flow of light between Metatron and each one of us begins to immediately stimulate our Crown Chakra and further awaken the facets of the Thousand-Petaled Lotus.

We feel this light permeate our entire being with a frequency that Metatron tells us was not possible to achieve before his gift and activation.

He tells us that by this vast light, all lesser lights shall be ignited.

As he says these words, we feel the light, love and activation of all of the major and all of the minor chakras within our entire 12-body system become charged and activated, accelerating our ascension process ten thousand fold.

We suddenly find ourselves being bathed in an exquisite sapphire-blue light.

We look up and before us stands Archangels Michael and Faith.

They, like Lord Metatron, are exceedingly tall.

They both are exquisitely beautiful, radiating a sublime blue glow from within and without.

Archangel Michael steps forward and encircles us one by one with his Blue Flame Sword of Protection.

He takes his sword and transfers it into his left hand, repeating the process again.

Passing the sword to Archangel Faith, she holds it within both hands and now again encircles each one of us with the Blue Flame Sword.

Archangel Michael tells us that this ritual has forever bonded us with the vibrational frequency of protection, will, and power.

As he takes his sword back from Archangel Faith, she places a magenta-red crystal into the center of each of our Crown Chakras.

Lord Michael tells us that the installment of this crystal completes the bonding between each one of us and Archangel Faith and himself.

He also tells us that we now not only have a deep and eternal bond with himself and Faith, but that we have within our own Crown Chakras an eternal source of protection, strength, and will that we can call upon at any time.

We feel the increased power, strength, and will penetrate and blend with every cell, atom, and electron within us.

We feel stirring within each of us the essence of pure unconditional love, the likes of which we have never felt before.

We each notice that we are standing within the glow of a soft pinkish-blue light.

As we look up we are met by the intense blue eyes of the Archangels Jophiel and Christine.

Archangel Jophiel opens his left palm to reveal a powder-blue crystal in the shape of a heart.

Archangel Christine opens her right hand and reveals a shimmering pink-colored crystal, also in the shape of a heart.

Magically now, they both divide, so that in front of each one of us stands Archangel Christine and behind each one of us stands Archangel Jophiel.

Both Archangels simultaneously place their crystals within each of our etheric Heart Centers.

The radiance of love that we now feel as the blue and pink crystals merge and blend within our Heart Centers is staggering.

We now know the height, depth, and breadth of the enormous love of the Archangels who hold the heartbeat of the Second Ray.

They tell us now, that we have been permanently gifted with an aspect of their love.

They go on to tell us that if ever we feel lonely, isolated, or in fear, or if ever we see any of our brothers and sisters of any kingdom or line of evolution in despair, all we have to do is to take a deep breath and call upon them.

Their crystal of eternal unconditional love will immediately be activated and any sense of loneliness, separateness, or isolation will be loved away by the light of their blessed heart crystal.

We stand for a moment and just drink in the grace of this most precious gift of love, as they tell us that by this sanctified act they have eternally bonded with us through the heart of everlasting love.

We notice a golden-yellow light where, but a moment ago, the light of the Archangels of the Second Ray glowed.

We look up into the wondrous eyes of Chamuel and Charity, the Archangels of the Third Ray.

Their eyes bespeak an unparalleled intelligence which blends with the joyous love that is characteristic of all the Archangels.

Archangels Chamuel and Charity split themselves into several forms so that the pair of Archangels stands before each one of us.

From a hidden pocket inside his golden robe, Archangel Chamuel takes out a tiny scroll.

He tells us that written on this scroll are the fire letters, key codes and sacred geometries that come straight from the Divine Intelligence of GOD.

Archangel Chamuel hands the small scroll to Charity, who installs it etherically within each of our Throat Chakras.

The Archangels of the Third Ray tell us that we have permanent access to the principle of active intelligence that governs all of Creation.

They tell us too, that by installing these scrolls within us they have established an eternal bond with each of us that will never be broken.

They also say that as they have placed these scrolls within our Throat Chakras, not only do we now have access to greater truths but that from this moment forward we will speak only truth to the highest potential possible.

We stand for a moment feeling a new and heightened intelligence moving through our beings, along with a new dedication to pure and absolute truth.

We notice that the yellow light now glows an exquisite shade of green.

We look up into eyes that shine with total harmony and beauty.

As we gaze into the windows of the souls of Archangels Gabriel and Hope, we feel as though we are gazing into the greenery of a lush summer forest.

The Archangels of the Fourth Ray each hold out a shimmering green crystal.

The crystal Archangel Gabriel holds is triangular, and of a rich emerald-green color.

The crystal Archangel Hope holds is circular and almost a golden-green, which sparkles like the leaves of early spring.

Like the Archangels before them, they split themselves so that the pair of them stands before each one of us.

Archangel Gabriel places his triangular crystal within the base of each of our etheric spines.

He tells us that this crystal will activate the principle of harmony within each of us so that from this moment forward, no matter what our particular spiritual and life path brings to us, we shall now bring harmony to it.

He goes on to say that as he now fully activates this crystal, not only will we feel a sense of harmony in all situations, but that we each have the ability to input and/or create this sense of harmony to those around us.

He also tells us to expect a new creativity to come into our lives.

Archangel Hope places her circular crystal into the base of each of our etheric spines.

As she does this, she tells us that she has activated our power to impart both hope and healing.

She tells us that in order for healing to truly occur on any level there must first be a sense of hope.

She goes on to say that one of the things we must each begin to hope for, with an attitude of expectation, worthiness, and a willingness to be of service to both self and others, is abundance.

The Archangels of the Fourth Ray now magically merge back into one of their individual forms.

As they walk away, we feel the base of our spines begin to tingle, and with that we feel a new sense of harmony, hope and abundance.

We also feel ourselves to be Co-Creator Gods.

We become aware that we are standing in the midst of a glorious orange light.

We look up, and there before us stands beloved Archangels Raphael and Mother Mary.

As we gaze into their eyes, it is as though we are looking into the face of kindness itself.

This kindness, however, is perfectly merged and blended with infinite knowledge and an understanding of the science of the Cosmos.

They tell us that what we sense about them is true, and it is these combined attributes that makes them the Archangels of Healing.

As did the other Archangels, Raphael and Mother Mary split into several aspects of themselves so that each one of us has the pair of them now standing before us.

Archangel Mary holds a heart-shaped, pink book within the palm of her hand.

Archangel Raphael holds out what appears to be an ancient manuscript bound in orange, that he holds within the palm of his own hand.

Beloved Mother Mary now installs her colored book of the heart within each of our Third Eyes.

Now Archangel Raphael does the same with his orange-bound manuscript.

We immediately feel great activity within each of our third eye areas.

They tell us now that they have jointly installed and activated the books of love and knowledge.

These books placed within our etheric third eyes allow us to see into the heart of all suffering.

The books also provide us with the concrete knowledge of how to effect healing upon all sentient beings as well as to give us the power to invoke the assistance of the legions of Healing Angels.

We feel the most gentle, sublime grace as it floods our entire beings with a sense of depth and profound knowledge.

We stand within the orange glow, which turns into a gentle rose-color pink, as the Archangels of the Fifth Ray blend back into their original form and take their leave.

As they depart, we know that we are eternally bonded with them and their holy work and that they are never more than a flicker of a thought or prayer away.

We notice now that we are standing in the midst of a beautiful indigo light.

It feels as if the light essence itself is embracing us with pure unconditional and unbounded devotion.

As we look up into the indigo eyes of Uriel and Aurora, the Archangels of the Sixth Ray, we know that we are looking at beings who are themselves the embodiment of devotion.

Uriel and Aurora split themselves into several aspects, so that each one of us stands individually before these glorious Archangels.

Uriel reveals that he holds in his hand a crystalline indigo heart that is no larger than the size of a small pebble.

As Archangel Uriel moves his hand over each of our solar plexus, Aurora places her hand on top of his.

Together now they install their crystalline heart within our etheric solar plexus.

We immediately feel the pure joy of devotion expand and envelop each of our entire 12-body systems, as an indigo glow radiates first from our solar plexus, and then directly into each of our hearts.

They tell us that we are permanently bonded with them and hold within us an aspect of their Archangelic devotion.

They tell us that this devotion will give us the ability to remain dedicated to our ascension mission and various puzzle pieces throughout any seeming obstacles or spiritual tests.

They also tell us that we are each being blessed with the ability to express love and devotion to all sentient beings in a depth and manner that we have never known before.

They now merge back into their individual forms.

As they take their leave, we stay for a moment enjoying the rapture of their pure boundless devotion.

Now we are each bathed in a glorious violet light.

We look up to see standing before us the Archangels of the Seventh Ray, Zadkiel and Amethyst.

As their violet eyes hold us in their gaze, we suddenly realize that they have also split themselves so that an aspect of them stands before each one of us.

Within each of their right hands burns a small violet fire.

Archangel Zadkiel anchors this fire within each of our sacral centers. Amethyst does the same.

Each of us immediately feels this violet fire spread throughout the core of us, of our beings; cleansing and purifying us not only throughout our entire 12-body systems, but also cleansing and purifying each of our 144 soul extensions.

As Archangels Zadkiel and Amethyst merge back into their original forms and begin to depart, they tell us that we each have the ability to immediately access the Violet Flame of purification and transmutation within each of our own etheric bodies.

We stand immersed in a violet glow, and silently give thanks to all of the Archangels who have so profoundly blessed us.

We once again hear in the distance the sound of the beating of wings.

We look up and see the beautiful diamond Merkabah slowly descending into our midst.

We see beloved Archangel Metatron standing by the door and inviting us back into the Merkabah.

We each take our seats as the Merkabah begins to rise.

Looking through the shimmering diamond windows, we each again give thanks for the tremendous grace, gifts, and blessings bestowed upon us.

The crystalline cathedral fades from our view as we begin to travel through the dimensions of time and space.

We feel ourselves descending through the various dimensions of the Cosmic Logic Plane.

Our diamond Merkabah continues to descend, now moving through the various dimensions and realms of the Cosmic Monadic Plane.

We continue traveling through the realms of the Cosmic Atmic Plane.

Now through the various dimensions and realms of the Cosmic Buddhic Plane.

Continuing our descent through the Cosmic Mental Plane.

Now through the various dimensions and frequencies of the Cosmic Astral Plane.

Our diamond Merkabah continues descending through the various realms of the Cosmic Physical Plane as we journey back towards the room where we first began our meditation.

We descend through all the various frequencies, tones, colors, and dimensions of our Cosmic Physical Plane.

We descend through the Logoic Plane.

Descending through the Monadic Plane and now, through the Atmic Plane.

Our Merkabah carries us through the Buddhic realm.

And the Mental realm.

Now, we pass through the Astral realm.

Archangel Metatron moves us within our diamond Merkabah into the etheric counterpart of the room in which we first began our meditation.

He gently and lovingly lowers each of us back into our physical bodies.

As we slowly feel ourselves re-entering our physical vehicles, we simultaneously feel an infusion of the Light of Metatron into every cell, atom and electron.

We become aware once again of our hands and feet.

As we integrate with our physical bodies more and more, we feel the joyous glorious Light of each of the Archangels within our own hearts.

We feel our breath get deeper, as we grow ever more aware of our physicality.

We flex our fingers and toes, and gently move our heads from side to side.

We are now fully and joyously grounded within our physical bodies.

When you are ready, you may open your eyes.

11

GOD, Christ, and the Holy Spirit Ascension Activation Meditation

To begin this meditation, close your eyes.

We call forth the Platinum Net from Lord Melchizedek, the Mahatma and Archangel Metatron, to sweep through each one of us in order to clear away any negative or unwanted energies.

We ask that these beloved Cosmic Masters sweep their Platinum Net across the entire room where we are gathered, as well

We call forth Archangels Michael and Faith.

We ask Archangel Michael to seal us with a sapphire blue dome of protective energy, which he now does with the motion of his Flaming Blue Sword.

We ask beloved Archangel Faith to add her strength of pure unwavering faith to our own.

She does this now, and we instantly feel our hearts open fully and with total trust to the Divine Will, Love and Light of GOD.

As we do this, we feel a soft, gentle, perfumed wind sweep across each one of us.

We become instantaneously aware that the Holy Spirit, Shekinah, has descended upon us.

We feel a sublime and joyous love as the Holy Spirit begins to move like a playful breeze within our Heart Centers.

As we sit within this joyous love, we behold a soft golden Merkabah in the shape of the six-pointed Star of David, descending upon us.

One by one now, each of us enters this radiant Merkabah.

We find that we are each led to a golden cushion, where our names have been written in the Fire Letters of GOD.

We notice that each seat contains two names that belong to us.

We easily recognize the first name, as that is the name by which we identify ourselves within our earthly existence.

The second name, which is scrolled next to the first one, is written in geometrical symbols that we are not yet able to decipher.

We know, however, that this is the name by which God knows us and we feel a deep and penetrating resonance with the name of geometric symbols.

We each now take our seats feeling completely at ease and at peace.

The Merkabah begins to rise.

We feel ourselves gliding gracefully through interdimensional space.

Our Merkabah lands in a most magnificent garden of multi-colored flowers.

Each of the flowers bends forward to greet us as we now, one by one, exit the Merkabah.

We notice that although each of the flowers is adorned in its own unique color and hue, the aura that all of these radiate is a glorious golden-white.

We realize, through a deep inner knowing and a sense of sublime and all-embracing love, that we have been brought to the "Ashram of the Christ."

We walk upon a garden pathway towards a most magnificent golden-white crystalline house.

As we continue walking toward it, we see a figure emerge from within.

The vibration of pure unconditional love merged in total balance with pure absolute wisdom lets us know immediately that it is Lord Maitreya himself!

Lord Maitreya walks towards us, dressed in robes of pearlescent white.

Every aspect of his countenance seems to glow with the same golden radiance.

Lord Maitreya now stands right in front of our group and extends his arms open, to welcome us into the sanctity of his private retreat within his ashram.

As he does this, we notice a soft pink glow flowing from his Heart Chakra directly into our own Heart Chakra and from the palms of his hands into the palms of our own hands.

Lord Maitreya now silently motions us to follow him.

We do so gladly and seat ourselves now upon golden rocks that form a semi-circle near a river of indigo water.

We cannot help but notice how soft and yielding the rocks are, and how comfortably they support each one of us.

We realize that all that exists within this hallowed realm is composed of pure Christ essence, which is pure love and light.

We allow ourselves to completely relax into this Divine Love essence, as the rocks embrace each of us with their own radiance of love.

We sit motionless as Lord Maitreya raises his arms upward toward the heavens.

We watch as the most refined platinum light, so refined that it is almost colorless, descends from the vast reaches of infinity, and falls like a mist around our group.

As we are all enveloped within this glow, we realize that we are being overlighted by the very Presence of GOD Himself!

We feel the Light of GOD penetrate our etheric forms.

We feel the pure Light Essence of GOD blend and merge within the golden-white light of the Christ, and the joyful, loving, light breeze of the Holy Spirit.

We remain motionless now, as every cell, atom, and electron of each of our entire 12-body systems drink in the combined grace of GOD, Christ, and the Holy Spirit.

We take a moment to enjoy the unconditional and eternal love that grows ever more expansive as we blend and merge with it.

As we again open our etheric eyes, we notice that there are two figures sitting on rocks on either side of Lord Maitreya.

To his left sits beloved Master Jesus/Sananda.

To Lord Maitreya's right sits beloved Master Kuthumi.

Kuthumi and Sananda telepathically tell each of us that they have come to assist Lord Maitreya in fully opening us up to attaining total Christ Realization.

Lord Maitreya tells us that until Christ Consciousness is achieved, integrated, and maintained in all circumstances and situations, total unbroken God Communion cannot be maintained.

He tells us that this is so because if any thought, word, deed or action be not of the Christ Consciousness, then it is of the negative ego consciousness of the lower-self, which automatically takes one out of God Communion, if only temporarily.

We are asked by Lord Maitreya to look within and notice the first situation that comes to mind where each of us has the most difficulty in.

Lord Maitreya asks us to observe the particular thoughts or emotional reactions of the negative ego that interferes with unconditional love.

As we each observe our own particular negative ego within a given situation, we simultaneously become aware of a soft pink glow flowing from Lord Maitreya's heart into our own.

He asks us to breath in this gentle, pink light of love.

As we do so, we are each individually guided to direct this light into whatever negative ego situation we are each caught up in.

As we do this, we notice that all negative ego feeling, emotions and psychological patterns begin to dissolve.

We continue to infuse our own personal situations with the pink glow of pure unconditional Christ love.

We notice that the golden-white energy field of Lord Maitreya begins to enter our visualization.

The golden-white light forms a halo around each of our heads.

The combined effect of the golden-white and pink light fills us now 100% with Christ light and love.

Our thoughts are now 100% totally and completely of the Christ mind.

Our feelings are also completely and totally 100% pure Christ love.

We are able to see our most negative ego challenges in all situations with the pure love of the Christed heart and the clarity of wisdom of the Christed mind.

We know now that we are able to totally and completely transform every situation through Christed thinking and feeling.

Placing our attention within our Heart Chakras, we see and feel the radiant splendor of pure unconditional Christ love.

We notice that each of our own Heart Chakras is radiating the same pink glow that is coming from Lord Maitreya's, Kuthumi's, and Sananda's Heart Chakras.

We are telepathically told that while we were each immersed in our visualization of the negative ego feeling versus the Christed love feeling, a small pink crystalline crystal was etherically placed in each of our Heart Chakras.

We are told now that this crystal is made up of the very essence of Christ love itself.

It has been placed there by Lord Maitreya himself, who raises the palm of his hand and fully activates the Christed crystal to its highest potential.

He tells us that it is his eternal gift to us, for we are true lightworkers who seek to feel and demonstrate the highest Christ vibration.

Lord Maitreya goes on to tell us that all we need to do to activate our individual full frequency is to call upon this pure Christ essence.

In essence, all we need to do now to fully demonstrate Christ feeling is to choose to feel love rather than fear.

Lord Maitreya stands up and walks over to each one of us.

He takes from the ethers around his head a tiny diamond crystal that glows with the glorious golden white-light that Lord Maitreya himself radiates.

As he walks over to each of us, a golden-white crystal appears for each one of us.

He places one of these crystals directly within each of our etheric Crown Chakras.

Lord Maitreya tells us that if we ever feel trapped by negative ego thinking all we need to do is to request Christed thinking and our thoughts will immediately become Christed thoughts.

As he says this we see and feel the aura around Lord Maitreya's head expand until each one of us is sitting within the very aura of pure Christed mind.

He tells us that these crystals have also been fully activated and that the power for thinking is ours eternally.

As we sit within this most resplendent aura of divinity, pure Christ light and pure Christ love rearrange our very cellular structure as each one of us becomes fully Christed in thought, feeling, action, and intention.

Receive this most profound blessing now.

As a special dispensation from GOD and the Cosmic Christ principle, or essence, for this meditation, a special anchoring and activation of the different levels of Christ Consciousness Realization will now take place.

GOD and the Cosmic Christ first anchor and fully activate the Anointed Christ Overself Body on the Planetary level.

Be still and receive this blessing now.

GOD and the Cosmic Christ fully anchor and activate the full Christ Consciousness on the Solar level.

Be still and receive this blessing now.

GOD and the Cosmic Christ fully anchor and activate the Christ Consciousness on the Galactic level.

Be still and receive this blessing now.

GOD and the Cosmic Christ fully anchor and activate the Christ Consciousness on the Universal level.

Be still and receive this blessing now.

GOD and the Cosmic Christ fully anchor the Cosmic Christ on the Multiuniversal level.

Be still and receive this blessing now.

GOD and the Cosmic Christ fully anchor and activate the Christ Consciousness on the full Cosmic Christ level.

Be still and receive this magnificent and profound blessing now.

We once again become aware of the perfumed scent of Shekinah, or the Holy Spirit.

We are immediately uplifted by the combined scent of jasmine and lilac.

The Holy Spirit now stands before each one of us, having divided itself into an equal number of forms, to work individually with each of us gathered in this sacred grove.

The Holy Spirit telepathically tells us that there is nothing done that cannot be undone, or more precisely, removed from cellular and Akashic memory.

The Holy Spirit tells us that it is its most important mission to assist all people in the removal of any and all thought forms, feelings, deeds, actions, or experiences that have lodged themselves in any part of the 12-body system.

The Holy Spirit continues to tell us that this is its reason for being, as it is these old, disturbing remnants of the past that keep humanity experiencing a sense of separateness from GOD!

The Holy Spirit asks us to allow ourselves to think upon any situation or experience, no matter how painful or how negative, and to invite it to come into whichever body or aspect of a body the cellular memory of this experience is lodged in.

The Holy Spirit tells us that by virtue of the Law of Free Will, it cannot perform its work without our individual consent and invitation.

For those of us who choose, we open our minds and hearts to all that we perceive as the most negative experience that we have individually participated in.

As we do this the scent of lilac and jasmine grows stronger and stronger, as the gentle breeze of the Holy Spirit grows more powerful.

We allow this beautiful scent to blow through our entire 12-body system.

As we do this we each feel as if iron bands that have kept us in bondage through guilt, shame and fear are breaking up and thawing out, like ice castles melting in a warm summer shower.

We each feel the birth of a new freedom, as that which has been our biggest guilt and shame is dishonored into pure nothingness, by the grace and power of the Holy Spirit.

The Holy Spirit asks each of us if it may continue to undo all the negative memories that have lodged in our 12 vehicles due to mistakes made during our process of evolution.

With our free will, we make the choice to accept its gracious offer.

The scent of its perfume grows stronger, and the force of its wind more powerful as it goes into every nook and cranny of our conscious and subconscious minds, our cellular structure, our permanent atoms, and our personal Akashic records.

The Holy Spirit magically undoes all negative memories, guilt, and shame for any thought, word, deed or feeling that we have had during the span of our incarnations which is not of the Christ mind and heart.

We now feel lighter and freer than we have ever felt before.

The Holy Spirit tells us that although certain memories of negative ego past deeds, thoughts or feelings might come to mind from time to time, they have been thoroughly removed from cellular and Akashic memory and their charge is 100% inactive.

All that remains, the Holy Spirit now tells us, might be the merest flicker of a thought and nothing more.

The Holy Spirit asks us to invite our 144 soul extensions to telepathically link with it at this time, and to let it know if they too would like this clearing and undoing of all negative ego processes.

We sit in silent reverence and gratitude as it performs this rite upon all of our 144 soul extensions, if they give permission in this moment.

As this is done, we feel a growing joy, lightness, and freedom that even now surpasses the freedom we felt mere moments ago.

The Holy Spirit stands once more before each one of us.

The Holy Spirit takes a spherical platinum-gold crystal and places it within the high point of the neck where the skull and neck converge.

It tells us that by the gift and grace of this crystal, if we ever find ourselves in need of disengaging the charge of a potentially volatile situation, we can activate its power simply by calling upon it.

The Holy Spirit tells us that all we have to do is say, "In the name of the Holy Spirit, I call forth the deactivation and the undoing of whatever you want," and it will be done to the greatest degree that Karmic Law permits.

The Holy Spirit tells us that if, for example, a letter was written in haste from the perspective of the negative ego rather than the Christ Consciousness, all we need to do is to call upon it and request the undoing of the effect of the letter.

The Holy Spirit tells us that if karma permits, the letter will be lost or mysteriously disappear. If not, the negative charge will be taken out of it and the letter rendered harmless.

The Holy Spirit gives its promise that it will do these things; however, only when it is permitted for our "highest good."

The Holy Spirit does give us its word that we are each bound to it through the Sacred Crystal and that it has now given us the inner power to "undo" much of what requires undoing by simply letting go and letting in GOD.

Before departing, the Holy Spirit also reminds us that we have each been greatly blessed by the Christ.

The paths we walk and the interactions we have can very easily be brought forth through the Christed mind and the Christed heart, both of which are now fully activated within each of us.

Before blending back into the wind, the Holy Spirit lightly touches us simultaneously on the forehead and the back of the neck, where it places its platinum-gold sphere-shaped crystal.

We watch now as the many forms of the Holy Spirit merge back into one form.

The Holy Spirit spreads open its arms and merges with the breeze.

We give silent gratitude as we feel the Holy Spirit riding with the wind, and smell now the perfume of jasmine and lilac within our own aura again.

We notice that the beloved Masters Lord Maitreya, Sananda, and Kuthumi walk toward us.

They telepathically ask us to follow them.

We find ourselves once again standing in front of our crystalline Star of David Merkabah.

Master Kuthumi walks toward us and raises his hand now in blessing.

He tells us that we are fully realized Christed beings.

Touching each one of us simultaneously on the Heart and Crown chakra, he gives the blessing to go forth to serve and teach in the name of the Christ.

Master Sananda walks toward us.

He individually touches each of us on the Heart Center.

As he does this, he places an indigo-colored rose etherically within our Heart Chakras.

Sananda tells us to go forth to serve and to teach.

Lord Maitreya now divides himself as did the Holy Spirit.

Standing before each of us at once, Lord Maitreya takes both our hands into his own.

He looks heavenward now and speaks the words, "Lord, let the Rain of Blessings fall."

We now find ourselves standing within a "light, love, and power shower" coming straight from the Godhead Itself.

The light, love, and power at first seems to be totally colorless.

It now takes on a distinctly platinum hue.

Now platinum-gold.

Now gold.

We find ourselves immersed in a "light, love, and power shower" of the most sublime and magnificent array of colors beyond imagination.

We now feel at once both comfortably cool and comfortably warm.

Our individual hearts seem to fill all of Creation and beyond.

Our love knows no bounds nor does the light, which we are drinking in with every particle of our beings.

We look down at ourselves and at one another and notice that we ourselves are now emanating the rainbow light.

Each of us also has a golden-white aura, much like Lord Maitreya's, with a radiance of pink coming forth from our individual Heart Chakras.

Lord Maitreya, who is still bilocated in various bodies and holding each of our hands within his own, looks deep into our eyes.

With a penetrating gaze that defies description, he says the words, "I and my Father are One."

We realize that we are saying the words with him.

Letting go of our hands, the many forms of Lord Maitreya merge back into one form.

Intuitively we know it is time for us to go.

We watch now as Lord Maitreya walks down the floral pathway and into his crystal retreat.

We once more enter our Star of David Merkabah.

Moving interdimensionally through time and space, we travel back to the place where we have begun our meditation.

We now feel 100% cleansed and purified.

We feel totally and completely that the mind and heart that is of Christ is also within each of us.

We feel, as we settle more and more deeply within our physical vehicles, that there is no separation between GOD and each of us.

As we fully integrate into our physical bodies, we still smell the faint scent of jasmine and lilac permeating our aura.

When you are ready, you may open your eyes.

12

GOD and the Godforce Golden Chamber of Melchizedek Ascension Activation Meditation

---

To begin this meditation, close your eyes.

We call all the masters of the Planetary and Cosmic Hierarchy to help in this meditation.

We call forth Melchizedek, the Mahatma, Metatron, and Archangel Michael, to bring forth a Platinum Net to remove any and all imbalanced energies.

We now call forth to His Holiness Lord Melchizedek, the Seven Chohans, Djwhal Khul, Lord Maitreya, and Lord Buddha, to provide a gigantic golden crystalline Merkabah for all in attendance.

We ask now to be taken spiritually to the Golden Chamber of Melchizedek in the Universal Core.

We call forth from Melchizedek each person's 144 soul extensions, from their Monad, or Mighty I Am Presence, to join us if they choose to for this meditation.

For our first ascension activation in the Golden Chamber, we call forth the Earth Mother, Pan, Archangel Sandalphon, and the mountain of Mt. Shasta, who now combine together for a special ascension attunement and alignment to the vortex of Mt. Shasta, so that all in attendance may be similar vortexes for the Light and Love of GOD in our daily lives.

We call to the Seven Chohans, for the opening of all chakras, the Ascension Chakra, all petals, chambers, and facets of all chakras.

We call to the Seven Chohans, Djwhal Khul, and Helios and Vesta, for an anchoring of an "ember of the nine Sacred Flames" of each of the Seven Rays, plus the Ray of Synthesis, and the ray and flame from the Solar Core, into each person's Heart Chakra.

Be still and receive this blessing now if you would like to receive this blessing and activation.

We call to the Lord of Sirius for the anchoring and activation of the "Scrolls of Wisdom and Knowledge," from the Great White Lodge on Sirius.

We call forth Sanat Kumara, Vywamus, and Lenduce, for help in establishing each person's planetary and cosmic Antakarana, back to each person's oversoul, Monad, and to GOD.

We call forth the Lord of Arcturus and Commander Ashtar and the Ashtar Command, for the complete illumination of each person's etheric nadis and acupuncture meridians for full planetary and cosmic ascension realization.

We call to the Archangels, for the full anchoring and activation of our fifty chakras, which takes us through planetary ascension.

We also request, from the Archangels, the anchoring and activation of our 330 chakras, helping us to move in the direction of fully realizing cosmic ascension on earth.

We call to Melchior, the Lord of Arcturus, Osiris, and Vywamus, for the permanent anchoring and activation of our 12 bodies, including the Solar, Galactic, and Universal bodies.

We call forth to the 14 Mighty Elohim, for the anchoring and activation of the Yod Spectrum and the Ten Lost Cosmic Rays.

We call forth to the Mahatma, for the anchoring and activation of the Deca Delta Light Encodements and Emanations from the Ten Superscripts of the Divine Mind.

We call forth to Melchizedek, the Mahatma, Metatron, and the Divine Father, for the highest possible building of our Light Quotient at this time.

We call forth to the Divine Mother, Sai Baba, Mother Mary, Quan Yin, Isis, Lord Maitreya, and Sananda, for the highest possible anchoring of our Love Quotient at this time.

We call forth to Helios and Vesta, Allah Gobi, and Sai Baba, for the highest possible integration and cleansing of our soul extensions from our Monad and our Higher Group Monadic Consciousness, that is available to us at this time.

We call to the Mighty Archangels, for a permanent anchoring and activation of the Twelve Heavenly Houses and Twelve Cosmic Stations.

We call forth to Melchizedek, for the anchoring and activation of the Star Codes of Melchizedek.

We call forth the anchoring and activation of the Light Encodements of the Mahatma.

We call forth the anchoring and activation of Melchizedek's transmitting system into our chakras, and ask that it be tuned-up to each person's highest potential.

We now call forth the seven Planetary Logoi, and the six Buddhas of Activity, for a special ascension acceleration for all that are gathered here in the Golden Chamber.

We now call forth the Great Divine Director and the Lords of Karma, for a special dispensation of cleansing and clearing of all our karma.

We now call forth Commander Ashtar and the Ashtar Command for a cleansing and clearing of our Monad.

We ask Lord Buddha, Lord Maitreya, Allah Gobi, and St. Germain, to now step forth and balance each person's chakra system, entire 12-body system, and remove now all negative implants, elementals, and any and all negative energy.

We now call forth Melchizedek, the Mahatma, Metatron, and Archangel Michael, for a cleansing and clearing back to our original Covenant with GOD.

We now call forth Archangel Michael, for the anchoring and activation of the "Language of Light," for each person in attendance, from the 352nd level of Divinity.

We call to Lord Buddha, Lord Maitreya, St. Germain, Allah Gobi, and the Seven Chohans, for the permanent anchoring and activation of the Great Central Sun into the core of our being.

We call forth to the Source of our Cosmic Day and to Melchizedek, for the anchoring and activation of the "43 Christed Universes."

We call forth to the Divine Mother, Mother Mary, Quan Yin, Isis, Pallas Athena, Lady Nada, Portia, the Goddess of Liberty, Lakshmi, Lady of the Sun, and Vesta, for the permanent anchoring of the greater flames of the Oversoul, our Monad and Mighty I Am Presence, into the lesser flame of the personality and/or soul incarnated on earth.

His Holiness Lord Melchizedek now takes the entire group into a secret chamber, within the heart of the Universal Core, where no large gathering of initiates and masters from earth has ever entered before.

As we now collectively step into this secret chamber, we see before us the Sacred Fire of the Universal Core, burning brilliantly on a golden altar.

This is the sacred fire that is the core and very center of the Melchizedek universe we all live in.

Melchizedek, with a wave of his sacred rod, gifts all in attendance with an "ember" of his Sacred Fire, and places it very gently and delicately in each person's Third Eye.

This most blessed and sanctified gift of Melchizedek is now being given, he says, for the purpose of solidifying each person in attendance in eternal connection with him.

Receive this most sacred blessing now, from Melchizedek himself.

Melchizedek has a seven-part final surprise and gift for all in attendance.

This surprise might be called the "seven-part Revelation from GOD," as Melchizedek's and GOD's final gift and blessing.

To begin this seven-part revelatory surprise, His Holiness Lord Melchizedek gathers us all up now in his golden crystalline Merkabah and takes us as a group, with the help of the Mahatma, Metatron, and Archangel Michael, back to the Throne of Grace at the 352nd level of Creation.

As we arrive again, we are greeted by the Cosmic Council of Twelve and the Twenty-Four Elders that surround the Throne of Grace, as well as the Divine Mother, the Divine Father, the Elohim Councils, all the Archangels, the Holy Spirit, and the entire Planetary and Cosmic Hierarchy.

The first revelatory surprise GOD, Melchizedek, the Mahatma, Metatron, and Archangel Michael have in store for us, as an initial purification directly from GOD, is the anchoring of a "match stick's amount" of Cosmic Fire directly from GOD around each person here and the entire group.

The purpose of this Cosmic Fire is to burn away any last remnants of astral, mental, etheric and/or physical dross that is not 100% of the Melchizedek/Christ/Buddha Consciousness.

Be still and receive this ray of Cosmic Fire directly from GOD now if you would like to receive this purification.

The second revelatory surprise and gift from GOD and the Godforce is an anchoring and activation from the "Cosmic Treasury of Light."

GOD and the Godforce now anchor and activate the "Light Packets of Information" from the Tablets of Creation, the Elohim Scriptures, the Torah Or, the Cosmic Book of Life, and the Cosmic Ten Commandments.

Be still and receive these "Cosmic Light Packets" now to each person's highest spiritual potential if you would like to receive this gift.

The third revelatory surprise and gift from GOD and the Godforce is to now call forward the entire Planetary and Cosmic Hierarchy.

We now ask from GOD and the Godforce for the merging of the Light Bodies of this entire celestial group with the group body of all earthly participants here, for the purpose of greater planetary world service.

If you choose to receive this cosmic merger, then be still and receive this blessing now.

The fourth revelatory surprise and gift now comes directly and singularly from GOD Himself.

GOD's gift is to give each person here the anchoring and activation of the Light Body of GOD.

If you would like to receive this gift of all gifts, and blessing of all blessings, be still, and receive this blessing now.

We now ask that this gift also be given to the Earth Mother, to help her in her physical and spiritual evolution.

The fifth revelatory gift and blessing comes directly from GOD, Melchizedek, the Mahatma, Metatron, Archangel Michael, the Twenty-Four Elders, the Cosmic Council of Twelve, the Divine Mother, the Divine Father, the Elohim Councils, Sai Baba, the Archangels, the Cosmic Christ Essence, and the Holy Spirit.

These great and noble beings, led directly now by GOD, raise their combined light rods into the air and bring them forward in a sweeping fashion.

This sweeping motion of the light rods clears the spiritual and energetic way for planet earth and all sentient beings to move with Godspeed within the new millennium.

GOD now steps forward for His last individual and singular gift and blessing, which is His sixth revelatory anointment that He will be giving during this meditation.

GOD steps forward now to anchor and fully activate from the "GOD Core of Creation" for all here, that which has esoterically been spoken of as "the Light, Love, and Power Packets of GOD."

If you would like to receive this gift of all gifts, and blessing of all blessings, be still, and receive this ultimate cosmic ascension activation now.

GOD and the GOD Force, and the entire Cosmic and Planetary Hierarchy, now have one final gift for all here and for the earth and all sentient beings.

This final and seventh gift from GOD and the entire GOD Force is one final "Light and Love Shower," infused by the full Power and Will of GOD, and the entire GOD Force.

Let us receive this "Light and Love Shower" of all "Light and Love Showers" now.

GOD and the entire GOD Force now has one final loving and humble request to make of all light, love, and power workers here who have received these blessings.

GOD and the GOD Force hereby officially and lovingly requests that each person receiving these gifts make the firm commitment on your return to earth to act as "Transmitters and Resolute Masters," to give forth to your brothers and sisters in an unceasing fashion the unconditional love and light, you have received so generously and graciously from GOD and the entire GOD Force today.

Let us all now take a few moments of silence to answer this request from GOD and the GOD Force, in the silence and sanctuary of your own heart, as you personally feel comfortable doing.

In this poignant period of silence where we have the rapt attention of GOD and the Godforce, is now also a perfect time to say any personal prayers for yourself, your spiritual mission, for family, friends, students, pets, and for the entire planet.

We will now take one minute of silence to do this.

We now call forth our inner plane spiritual hosts and request to now reenter Lord Melchizedek's golden crystalline Merkabah.

Let us feel ourselves now very slowly and gently begin to leave the Throne of Grace and begin moving from this Cosmic level of GOD, to the Multiuniversal level of Divinity.

Feel the Merkabah continue to descend now, back through the Universal Core and level of Melchizedek's ashram and sanctuary.

Continuing to descend now, through the Galactic Core level of Melchior.

Descending further now, through the Solar Core and Solar regions of Helios and Vesta.

Descending further still now, through the Planetary Core and Planetary levels of Lord Buddha and Sanat Kumara.

Gliding now back towards earth, where Pan and the Earth Mother welcome us with a loving embrace.

Let us now take one last moment to inwardly thank His Holiness Lord Melchizedek, for being our celestial guide and caretaker on our journey back to Source today.

Feel yourselves now easily and comfortably enter your physical body, bringing with you total recall and complete integration of all the Light and Love received from GOD and the Masters in the celestial heavens of GOD.

When you are ready, open your eyes and take a moment to share all the love and light you feel with your brothers and sisters here.

13

GOD and the Actual Wesak Ceremony Meditation

To begin this meditation, close your eyes.

We begin by calling forth the entire Planetary and Cosmic Hierarchy, including all the Archangels, Angels, and Elohim, to help in this meditation.

We also call forth the anchoring and activation of our 12 Higher Bodies, including the Zohar Body of Light and the Anointed Christ Overself Body.

We call forth the full opening now of all our chakras, all the petals in all the chakras, and all the facets of each individual chakra.

We are now literally going to soul travel together, to the Wesak Valley in the Himalayas.

There we will experience the actual Wesak Ceremony conducted by the inner plane Ascended Masters.

This ceremony has been going on every year at the Taurus full moon for eons of time.

Let us now prepare ourselves for this holy and sanctified experience with a moment of silence.

We now call forward our inner plane spiritual hosts, and ask for the creation of a group Merkabah in the shape of a gigantic holographic crystalline sphere of light.

We ask now to be taken to the Wesak Valley, in the Himalayas, to experience the actual Wesak Ceremony.

As we travel now through time and space, feel your energies blending with all the other groups that are participating in the Wesak Ceremony around the globe this night.

Let us feel ourselves now descending into the actual Wesak Valley, joining all the other Ascended Masters, initiates and disciples.

See and/or feel the presence of Lord Maitreya, St. Germain, and Allah Gobi.

See these three masters standing in a triangular formation around a bowl of water that sits upon a very large crystal.

See, feel, and/or visualize all the rest of the masters of the Spiritual Hierarchy standing in a circular fashion around these three masters.

Just prior to the precise moment of the rising of the full moon, which is now upon us on the inner plane, the expectancy and excitement begins to build.

We now begin by calling forth a permanent anchoring of our Higher Self and Mighty I AM Presence.

We watch in profound joy as Helios and Vesta, our beloved Solar Logos, make their descent toward the Wesak Valley.

Helios and Vesta now take their place as one, just above the sacred spot where Lord Buddha will soon descend.

All in attendance hold silent reverence, as Helios and Vesta now anchor and activate a "Golden Halo of Light" around each person's Third Eye and Crown Chakra.

This Divine dispensation will serve as a baptism of Light for this entire incarnation and beyond, to connect you permanently with your solar Source.

Now descending from the Galactic Core is our beloved Galactic Logos, Melchior.

He comes with the specific mission of assisting us to fully anchor and utilize our Light Bodies upon the physical plane.

Melchior does this now by bringing forth a special spiritual current and electrical charge of energy into our chakra column and 12-body system.

This Divine dispensation is now also being fully anchored into the etheric/physical vehicle.

Melchior now takes his place next to Helios and Vesta.

Now from the Universal realm comes His Holiness Lord Melchizedek.

Melchizedek forms the third part of the "Cosmic Trinity," which floats just above the sacred place where Lord Buddha will appear shortly.

Melchizedek comes not only to honor Lord Buddha and the sacred ceremony of Wesak, but also to honor and assist the 144,000 who have come forth from his sacred heart to assist in earth's evolution.

He comes also to honor and bless all the Cosmic and Planetary Masters in attendance, as well as planet earth herself.

As a special activation for the Wesak Ceremony to institute this purpose, Melchizedek brings forth now his Rod of Light, and touches each person's Crown Chakra.

This causes an instantaneous "ring of fire," in the form of a figure-eight, to appear in each person's chakra column and entire auric field.

This "ring of fire" in the form of an infinity sign, serves to activate on a permanent basis each person's entire chakra system, and enormously enhances each person's auric field and Light Body on all planes of existence.

This Melchizedek infusion fills and bonds each person eternally, with an impenetrable field of Melchizedek light, love, and power.

Feel now the added energies of the "Silent Watchers"—on a Solar, Galactic, and Universal level—come pouring in to add to this sanctified moment.

Take a few moments now to bathe in these glorious blessings given forth by our Universal Logos and the "Silent Watchers."

Sacred ritualistic movements and mantras now sound forth under the guidance of the seven Chohans of the Seven Rays.

As the moment of the rising moon now takes place, a supreme and unparalleled stillness, settles down upon all in attendance.

All Cosmic and Planetary Masters, initiates, and disciples turn with great expectation toward the northeast.

In the far, distant northeast, a tiny speck can be seen in the sky.

This speck gradually grows larger and larger, and the form of the Buddha, seated in a cross-legged position, appears.

He is clad in a saffron-colored robe and bathed in light and color, with his hands extended in blessing.

While hovering above the bowl of water, a great mantra is sounded forth by Lord Maitreya that is only used once a year at Wesak.

This invocation sets up an enormous vibration of spiritual current. It marks the "supreme moment of intensive spiritual effort" of all initiates and masters in attendance, for the entire year.

In this moment, let us watch Lord Buddha hovering over this bowl of water transmitting his Divine and Cosmic energies into this water.

Lord Buddha, our Planetary Logos, brings forth his Rod of Initiation.

He now anchors into each person in attendance the Divine attributes of "peace" and "tranquillity."

Lord Buddha now states that these Divine attributes that are now being anchored are two of the most powerful Christ/Buddha qualities in the universe.

Feel the "peace" and "tranquillity" now begin to permeate every atomic particle of your being.

These two qualities, Lord Buddha now states, will serve as a type of spiritual anchoring and activation for all in attendance, on the inner and outer planes.

Helios and Vesta, Melchior, His Holiness Lord Melchizedek, and the Silent Watchers now add their combined outpouring of energy into this already sanctified bowl of water.

This water now takes on an intensity of cosmic vibrational frequency never before given forth.

The frequency of grace itself keeps building and building, flowing both into the water and through Lord Maitreya.

The energy is then sent forth by Lord Maitreya to the entire Spiritual Hierarchy, and into all of us who form a part of this hierarchy on earth.

Feel this massive downpouring of cosmic energies from the Planetary and Cosmic Hierarchy now flow through us.

As these energies move through us, we feel ourselves being transformed into pure vessels of Divinity.

We now allow these most rarefied and holy frequencies of Divinity to flow out into the world and into the very core of the earth herself.

As these energies continue to pour in, see the bowl of water that sits on the large crystal, being passed around the gathered crowd.

See and feel yourself taking a sip of this most holy, blessed, and sanctified water.

Take the essence of light and love from this water and allow it to integrate into every cell, molecule, atom, and electron of your being.

See yourself now walking toward Lord Buddha, Lord Maitreya, and Sanat Kumara.

Feel the radiance of pure love flowing to you from them, as well as the Cosmic Trinity of Helios and Vesta, Melchior, and His Holiness Lord Melchizedek.

Stand now before these glorious masters, and share with them on the inner plane as to what you feel your service work, mission, and puzzle piece is in God's Divine Plan on earth.

Take this time also to make any prayer requests to GOD and these masters, for help in manifesting your mission.

Also, make any personal prayer requests, on behalf of yourself or others.

Let us now take thirty seconds of silence to allow you to make these prayer requests.

Feel and visualize these prayers being answered.

Know that you have the full love and support of GOD and these most beloved Cosmic and Planetary Masters.

You now move away from the crowd, almost gliding rather than walking.

You find yourself by a small lake surrounded by magnificent flowers of every color.

Appearing above you now are the 14 Mighty Archangels and the 14 Mighty Elohim.

Feel now these Archangels and Elohim surround and caress your auric field with the touch of their gentle wings and arms.

Immediately feel a downpouring of cosmic current, directly from the Archangelic and Elohim realms.

Feel your entire 12-Body System now become illuminated with unconditional love and translucent light.

This Divine dispensation will have an enormous accelerating effect on each person's path of initiation and ascension, as a special gift from the Archangels and the Elohim.

Bathe and completely soak in these blessings given forth by the 14 Mighty Archangels and the 14 Mighty Elohim for this Wesak Ceremony.

As a final Divine dispensation for this actual Wesak Ceremony, the Beloved Presence of GOD steps forth and now anchors and activates within each person's heart a thousandfold increase of the radiance of each person's Threefold Flame, as His gift on this most holy and sanctified occasion.

Be still and feel a most rarefied "Divine Shaft of Light" now enter your Crown Chakra and move down your chakra column to ignite your own personal Threefold Flame, with this most sublime and sanctified blessing from the Beloved Presence of GOD Himself!

Now allow yourself to integrate into the core of your being the full totality of all the Wesak energies set in motion by GOD, Lord Buddha, and this sanctified gathering of Planetary and Cosmic beings.

Find yourself once again magically standing within the ceremonial circle and gathering where the large crystal and bowl stand.

See, feel, and visualize Lord Buddha begin to rise and make his ascent in the lotus posture, and begin to now float back to the northeast to the realm from whence he came.

As Lord Buddha leaves, he raises his right hand, palm face up in blessing and love to all who are gathered here on this most joyous and sanctified occasion.

As Lord Buddha again becomes a small speck in the distance, watch now as Helios and Vesta, Melchior, and His Holiness Lord Melchizedek also make their ascent.

Feel again the depth of the blessings given forth, as these glorious beings once again return to the vast cosmic realms wherein they dwell.

See and feel the arrival of our inner plane spiritual hosts, with their gigantic holographic, crystalline sphere of light Merkabah.

Feel yourself now entering this Merkabah; in total oneness, joy, and love.

Feel again the tremendous illumination of energies in your auric field, which has been vastly expanded by your participation in this experience.

Also feel an enormous expansion of love and unity for all your brothers and sisters who have shared this experience with you.

Feel now the group Merkabah begin to rise into the air above the Wesak Valley.

See and feel the Merkabah floating now, high above the Himalaya Mountains, and begin its journey back.

Feel the Merkabah traveling through time and space, and magically now beginning to descend toward the earth once again.

Mother Earth now welcomes us back with open arms and an open heart to her sacred ground, and into this room.

Feel yourself now gently entering your physical body, bringing all the light and love you have just experienced, fully and permanently with you.

When you are ready, you may open your eyes, as the energies continue to pour in…

14

GOD
and the Construction of your Light Body, Love Body and Power Body Ascension Activation Meditation

---

To begin this meditation, close your eyes.

We now call forth the entire Cosmic and Planetary Hierarchy to help in this meditation.

We call forth from the Cosmic and Planetary Hierarchy a Platinum Net to cleanse and remove all negative and imbalanced energy.

We now focus this meditation first on the construction of our Light Body.

To do this, we call forth Archangel Metatron to bring forth his platinum crystalline Merkabah for all in attendance.

We ask now to Archangel Metatron to take us in our spiritual bodies to his platinum temple at the 352nd level of Divinity.

As we arrive in our Merkabah, we are infused and surrounded in the most brilliant, platinum, sparkling light you have ever seen or experienced.

The entire temple is made up of this most rarefied, sparkling substance.

This is the first time in earth's history that disciples, initiates and ascended beings have been allowed into this sanctified, holy abode of Archangel Metatron.

Here Archangel Metatron begins the advanced construction of building each of our Light Bodies by fully anchoring and activating the Anointed Christ Overself Body, the Zohar Body of Light, and the Overself Body.

Metatron also now activates each of our Electromagnetic Bodies, Gematrian Bodies, Epi-Kenetic Bodies and Eka Bodies.

Master Kuthumi now steps forward with Djwhal Khul to anchor each person's Oversoul and Monadic Body permanently into each person's soul and personality on earth.

Lord Buddha steps forward in golden, radiant form to anchor and activate each person's Buddhic Body.

Master Hilarion steps forward to fully anchor and activate each person's Atmic Body.

Sananda now steps forward to anchor and activate each person's Monadic Blueprint Body.

Lord Maitreya steps forward to anchor and activate each person's Logoic Body.

We call forth Portia and Lady Nada to fully anchor and activate each person's Higher Adam Kadmon Body.

We call forth now to Helios and Vesta to fully anchor and activate our Solar Body.

We call forth to beloved Melchior, our Galactic Logos, to fully anchor our Galactic Body.

We call forth to Lord Melchizedek, our Universal Logos, to fully anchor and activate our Universal Body.

We call forth to Isis, Osirus, Thoth, and Serapis Bey to fully anchor and activate our entire 12-Body System.

We call forth to the 14 Mighty Archangels of the Seven Rays, to fully anchor and activate our Multiuniversal Body.

We call forth to the 14 Mighty Elohim to fully anchor and activate each of our Elohistic Lord's Bodies.

We call forth now to the Paradise Sons to anchor our Paradise Son's Body.

We call to His Holiness the Lord Sai Baba to fully anchor and activate our Causal Body, which surrounds our Oversoul, and ask Sai Baba to fill it with good karma.

We call forth to El Morya now to fully anchor and activate each person's Mayavarupa Body.

We call forth to Paul the Venetian to anchor and activate each person's Ascension Body of Light.

We call forth Mother Mary, Quan Yin, Isis, Vesta, and Lakshmi to fully anchor and activate each person's Cosmic Astral Body.

We call forth Sanat Kumara, Vywamus, and Lenduce to fully anchor and activate each person's Cosmic Mental Body.

We call forth now the Lord of Sirius, the Lord of Arcturus, and Commander Ashtar to fully anchor and activate each person's Cosmic Buddhic Body.

We call forth Archangels Michael and Faith to fully anchor and activate now, each person's Cosmic Atmic Body.

We call forth to the Cosmic Council of Twelve to fully anchor and activate each person's Cosmic Monadic Body.

We call forth the "24 Elders that surround the Throne of Grace" to fully anchor and activate each person's Cosmic Logoic Body.

We call forth the Heavenly Father and Divine Mother to fully anchor and activate each person's 48 dimensional bodies, in preparation for eventual full cosmic ascension realization.

We call forth Metatron, our gracious host for this phase of our meditation, to fully anchor and activate the Garment of Shaddai, also known as the Light Body of Metatron.

Now we call forth the entire Cosmic and Planetary Hierarchy, and we humbly request a complete merger of the Light Bodies of this auspicious group with the Light Bodies of all in attendance from earth for this meditation.

We humbly request to receive this blessing now…

We call forth His Holiness the Mahatma, also known as the Cosmic Avatar of Synthesis.

We request of you, beloved Mahatma, to help us synthesize all the bodies that have been anchored and activated in this meditation, so they may function as one unified whole in perfect integration, synthesis and balance.

Archangel Metatron again steps forward, and has one final surprise for us.

Archangel Metatron now takes us collectively in his platinum crystalline Merkabah to the Crystal Cathedral of GOD that exists beyond the 352 levels of Divinity.

As we arrive here in Metatron's Merkabah, we bear witness to the cathedral of all cathedrals.

The light is so brilliant and clear that it seems to envelop, consume and live in all space and time.

We find ourselves now inside this cathedral that can only be described as stepping into the Heart Center of GOD.

It is here GOD steps forth with His invisible hand, with the "crown jewel of crown jewels" of Light Body construction.

It is here, now, in this sacred moment that GOD steps forth and fully anchors and activates what can only be esoterically called the "Light Body of GOD" and/or "The Lord's Mystical Body."

If you are open to receiving this blessing of all blessings, be still, and receive this anointing and GOD merger now…

This incredible blessing manifests in each person's Heart Chakra as a luminous, platinum-gold flame.

This blessing of all blessings also manifests as a luminous, platinum-gold light radiance throughout the aura of each person in attendance, on a permanent basis.

As a final blessing now from GOD and the GOD Force, for a final building of our Light Bodies, we call forth a Light Quotient-building shower infusion, directly from GOD and the entire Cosmic and Planetary Hierarchy.

Let this light completely penetrate and infuse all the bodies that have now been fully anchored and activated.

Be still, and receive this enormous cosmic grace and blessing now...

My beloved brothers and sisters, we now move to the Love Body building phase of this meditation.

Our hostess for this phase of our Love Body building program is the Divine Mother.

The Divine Mother steps forward with Her platinum-gold pink Merkabah, and Archangel Metatron now graciously merges his Merkabah with the Divine Mother's Merkabah for the second stage of this journey.

The Divine Mother takes us to Her heavenly abode at the 352nd level of Divinity.

She takes us specifically to Her ruby-rose Cathedral of Unconditional Love.

This ruby-rose Cathedral of Unconditional Love could be seen as the Heart Chamber of the Cosmic Goddess throughout the infinite Omniverse.

To begin the process of constructing our Cosmic and Planetary Love Body, the Divine Mother initiates this process by merging Her sacred immaculate Heart with each person in attendance, on a permanent basis for the rest of eternity, for those who choose to receive this blessing now...

Mother Mary steps forward in radiant splendor and places a ruby-red rose in each person's etheric heart Chakra to activate each person's Heart Chakra to its highest potential.

Quan Yin steps forward in a flowing white robe and places within each person's Heart Chamber a "lotus blossom of compassion."

Quan Yin says that this lotus blossom will open and stream forth her energy every time an opportunity for compassion presents itself to you within your daily life.

His Holiness Lord Maitreya, the Planetary Christ, now steps forward and places within all in attendance a "rod of love," which extends through all seven chakras.

Lord Maitreya states that this "rod of love" will help you to manifest unconditional love at all times, regardless of which chakra you are expressing and demonstrating GOD from.

His Holiness Lord Sananda now steps forward with an exquisite gift to all in attendance of a "winged-cross necklace," which he places around your neck.

Sananda says that this winged cross, which is being placed around your etheric body, will serve to help you be unconditionally loving at all times, even under the most extreme situations.

The cross is winged to symbolize the rising and ascending power of love, and to symbolize the transcendent nature of unconditional love, which can be given forth even when other people are negatively attacking.

His Holiness the Lord Sai Baba now steps forward with a profound gift, providing each person in attendance with an orange robe of Sai Baba's love.

This robe, Sai Baba says, is for the purpose of protecting you from the attacks of others so that you are able to respond to others in love in all situations, rather than react.

This robe prevents other people's attacks or negative ego energies from getting into your subconscious mind and/or auric field.

Isis steps forward with the gift of a golden-pink halo of love, which she now places upon each person's head. She says it will serve to keep your mind attuned and magnetized only to Christ thinking and not negative ego thinking.

Pallas Athena now steps forward with a rainbow-colored globe of light, which surrounds your entire auric field.

Pallas Athena says that this gift is for the purpose of attuning each person on a permanent basis with their wholeness, within their relationship to self and GOD.

This gift will hence allow each "loveworker" to only think, feel and demonstrate preferential and mutually independent love, rather than addictive love, attachment-oriented love, or co-dependent love.

We now call forth Vesta, from the Solar Core, who places an "ember of the Solar Sun" in each person's etheric Heart Center, which will serve to help each loveworker shine their unconditional love equally and at all times upon all who you encounter.

This gift from Vesta will help you, in essence, to stay in unconditional love rather than conditional love.

Lakshmi now steps forward with a gift of a pinkish-blue gemstone ring with an infinity sign exquisitely carved into the face of the gemstone.

Lakshmi states that this gift is a symbol to help you attune to the limitless and abundant flow of love that comes to you from GOD, and that you give limitlessly to GOD, self, and to all sentient beings.

We call forth Lady Nada and Lady Portia, who now place a wreath of seafoam-green upon your head, and this wreath has a symbol of the Third Eye in gold at the front of the gift.

The purpose of this gift, they are saying, is to help magnetize and attune your consciousness at all times to the "Holy Encounter."

The "Holy Encounter" is that every meeting with a brother and sister, whether you know them or not, is Christ meeting Christ and/or GOD meeting GOD.

This gift will help you always see and remember the essence and not just the form of each person you meet, which is essential to do if you are going to remain in unconditional love at all times.

We now call forth His Holiness Lord Melchizedek, who steps forward with a gift of a golden heart, which he places around your entire auric field.

Melchizedek says that this golden heart is for the purpose of reminding your consciousness to never, ever indulge in attack thoughts, words or deeds to another brother or sister of GOD.

Melchizedek is saying that whenever there is a tinge of this energy beginning to manifest, this heart which is connected to his heart, will give you a gentle, loving reminder to remain in unconditional love, if you choose to receive this gift now.

Master Kuthumi steps forward with the gift of a "three-dimensional spinning star Merkabah" that he now places in your third chakra.

Master Kuthumi says that this beautiful, white star Merkabah is for the purpose of attuning and magnetizing your consciousness to only express and demonstrate Christed feelings and emotions and not to indulge in lower-self, negative ego, separative, fear-based feelings and emotions.

Master Kuthumi is now saying that whenever negative ego-based feelings and emotions begin to surface in your consciousness, this Merkabah will begin to spin faster to help transmute these feelings, and will also serve as a telepathic reminder to either attitudinally heal these feelings and/or express them in some spiritualized, cathartic manner.

Archangels Jophiel and Christine step forward with a gift of a yin/yang symbol necklace, which will help you to always keep your feminine/masculine, God/Goddess, yin/yang balance so your unconditional love can remain steady and even at all times.

Now stepping forward are Melchizedek, the Mahatma, and Metatron, who come forth with a gift of a "spinning rainbow platinum-gold diamond miniature Merkabah," which they place within your Third Eye chakra.

They collectively are saying that this gift will serve to permanently remind you to always choose love over fear.

To always choose GOD over negative ego.

To always choose oneness over separation.

Lastly, to always be a love finder, rather than a fault finder.

This spinning, diamond Merkabah will spin faster any time negative ego has been unconsciously chosen.

It will help to transmute this energy, and will serve to telepathically remind your conscious mind to choose once again GOD, instead of negative ego.

We now call forth Paramahansa Yogananda, who steps forward with a gift of golden-red sandals.

Paramahansa Yogananda says that these sandals will serve as a tuning agent and catalyst to remind you to love GOD with all your heart and soul and mind and might and to love your neighbor as yourself.

These sandals will also serve to help you walk the path of devotion, full all-out spiritual passion, and Divine fiery love for GOD and all aspects of His Creation.

Lastly, these sandals will also serve to help inspire you to seek GOD with full focus and spiritual commitment, like a drowning man seeks air.

Jesus/Sananda steps forward again to offer a second gift in the process of building your Love Body, which is a dove of pure white love descending downwards, anchoring above your Crown Chakra,.

Sananda is saying that this ever-present dove, descending into your crown, is a symbol and reminding agent and catalyst to help you always to remember to forgive self and others for mistakes.

Lord Sananda reminds us now of his famous words in his life as Jesus when he said, "Forgive them Father, for they know not what they do."

He also said, "He that hath no sin, let him cast the first stone."

As well as, "Judge not, that ye not be judged."

This descending dove will serve as a telepathic reminder to your conscious mind to demonstrate these noble truths at all times.

The Earth Mother, Pan, and Archangel Sandalphon step forward and offer collectively a most wondrous gift of an "etheric bonsai tree," which they are placing now in each person's earthly home, who is in attendance here.

The combined voice of the Earth Mother, Pan, and Archangel Sandalphon are collectively saying now that this gift will serve as a connection and telepathic reminder to not only love GOD, the Masters, and your brothers and sisters, but to also love with all your heart your animal brothers and sisters, the plant kingdom, the mineral kingdom, the nature spirits and devas, your physical bodies, the physical earth, the physical universe, and the overall Material Face of GOD!

His Holiness the Lord Sai Baba and Paul the Venetian step forward and offer to each loveworker in attendance a golden-platinum ring with a small picture of disciples and devotees singing bhajans and devotional songs.

Sai Baba and Paul the Venetian are collectively saying that this special ring is a symbol and catalyst to help remind you to always repeat, chant and sing the names of GOD.

They are saying that engaging the emotional body and mental body in this process is one of the best ways to keep these vehicles' attention on GOD and Unconditional Love, rather than the temptations, fears and lack of love of the negative ego thoughts and negative emotions.

Now stepping forward are the Second Ray Mighty Elohim Divine counterparts Apollo and Lumina.

They step forward with a gift of a platinum-silver bracelet with an exquisite emblem of a golden brick, like a golden bar from the Cosmic Treasury of Limitless Love.

This golden bar and/or brick, Apollo and Lumina are saying, is a symbol and reminder of the importance of manifesting and building a life of unconditional love in all your relationships and in every aspect of your life.

The Divine Mother steps forth again, in Her ruby-rose cathedral of love, to give Her final gift on this auspicious occasion.

Her final gift as our hostess for this phase of our meditation is to anchor what has only been esoterically described as "The Garment of the Goddess," also known as "The Love Body of the Divine Mother."

Be still and receive this blessing now...

We now call forth all the Masters of the Cosmic and Planetary Hierarchy to join us in the ruby-rose cathedral of the Divine Mother.

It is here again that we ask all the Masters gathered for a stupendous love blessing.

We ask all the Masters gathered to collectively anchor, activate, and merge their Love Bodies with all the earthly disciples, initiates and ascended beings in attendance.

My beloved brothers and sisters, the final singular gift to help you build your Love Body will now come directly from GOD.

The Divine Mother lifts us in Her platinum-gold pink Merkabah from Her ruby-rose Cathedral of Love.

The Divine Mother, who is merged with Metatron in the Merkabah, takes us back to the Crystal Cathedral of GOD.

Again we enter the Heart Center of this crystal cathedral where GOD has one final gift for this phase of the meditation.

GOD now anchors and activates in this poignant and sacred moment what can only be esoterically called "GOD's Mystical Heart," into each person's etheric Heart Center.

This appears etherically as an eternal, luminous, pearlescent pink flame within your Heart Chakra, and this anchoring also creates a luminous pearlescent pink color throughout your entire aura.

The final gift to conclude this second phase of this meditation to build our Love Bodies comes directly from GOD and the entire Cosmic and Planetary Hierarchy.

GOD and the entire Cosmic and Planetary Hierarchy do not give us a Light Shower, but instead give us a "Love Shower" directly form GOD's own Heart and the hearts of all of the Masters gathered.

Be still and receive this cosmic love infusion now, from GOD and the GOD Force, and allow it to penetrate, infuse, and build Love Quotient within your fully anchored and activated 12-Body System and all your bodies now...

Now stepping forward out of the cosmic mist is Archangel Michael, who has graciously taken on the mantle of spiritual leadership to host the final phase of this meditation, which is to build and construct our Power Body.

Archangel Michael now, with a wave of his mighty sword brings forth his opalescent-blue Merkabah, which we all gather into.

Archangel Michael merges his Merkabah with the Merkabah of the Divine Mother and Archangel Metatron, and carries us off to the heavenly abode of the Heavenly Father, at the Right Hand of GOD.

As we arrive, we see the most exquisite magenta-blue crystal cathedral you could possibly imagine.

As we now enter into the heart of this magenta-blue cathedral, we see before us on the altar of the "Church of the Heavenly Father" the eternal cosmic blue flame, which is one of the Three-Fold Flames of GOD's own Heart.

This cosmic flame has been burning here throughout eternity, as the causal point and catalyst of the flame of power for all sentient beings throughout Creation.

Our first gift for the building of our Power Bodies comes directly from the Heavenly or Divine Father.

The Divine Father now reaches forth His hand, like the Michelangelo fresco depicting GOD awakening Adam.

The Divine Father or Heavenly Father takes an ember or miniature flame from this cosmic flame and places it in each person's own heart to ignite and empower the blue flame that already exists there.

Be still, and receive this incredible gift of the Divine and Heavenly Father now...

Archangel Michael now steps forward and hands each person in attendance a replica of his Flaming Blue Sword of Personal Power and Protection.

See this flaming blue sword appear in your right hand now.

Feel the spiritual current of Archangel Michael and his flaming blue sword move up your arm and all the meridians and nadis of your entire being to electrify, revitalize and empower them, with his First Ray cosmic current.

We now call forth Archangel Faith, who complements her Divine counterpart Archangel Michael with a feminine gift of power to help build your Power Body, with a magenta etheric wreath that sits on the head like a crown.

Archangel Faith says that this magenta wreath will help disciples, initiates, and ascended beings carry the resonance of humble GOD/GODDESS dignity.

Now stepping forward out of the cosmic mist are the Mighty Elohim of the First Ray: Hercules and Amazonia.

They offer to all in attendance a "rod of power," which now appears in each person's left hand.

Hercules and Amazonia are saying that this "rod of power" will bring forth a thousandfold increase in your power to manifest your Christ/Buddha ideals and spiritual mission, on each and every level of your being.

They are also saying that this power will manifest on a superconscious, conscious, subconscious and physical body level.

The affirmation that they bring forth as an added gift is "GOD, my personal power, the power of my subconscious mind, and my physical body power are an unbeatable team!"

Now stepping forward is Master El Morya, the First Ray Chohan of the Power Ray and Flame on earth.

El Morya steps forward with the gift of Divine shaktipat, which he is going to transfer through his eyes to all assembled.

El Morya is saying that this Divine shaktipat will serve to help each individual fully own their personal power and self-mastery at their highest potential if, in this moment as you receive this gift, you fully "claim it" as your own.

Let us all be silent and receive this First Ray shaktipat blessing from Master El Morya now...

As we have received this shaktipat, El Morya telepathically asks each individual, if you are now willing to claim your full personal power at all times, inwardly and outwardly in service of GOD, at the 100% level.

If you are, then in this moment Master El Morya requests that you place your left hand, palm open, arm stretched out in front of you.

He asks now, also, that you raise your right hand straight up into the air, fists closed for seven seconds. This can be done inwardly or outwardly.

The act of doing this First Ray mudra demonstrates with your left hand that you are willing to receive the full Power of GOD and the GOD Force.

The act of raising your right hand into the air with a closed fist shows that you are willing to fully 100% claim your personal power and never give it to another person, and never give it to your mental body, emotional body, etheric body, physical body, subconscious mind, inner child, desire body or negative ego ever again.

The holding of this First Ray mudra for seven seconds is to insure that your power will manifest at all times equally and evenly, through all seven chakras.

If you are now willing to make this commitment and fully claim your power at the 100% level on a permanent basis, in front of Master El Morya and the entire Cosmic and Planetary Hierarchy, then Master El Morya asks you to make this mudra fully and completely now.

Now stepping forward is Master Allah Gobi, who is the Manu and/or department head of the First Ray for planet earth.

He steps forward with a gift for all in attendance of a "platinum headband," with a perfect GOD-Diamond that fits exactly right over your Third Eye on the etheric plane.

This gift, Allah Gobi is now saying, is a symbol and catalyst to help all powerworkers develop perfect spiritual discernment at all times, as GOD would have it be.

Receive this gift now...

Now stepping forward is Pallas Athena again, with a gift of a "breastplate of platinum-gold armor," for all in attendance.

This Divine Breastplate of GOD will serve to also create in the aura a semi-permeable Bubble of Light.

This semi-permeable Bubble of Light, which is permanently in place, will allow only thoughts, feelings, emotions, and energy of GOD to enter your auric field. All other energies will not be able to move through this protective field of energy.

All that Pallas Athena asks is that every morning when you get up from sleeping, you take 10 seconds to consciously put on this "Breastplate of GOD" and see the golden, semi-permeable bubble in place.

The breastplate and bubble are always there; however, it is important that you take a few seconds each morning to claim it to make sure the conscious mind is connected to it as well.

Now stepping forward is Master Sananda, who comes forth with a gift of a ruby-metallic shield that you will hold in your left hand.

See yourself placing your previous gift of your "rod of power" in a sheath connected to your belt.

Now take this ruby-metallic shield that Master Sananda is giving you.

This ruby-metallic shield is symbolic and serves as a telepathic reminder from Sananda to at all times "deny any thought that is not of GOD to enter your mind."

This proper and spiritual use of denial, Master Sananda is saying, is essential to the retaining of your inner peace and causing only a GOD-Reality for yourself.

Sananda also gives a second gift, which is to add to your shield a crystal-blue gemstone, which serves to remind, activate and stimulate you to not only deny negative thoughts, but to also, at all times, affirm positive Christed thoughts.

Sananda reminds us in this moment that, "an idle mind is the devil's workshop," so keep your mind filled at all times with positive and spiritually uplifting thoughts.

Now stepping forward is the Master Djwhal Khul, who brings forth the gift of a "radiant sun," which he places eight inches above the Crown Chakra.

Master Djwhal Khul is saying that this permanently anchored sun will serve as a telepathic reminder from him to always "keep your mind steady in the Light."

Now stepping forward is St. Germain, who places on each person's head a golden-white crown, with three violet amethyst gemstones that adorn the front of the crown.

St. Germain is saying that this gift will serve as a telepathic reminder from him to always retain mastery over your "attention," and to always keep your attention focused on the Mighty I AM Presence and the Christ/Buddha ideal in your every thought, word and deed.

Now stepping forward is Master Serapis Bey, who brings forth the gift of a golden hammer.

Master Serapis says that this golden hammer will serve as a telepathic reminder from him to always own your personal power in a way that demonstrates it fully and completely upon the physical plane.

Master Serapis reminds us of the famous quote of Sai Baba who states, "Hands that help are holier than lips that pray."

Now stepping forward is my dear friend, Paul the Venetian, who comes forth with the gift of a paint brush with twelve jars of individualized paint colors, signifying the Twelve Rays.

Master Paul says that this gift will serve as a permanent telepathic reminder to remain enthusiastic at all times in the manifestation of your mission on earth.

Paul is now saying that this is the engaging of your personal power with your emotional body; with full motivation, commitment, joy, and excitement, which becomes infectious to others in a positive sense. This is true because the subconscious mind, inner child, emotional body, conscious mind, Oversoul, and Monad are all involved in the process.

Master Kuthumi now steps forward with the gift of a "Staff of GOD."

This gift, Master Kuthumi is saying, will serve to help you to own your power in the vein of always sticking to your ideals, practicing what you preach, keeping a flawless character, maintaining absolute integrity at all times, never saying anything that you are not going to do, and never giving in to temptation or weakness.

Master Hilarion now steps forward with the gift of a golden scale.

Master Hilarion is saying that this golden scale will serve as a telepathic link with him, to remind you to always be decisive in everything you do.

Master Hilarion states that decisiveness is the first cousin of personal power.

If you are going to own your power, you must be decisive at all times.

We all know the sayings: "fish or cut bait" and "do not sit on the fence."

It is better to be decisive and make the wrong decision than to live in the "twilight zone" in a state of lethargy, confusion, and psychological indolence.

Master Hilarion now gives you a rainbow-colored "stone of decisive decision making," so when this is placed on the scale it goes one way or the other, and is not fickle.

This way, once a decision is made you stand behind it and don't look back, unless a new decision needs to be made, where the same principle applies.

Now stepping forward are Melchizedek, the Mahatma, and Metatron, who offer a gift of a "pillar of protective power" directly from the Cosmic realms.

This "cosmic pillar of protective power and light" will serve as a type of cosmic spiritual immune system and spiritual cell wall to keep out unwanted and unhealthy particles of misqualified energy.

We call forth His Holiness the Lord Sai Baba, who comes with a gift of the sprinkling of his Virbutti ash over your entire Crown Chakra, and he also now places some Virbutti directly on your Third Eye.

Sai Baba is saying that the purpose of this two-fold gift is first to help you focus your power in the vein of remaining evenminded and even-emotionally at all times.

Sai Baba reminds us that it is our thoughts, beliefs, and interpretations that we project onto people and circumstances that determines whether we are evenminded or have lots of highs and lows.

Sai Baba's second gift is a telepathic reminder from him to strive at all times to transcend duality.

By this he means to remain in power, equanimity, peace, love and joy whether you have profit or loss, pleasure or pain, sickness or health, and whether people praise you or malign you.

Sai Baba is now saying that the ultimate GOD ideal is to remain the same through all the various dualities of outer existence.

Now stepping forward is Lord Buddha, who comes with a gift of Mala Prayer Beads, which he places around each person's neck.

Lord Buddha says that these prayer beads will help you use power to have the proper detachment in life, and to not be overly emotionally sensitive.

Lord Buddha reminds us of one of his more noble truths that states, "All suffering comes from attachment."

Lord Buddha guides us now to use our power to only have preferences and not attachments. This way you may retain happiness, joy, and inner peace at all times.

Now stepping forward is Vywamus, who brings a dual gift of providing a "golden dome of protection" over each person in attendance on a permanent basis, and a second golden dome over each person's home.

Vywamus is saying that these gifts will provide added protection so that all may enter the world of form with confidence.

We now call forth Melchizedek, who comes forth with a gift of a golden robe with a beautiful embroidered emblem of a golden lion on the back of the robe.

Melchizedek states that this gift will provide directly from him telepathically the added Christed quality of "courage" to your auric field.

Melchizedek reminds us that the main theme of the Cosmic Day of Brahma for our universe is "courage," and he will now help you increase that resonance.

Now stepping forward is Lord Maitreya, who comes with a gift of a golden bracelet with a winged, golden-pink heart.

Lord Maitreya says that this gift will serve a dual function to help you transcend and conquer all fear.

The wings on the heart will give you the transcendent quality needed, backed with full Christed power, and the heart will give you the unconditional love needed to conquer fear.

Lord Maitreya reminds us that to conquer fear it takes full personal power focused only on unconditional love. Love alone won't work, and power alone won't work.

It is when these two Christed qualities are combined in the form of the gift he has given you that success is inevitable.

Now stepping forward is Mother Mary and Quan Yin, who bring forth the gift of an "invisible mist" from them that spiritually permeates the auric field.

Mother Mary and Quan Yin now remind us that "faith is the substance of things not seen, and the evidence of things not known."

This gift, they collectively state, will help you channel your personal power into faith rather than doubt, and in time, even beyond faith into absolute knowingness that "if GOD be for me, who or what can be against me?"

Now stepping forward is the Lord of Arcturus, who brings forth a gift of a torch, much like the type that runners carry to start the Olympic games.

The Lord of Arcturus is saying that the development of perseverance over the duration of one's earthly service mission is essential because of the nature of physical existence and third-dimensional reality.

In a similar vein, Lady Nada, Lanto, and Lady Portia step forward with the gift of an "etheric hourglass" with spiritual sand running through it.

Lady Nada, Lanto, and Lady Portia now are collectively saying that this gift will serve to help you at all times to remember to use your personal power and self-mastery in the focus of patience in all ways and all things.

They collectively remind us that every situation and interaction in life is a spiritual test.

One of the spiritual tests that comes up most often within self and with others is "patience."

Now stepping forward is Commander Ashtar of the Ashtar Command, who offers a gift of a golden lantern.

Commander Ashtar states that this golden lantern will serve as a telepathic link with him to remind you at all times to be vigilant against negative ego thoughts, emotions, and energy that will try to enter your consciousness from within and without.

Commander Ashtar reminds us of the famous quote from Sananda in *A Course in Miracles* where Sananda states, "Be vigilant for GOD and His Kingdom."

Commander Ashtar adds to this by reminding us to be vigilant and not allow our consciousness to slip into automatic pilot.

Stepping forward now is Lord Krishna, who comes with the gift of a platinum-gold flute for all in attendance.

Lord Krishna is telling us that this gift is for the purpose of telepathically reminding you and helping you to be a spiritual warrior on earth, in service of GOD and love at all times.

Lord Krishna now reminds us of his famous quote in the *Bhagavad-Gita* where he says to Arjuna on the battlefield, when Arjuna was becoming weak and mentally and emotionally confused, "Get up and give up your unmanliness and get up and fight, this self-pity and self-indulgence is unbecoming of the great soul you are."

Now stepping forward is Sri Yukteswar, the guru of Paramahansa Yogananda, who comes with a gift of an exquisitely bound, golden-brown manuscript, with golden lettering on the cover in ancient script writing which spells out the words "GOD's Laws."

Sri Yukteswar is now telling us that this gift is a telepathic reminder and link with him to help you to always be disciplined in your spiritual practices and service to GOD.

Sri Yukteswar states that when you own your personal power over an extended period of time, in an evenminded manner, you have discipline.

Self-discipline is the "first cousin" of self-mastery, and it is essential for all "powerworkers" to develop this gift. Sri Yukteswar himself will help you in this goal.

We call forth Helios, Vesta, and Melchior, who bring forth a dual gift of an "ember of solar fire" from the Solar Core and an "ember of galactic fire" from the Galactic Core.

Helios and Vesta place their ember in each person's solar plexus.

Melchior now places his galactic ember in each person's Crown Chakra.

Helios and Vesta and Melchior collectively state that this combined gift is to help each person learn to not only own 100% of their personal power, but to also simultaneously completely surrender to GOD's Will.

Helios and Vesta and Melchior state here that some powerworkers own their power, but do not surrender to GOD's Will and instead use the power for negative ego will, or self-centered will.

Other powerworkers have learned to surrender to GOD's Will; however, they do not fully own their personal power and are hence knocked off-balance by their own subconscious mind and other people's energy.

This extremely profound gift of Helios and Vesta and Melchior will help you to perfectly integrate these two aspects of power that are embodied in the First Ray of GOD!

Now stepping forward is the Lord of Sirius and Dr. Lorphan, from the Great White Lodge on Sirius.

They come forward with a dual gift for all in attendance.

The Lord of Sirius comes forward with the gift of a golden-white "rod of power and light," which he scientifically places to fit perfectly into each person's physical/etheric spinal column.

The Lord of Sirius now states that this gift will serve to fully empower each person's physical posture, which will have a reciprocal effect of helping to re-empower the psychological and spiritual selves as well.

Dr. Lorphan, who is the director of the Healing Academy in the Great White Lodge on Sirius, now places two clear etheric crystals into each person's pituitary gland and pineal gland.

Dr. Lorphan states that these gifts will serve as a telepathic reminder and direct link to him, the Lord of Sirius, and the Galactic Healing Team on Sirius, which he trains, to remain in your full personal power even when the physical body starts getting sleepy or is having chronic health problems or is just sick, ill and going through a cleansing crisis.

Dr. Lorphan reminds us that a great many powerworkers equate personal power with their physical energy level and health.

In doing this, they often give in to the lower-self and temptation when their physical energy gets low. Dr. Lorphan's gifts will help powerworkers remain in full, empowered consciousness at all times, even when the physical body is going through its various highs and lows.

When a powerworker can remain in full power and self-mastery regardless of what is going on in the physical vehicle, this is one of the signs of a true, full-fledged Ascended Master.

Now stepping forward is Archangel Michael, who has one of the power blessings of all power blessings, which he has organized for us in the Heavenly Father's magenta-blue crystal cathedral.

Appearing now in the Heavenly Father's magenta-blue crystal cathedral are the entire Cosmic and Planetary Hierarchy of Masters, Archangels, Angels, Elohim Masters and Christed Extraterrestrials.

As the Cosmic and Planetary Hierarchy's collective gift, they now fully anchor and activate their combined Power Bodies with all in attendance.

Be still, and receive this stupendous power blessing and activation now...

Now stepping forward again within his magenta-blue crystal cathedral is the Heavenly Father.

The Heavenly Father has one final personal gift to share.

The Heavenly, or Divine Father now fully anchors and activates to all in attendance what can only be esoterically called "The Robe of the Divine Father," also esoterically called "The Power Body of the Heavenly Father."

If you would like to receive this incredible blessing, be still and receive this blessing now...

The Divine Father and Archangel Michael have another surprise in store for us.

They both lift us up collectively in Archangel Michael's Merkabah to ascend ever higher into the Seventh Heaven of GOD.

We find ourselves in the "Crystal Power Cathedral of GOD"!

This cathedral we now find ourselves inside of has a reddish-blue luminescent glow pervading the Clear Light of GOD crystals that make up the structure of this hallowed sanctuary.

This Crystal Power Cathedral of GOD is literally the power center of the Infinite Universe.

If you remain quiet and still, you can not only hear, but actually *feel* reverberating through your being the "Cosmic Pulse of GOD."

GOD has one final personal gift to share with all in attendance.

GOD now fully anchors and activates what can only be esoterically called the "Power Body of GOD"!

If you wish to receive this power blessing of all power blessings to help construct your power body, be still and receive this blessing now...

GOD has one final collective gift and blessing for all in attendance.

God and the Cosmic and Planetary Hierarchy anchor what can only esoterically be described as a "Cosmic Power Shower."

Although sounding quite humorous and funny, we have had a Cosmic Light Shower, Cosmic Love Shower, and now it is time for the "Cosmic Power Shower of All Cosmic Power Showers."

This Cosmic Power Shower will build each person's Power Quotient as nothing you have ever done before.

If you wish to receive this "Power Shower of all Power Showers," be still and receive this blessing now...

Appearing now, out of this reddish-blue luminescent mist, is the Avatar of Synthesis, also known as the Mahatma.

The Mahatma merges his Merkabah with the Merkabah of Metatron, the Divine Mother, and Archangel Michael.

He lifts and ascends us into a new region of GOD's Seventh Heaven.

We now find ourselves inside the Mahatma's rainbow-colored "Crystal Cathedral of Synthesis," at the 352nd level of Divinity.

As we find ourselves standing before the altar of this most sanctified cathedral, we behold luminescent rainbow-colored light, delicately shimmering, of all the Mahatma crystals that are the building blocks of this most sacred sanctuary.

Beginning our ceremony here, now appear the three department heads of the Planetary Hierarchy: Allah Gobi, the Manu; Lord Maitreya, the Planetary Christ; and St. Germain, the Maha Chohan.

These three great and noble masters have come together in unity and synthesis, as the department heads of the first three rays, to give forth a gift of a platinum-gold medallion, with the engraved picture of these three masters arm in arm on the front of the medallion.

Allah Gobi, Lord Maitreya, and St. Germain are now saying that this medallion is a symbol of synthesis of the first three rays, the first seven rays, and the first 12 Planetary rays, which we each must master to become full-fledged Ascended Masters in the highest sense of the term.

They collectively say that this medallion will serve as a telepathic link with each of them, and with all 12 rays, for the purpose of helping you to fully integrate and master all 12 rays in perfect synthesis, as GOD would have it be.

Now stepping forward is the Mahatma, who brings forth a similar gift as Allah Gobi, Lord Maitreya, and St. Germain just brought; however, the Mahatma brings the *Cosmic* equivalent.

The extraordinary gift that the Mahatma is now graciously offering to give to all in attendance, is to fully anchor and activate what can only esoterically be called "The Light, Love, and Power Body of the Mahatma," into each light, love, and powerworker.

My beloved brothers and sisters, please now understand the incredible profundity of that which is about to happen.

The Mahatma holds the "Three-Fold Flame of Synthesis" for the Infinite Universe within his body.

The Mahatma is now ready and willing to fully merge his Three-Fold Cosmic Flame Body with each one of us.

The Mahatma is saying that the purpose of this will be to not only help with the perfect integration of the 12 Planetary rays, but to help with the perfect integration of the Solar rays, Galactic rays, Universal rays, Multiuniversal rays, and the 12 Cosmic rays that form the matrix of all Creation.

This "synthesis gift of all synthesis gifts" will also help in the perfect synthesizing of all your bodies, chakras, meridians, psychology, three minds, astrological signs, archetypes, and, in truth, all aspects of self, including all 352 levels of Divinity back to the Godhead.

If you would like to receive this synthesis gift of all synthesis gifts then be still, and receive this blessing now...

My beloved brothers and sisters, if this were not enough, GOD and the Mahatma have another unfathomable blessing in mind for GOD's beloved sons and daughters.

The Mahatma, merged with Metatron, the Divine Mother, the Heavenly Father and Archangel Michael along with the Cosmic and Planetary Hierarchy, now lift us even higher.

We find ourselves ascending into the most refined regions of GOD one can possibly imagine.

We now find ourselves in the "Three-Fold Flame Crystal Cathedral Church of GOD."

As we stand in the center of the heart of this church, we see at the altar the "Three-Fold Flame of All-Creation."

The shimmering, luminescent color of this Three-Fold Flame reflecting in the GOD Crystals that make up this church is a religious experience in itself.

The colors of the Three-Fold Infinite Cosmic Flame within GOD's own Heart are platinum-gold, platinum-blue, and platinum-pink.

In the background, we can hear the "Music of the Spheres," and the celestial dance of the Archangels, Angels, and Mighty Elohim.

The first ceremonial blessing GOD has in store for us is the full anchoring and activation of the full Light, Love, and Power Bodies of all the Masters, Archangels, Angels, Elohim, and Christed Extraterrestrials of the entire Cosmic and Planetary Hierarchy.

If you wish to receive this three-fold synthesis blessing from the entire GOD Force, be still and receive this blessing now...

For our final singular blessing in this meditation and GOD experience, GOD now offers to all in attendance to fully anchor, activate, and merge with what can only esoterically be called "The Light, Love, and Power Body of GOD."

If you wish to receive this blessing then be still, and know and receive "I AM GOD"...

As we now prepare to conclude this meditation, let us take a few moments to thank GOD and all the Masters of the Cosmic and Planetary Hierarchy for their bountiful blessings and gifts...

As we complete this process, Metatron, the Divine Mother, Archangel Michael, and the Mahatma embrace the assembled participants in their "Merkabah of Light, Love, and Power," perfectly synthesized and integrated.

We begin the gradual and slow descent from the top of Creation back through the 352 levels of the Divinity of GOD.

Moving down now to the platinum Multiuniversal level.

Descending further into and through the refined golden realms of His Holiness Lord Melchizedek.

Descending further now through the soft golden-color frequencies of our Galactic Logos, Lord Melchior.

Descending further through the copper-gold dimensions of reality of Helios and Vesta, our Solar Logos.

Descending further still now, through the pure white light dimensions of Lord Buddha and Sanat Kumara in Shamballa, our Planetary capital.

Descending further as we move toward planet earth.

Here again, we are greeted by the Earth Mother, Pan, and Archangel Sandalphon.

As we descend further into their loving embrace, we now enter our physical bodies through our Crown Chakra.

The Earth Mother, Pan, Archangel Sandalphon, and the Mahatma help us to get properly anchored and balanced within our physical vehicle, and bring all the Light, Love and Power we have gained from celestial realms with us.

Let us take one last moment to thank our celestial hosts for this meditation; GOD, Archangel Metatron, the Divine Mother, the Divine Father, Archangel Michael, the Mahatma, and the entire Cosmic and Planetary Hierarchy for their noble service on our behalf...

As this moment of silence concludes, take a moment with your eyes closed to send your perfectly balanced Love, Light and Power through your Heart Chakra to all your brothers and sisters in this room that have shared this journey with you...

When you are ready, you may open your eyes.

15

Mt. Shasta 50 Point Cosmic Cleansing Meditation

To begin this meditation, close your eyes.

Let us all take a deep breath—exhale.

We call forth the entire Planetary and Cosmic Hierarchy for help in implementing this meditation for the entire group.

We call forth a Planetary and Cosmic axiatonal alignment.

The meditation we are about to do is extremely in-depth and will foster enormous ascension acceleration, so I want you all to just completely relax, be like a sponge, and let the Masters do their Divine handiwork.

We call forth Lord Michael to establish a golden dome of protection for all in attendance.

We call forth Vywamus and the Archangels, to bring forth their golden hands as a net to cleanse any and all negative energies in the field of each person individually, and in the collective group body.

We call forth from Melchizedek, the Mahatma, and Metatron, the anchoring of the Platinum Net, to cleanse the energy fields of each person in attendance in an even deeper fashion now.

We now call forth to the Lord of Arcturus and the Arcturians, for the anchoring of the Prana Wind Clearing Device individually and in our collective group body.

See this Prana Wind Clearing Device as a type of fan that is anchored into the solar plexus and blows and clears all unwanted energies out of the etheric body system.

Feel the Prana Wind Clearing Device now being lifted out of your field by the Lord of Arcturus and the Beloved Arcturians.

We now call forth from Djwhal Khul, the Seven Chohans, Lord Maitreya, Allah Gobi, Lord Buddha, and the Cosmic Masters, for the anchoring of the Core Fear Matrix Removal Program.

See this as a lattice work of light that is anchored into the four-body system, and hence highlights any negative energies or blockages in your energy fields.

We begin by calling forth the removal of all fear programming and blocks from every person so they may achieve their ascension at the highest possible level.

See this fear programming as black roots intertwined in your energy fields, now being pulled out by the Masters—as though by a vacuum cleaner—through your Crown Chakra.

Planetary and Cosmic Hierarchy, please now remove all separative thinking from the four-body system.

Please also remove all judgmental programming from the four-body system.

Please remove all lack of forgiveness from the four-body system.

Feel these negative aspects being pulled out of your energy fields, through the Crown Chakra like unwanted weeds being removed from a beautiful garden.

Planetary and Cosmic Hierarchy, please remove all impatience and negative anger.

Please remove all negative selfishness, self-centeredness and narcissism.

Please remove any negative thoughtforms, negative feelings and emotions, and/or imbalanced archetypes from the four-body system.

Please remove all superiority and inferiority thinking created by the negative ego.

Please remove all aspects of guilt and shame consciousness created by the negative ego.

Please remove all negative ego and fear-based programming in a generalized sense.

Please cleanse and remove all Extraterrestrial implants and negative elementals.

We call forth the cleansing and removal of all unwanted astral entities.

We call to Melchizedek, the Mahatma, and Metatron, for the Cosmic Viral Vacuum, to remove and pull out any clinical or subclinical viruses currently existing in any of our energy fields.

Please also remove and pull out all negative bacteria with the Cosmic Bacterial Vacuum Program.

We call to the Archangels and the Elohim to remove all disease energy from the physical, etheric, astral and mental vehicles.

We call forth each person's personal inner plane Healing Angels, to now heal, repair, and sew up any irritations, spots, and/or leaks in the aura.

We call forth to Melchizedek, the Mahatma, Metatron, Archangel Michael and the Archangels, for the removal of all improper soul fragments.

We also ask for the retrieval of all the soul fragments from the universe that belong to us in Divine order.

We call forth each person's etheric healing team, and now request that the etheric body be repaired and brought back to its perfect blueprint now.

We call forth the anchoring of each person's perfect Divine Monadic Blueprint Body and/or Mayavarupa Body to use from this moment forward, to accelerate healing and spiritual growth on all levels the rest of this lifetime.

We call forth a complete cleansing and clearing of our genetic line and ancestral lineage.

We call forth the Lord of Arcturus to now bring forth the Golden Cylinder to remove and vacuum up any and all remaining negative energy in our collective energy fields.

We call forth a clearing and cleansing of all past lives and future lives.

We call forth now the integration and cleansing of our 144 soul extensions from our Monad and Mighty I AM Presence.

We now call forth a clearing and cleansing of all karma. As you all know, one needs to balance 51% of their karma to take the beginning phase of their Planetary ascension.

We ask for the greatest possible cleansing of our karma now.

We call forth from Melchizedek, the Mahatma, and Metatron, for the anchoring of a "matchstick worth" of the Cosmic Fire, to very gently burn away all astral, mental and etheric dross and gray clouds, from our fields.

We now request a complete clearing and cleansing of our entire Monad and Mighty I AM Presence itself.

We now call forth the greatest cleansing process this world has ever known, from Melchizedek, the Mahatma, Metatron, Lord Michael, the Archangels, the Elohim Councils and from GOD.

We call forth the "ultimate Cosmic cleansing and clearing," back to our original covenant with GOD, upon our "Original Spiritual Creation"...

We will take a few extra moments of silence to receive this blessing and grace.

We now call forth from all the Cosmic and Planetary Masters gathered here, a downpouring and Light Shower of "Core Love" and the "Christ/Buddha/Melchizedek attributes," to replace all that has been removed and cleansed, by the grace of GOD and the Cosmic and Planetary Hierarchy.

We call forth Archangel Sandalphon, Pan, and the Earth Mother, to help us now become properly integrated and grounded back into our physical bodies.

We call forth our personal inner plane Healing Angels to now perfectly balance our chakras and four-body system.

When you are ready, open your eyes and enjoy the tremendous sense of well-being and crystal clear clarity in your energy fields.

16

Ultimate Cosmic Ray Ascension Activation Meditation

Close your eyes—let us begin by having everyone take a deep breath—exhale.

We call all the Masters of the Planetary and Cosmic Hierarchy to help in this meditation.

We call forth a Planetary and Cosmic axiatonal alignment.

We call to Melchizedek, the Mahatma, and Metatron for the anchoring of the Platinum Net to clear away any and all unwanted energies.

We call to Archangel Michael for the establishment of a dome of protection.

We call for the establishment of a Pillar of Light, and a Planetary and Cosmic Ascension Column.

We now begin the process of fully anchoring and activating the Planetary and Cosmic Rays.

We begin by calling forth the Ascended Master El Morya, the Chohan of the First Ray, to now fully anchor and activate the First Ray, representing the Will aspect of GOD, which is red in color...

Bathe in the positive effects of this red ray now.

We call forth Master Kuthumi and the Ascended Master Djwhal Khul to now fully anchor and activate the Second Ray of Love/Wisdom, which is blue in color...

Bathe in the positive effects of this blue ray now.

We call forth Master Serapis Bey, who is the Chohan of the Third Ray, to now fully anchor and activate the Third Ray of Active Intelligence, which is yellow in color...

Bathe in the positive effects of this yellow ray now.

We call forth Master Paul the Venetian, who is the Chohan of the Fourth Ray, to now fully anchor and activate the Fourth Ray of Harmony, which is emerald-green in color...

Bathe in the positive effects of this emerald-green ray now.

We call forth Master Hilarion, who is the Chohan of the Fifth Ray, to now fully anchor and activate the Fifth Ray of New Age Science, which is orange in color...

Bathe in the positive effects of this orange ray now.

We call forth Sananda, the Chohan of the Sixth Ray, who in one of his past lives was known as the Master Jesus, to now fully anchor and activate the Sixth Ray of Devotion, which is indigo in color...

Bathe in the positive effects of this indigo ray now.

We call forth St. Germain, the Chohan of the Seventh Ray, who also now just recently has taken over the position in the spiritual government known as the Mahachohan. We now request from St. Germain the full anchoring and activation of the Seventh Ray of Ceremonial Order and Magic, which is violet in color...

Bathe in the positive effects of this violet transmuting flame.

We call forth the seven Ray Masters and the Ascended Master Djwhal Khul, to clear all lower and/or negative attributes from these first seven rays, and replace them with the higher and positive attributes of the Christ/Buddha archetype and imprint.

We call forth the Ascended Master Lady Nada, to now fully anchor and activate the Eighth Ray of Higher Cleansing, which is seafoam-green in color...

Bathe in the positive effects of this seafoam-green ray now.

We call forth Mother Mary to now fully anchor and activate the Ninth Ray of Joy and Attracting the Light Body, which is blue-green in color...

Bathe in the positive effects of this blue-green ray now.

We call forth Allah Gobi, who holds the position in the spiritual government known as the Manu, which is a higher governmental position of the First Ray.

He has volunteered this evening to officially activate the Tenth Ray, which has to do with fully anchoring the Light Body, and this ray is pearlescent in color...

Bathe in the positive effects of this pearlescent ray now.

We call forth Quan Yin, the Bodhisattva of Compassion, to now fully anchor and activate the Eleventh Ray, which serves as a bridge to the New Age and is pink-orange in color...

Bathe in the positive effects of this pink-orange ray now.

We call forth the Ascended Master Pallas Athena, to now fully anchor and activate the Twelfth Ray, which embodies the full anchoring of the New Age and the Christ Consciousness, and is gold in color...

Bathe in the positive effects of this gold ray now.

We now move from the Planetary rays to the Cosmic rays.

We begin by calling forth Lord Buddha, our new Planetary Logos, to fully anchor and activate the Shamballic Ray of pure white light...

Bathe in the profundity and glory of this pure white light from Lord Buddha himself.

We call forth Helios and Vesta, our Solar Logos, to now fully anchor and activate the cosmic Solar Ray from the Solar Core, which is copper-gold in color...

Bathe in the wonderful positive effects of this copper-gold Cosmic ray now.

We call forth Melchior, our Galactic Logos, to now fully anchor and activate the Galactic Ray, which is silver-gold in color...

Bathe and soak in this exquisite silver-gold ray.

We call forth Lord Melchizedek, our Universal Logos, for the full anchoring and activation of the Universal Ray, which is the purest and most refined golden vibration available to earth...

Bathe and absorb into every cell of your being this golden radiation from Melchizedek.

We call forth Archangel Metatron, to fully anchor and activate the Ten Lost Cosmic Rays of the Yod Spectrum, which are all hues of platinum...

Bathe now and fully absorb these ten lost Cosmic platinum hues.

We call forth the Multiuniversal Logos, to now fully anchor and activate the Pure Core Platinum Ray itself.

Become like a sponge and soak in this Pure Core Platinum Ray.

We call forth the Mahatma, who is a Cosmic group consciousness being that embodies all 352 levels of the GODHEAD, to fully anchor and activate the Mahatma Ray, which is a cosmic white light containing all colors of the spectrum.

Soak in this rainbow-colored Cosmic white light into the very core and essence of your being.

We call forth the Cosmic Council of Twelve, who are the 12 Cosmic beings that surround the Throne of Grace, to now fully anchor and activate their 12 Cosmic Rays.

These 12 Cosmic Rays are so refined in nature that they are translucent and beyond all color.

Soak in these exquisite rays and translucent vibrations into the very core essence of your heart and soul.

Last, but not least, as a special dispensation we call forth the Presence of GOD and request an anchoring and activation of the "Clear Light of the Ray of GOD."

Let us enter the silence now...

Let us now come back into our bodies, while continuing to absorb and enjoy these most refined Cosmic Rays.

17

GOD Ascension Seat Meditation

Close your eyes—let us begin by taking a deep breath—exhale

We call forth all the Masters of the Planetary and Cosmic Hierarchy to help in this meditation.

We call forth a Planetary and Cosmic axiatonal alignment.

We call to our inner plane spiritual hosts to now completely balance the energies.

We call forth Melchizedek, the Mahatma, and Metatron, for the anchoring of the Platinum Net to clear away any and all unwanted energies.

We begin our ascension seat journey this evening by calling forth our inner plane spiritual hosts to now provide a group Merkabah, like a gigantic boat, for everyone in attendance.

We ask to be taken in this Merkabah to Shamballa, to sit in the ascension seat of Lord Buddha, our Planetary Logos.

Feel and absorb the energies of this Planetary ascension seat.

We call forth from Lord Buddha a special Divine dispensation of ascension activation for this beloved group.

As a final blessing from Lord Buddha, we call forth and request a Divine dispensation to now experience the "Light Rod" of Lord Buddha, which will ignite our ascension realization even further.

Let us receive this special blessing now.

We call to our inner plane spiritual hosts to now move our gigantic group Merkabah from the Planetary to the Solar level to visit Helios and Vesta and sit in their Solar ascension seat.

Feel and sense the difference between the ascension seat in Shamballa and the ascension seat of Helios and Vesta in the Solar Core.

Feel and absorb these energies.

We call forth from Helios and Vesta for the most accelerated ascension activation that is available to us at this time.

We also call forth a special Divine dispensation to experience the "Light Rod" of Helios and Vesta, which will ignite and catalyze our ascension growth even further.

Let us receive this special blessing now.

We now call forth our inner plane spiritual hosts, and ask to be taken in our group Merkabah to the Galactic Core and the ascension seat of Melchior, our Galactic Logos.

Feel the difference in frequency between the Solar ascension seat and the Galactic ascension seat you are now sitting in.

We call forth the merging of three other Galactic ascension seats with the one we are currently sitting in.

We call forth the ascension seats of the Lord of Sirius, Lenduce, and the Lord of Arcturus, to all blend together so we may experience the effects of combining these Galactic ascension seats together...

We now call forth and request from Melchior, the Lord of Sirius, Lenduce, and the Lord of Arcturus, for the greatest possible ascension acceleration that is available to us at this time...

We call forth a special Divine dispensation, to experience the combined "Light Rods" of these four great and noble Masters.

Let us receive this very unique and special blessing now.

We now call forth our inner plane spiritual hosts and ask to be taken in our group Merkabah to the Golden Chamber of Melchizedek at the Universal level, to sit in his ascension seat.

Notice again the difference in frequency and quality of energy between the Galactic ascension seat and the Universal ascension seat you are now sitting in.

We also call forth at this time while at this Universal level, a special Divine dispensation from the Archangels, Michael/Faith, Jophiel/Christine, Chamuel/Charity, Gabriel/Hope, Raphael/Mother Mary, Uriel/Aurora, Zadekiel/Amethyst, The Seven Mighty Elohim and their Divine Counterparts, and request an ascension acceleration for each person individually, and for the entire group body.

We now call forth from Lord Melchizedek for the greatest possible ascension acceleration that is available to us at this time.

We call forth from Melchizedek for a special Divine dispensation to experience the "Light Rod" of Melchizedek.

Let us receive this very special blessing and grace now.

We now ask to be taken in our group Merkabah by Melchizedek to the next level up which is the Multiuniversal level, to sit in the Multiuniversal level ascension seat, by the grace of the Mahatma and the Multiuniversal Logos.

Feel an even more refined frequency at this most rarefied vibration.

We call to the Mahatma and the Multiuniversal Logos for a Divine dispensation for the greatest possible ascension acceleration that is available to us at this time.

We now call forth to the Mahatma and the Multiuniversal Logos to take the group Merkabah up to the next level, which is the ascension seat of the Divine Mother, at the Left Hand of GOD.

Feel the sublime energies of this ascension seat that words fail to even describe.

We call forth to the Divine Mother for a Divine dispensation, of the greatest possible ascension acceleration that is available to each one of us individually and collectively at this time.

Bathe in the Divine Cosmic Love and acceleration of the Divine Mother at this 352nd level of Divinity.

We call forth to the Divine Mother and ask that our group Merkabah now be taken to the ascension seat of the Divine Father, at the Right Hand of GOD.

Bathe in these most exquisite and sublime energies of the Divine Father's ascension seat.

We call forth to the Divine Father for a Divine dispensation of the greatest possible ascension acceleration that is available to each of us individually and collectively at this time.

Absorb this Divine Father acceleration into the very core and essence of your being.

As a special dispensation, we lastly call forth the Divine Mother, the Divine Father, the Mahatma, Melchizedek, Metatron, and Lord Michael, to take us in our group Merkabah to the Throne of Grace itself, to sit in GOD's Ascension Seat.

Let us humbly receive this blessing now, as we enter into the silence.

From the bottom of our hearts we thank the Beloved Presence of GOD for this most sanctified blessing and grace.

We now call forth the Divine Mother, the Divine Father, the Mahatma, Melchizedek, Metatron, and Lord Michael, and humbly request to be taken in our group Merkabah back down through all the levels and dimensions of reality into our physical bodies and back into the room.

18

Divine Mother & Lady Masters Ascension Activation Meditation

Close your eyes.

We begin this meditation by calling forth the Divine Mother and all the Lady Masters of the Planetary and Cosmic Hierarchy. We call to the Divine Mother and Lady Masters to supply a group Merkabah in the shape of a gigantic lotus blossom, which will carry all in attendance like a giant ocean liner sailing through the heavens to take us up through the 352 levels of reality to the Throne of the Divine Mother.

The Divine Mother I speak of here is the Cosmic Feminine Being who, in truth, is the Left Hand of GOD and is the fount of which all feminine Goddesses and Deities spring forth. She is also the fount from which the feminine aspect of all beings springs forth including all of the Gods, Goddesses, Ascended Masters, initiates, disciples and, in actuality, every single manifested aspect of Creation.

So let us now, my beloved brothers and sisters, feel ourselves being lifted up in the Divine Mother's Merkabah embrace and carried upward through all the dimensions of reality to the very Throne of Creation itself. As our lotus blossom Merkabah ascends now to the top of Creation itself, at the 352nd level of Divinity, we first experience, at the very Core Heart of Creation itself, absolute stillness and absolute all-pervading love. We are enveloped in a translucent platinum-pink light that is now absorbing itself into every cell, molecule, atom and electron of our being and into our very soul and Monadic essence itself.

We are also immersed in the most sublime fragrance of the sweetest smelling roses you could possibly imagine. In the background can be heard the Music of the Spheres in the form of a radiant choir of Angels intoning the most magnificent melodies and harmonies you have ever heard. The light emanating from the Throne of the Divine Mother is so bright and magnificent that it takes a few moments for the eyes and senses to adjust to such splendor.

As our collective eyes focus upon the Throne of the Divine Mother, Her translucent lighted form can now be seen with Her arms open in embrace, gathering all into the center of Her very heart. It is as if the Merkabah with all of us gathered within it has entered and become one with the living, pulsating Heart of the Divine Mother. As we remain in this stillness, we can feel our entire beings and our own individual hearts now rhythmically beating to Her Cosmic Pulse.

Beloved brothers and sisters, know that Divine Mother and Divine Father are but two halves of the same whole that together comprise that which we call the GODHEAD. Feel the exquisite love, joy, warmth, tenderness, and nurturing as we are now merged with the Divine Mother.

Feel yourself transforming into both an anchor for, and a transmitter of, this Divine and hallowed Love.

Know the safety and the nurturing that exists within this most sacred gift, as Divine Mother continues to infuse you with the reawakening of that part of yourself that is the core of the Goddess within you, both in female and male alike.

Now see within this translucent, hallowed, platinum-pink aura, blessed Virgin Mary as she glides to you upon a golden crescent moon. Feel the absolute purity of her essence and the wondrous benediction of her all-embracing love, as she merges into this heart-space we now find ourselves in.

She holds within her hand a rose, pink in color, representative of love's tenderness, and individually hands one to each of you at this moment. She watches as you each place the rose within your own heart, thereby claiming the essence of the Feminine Spirit and of Unconditional Love for and within your very selves.

Take a moment to feel this love flood through your own being and then outward to touch all of life.

Now see Quan Yin as she emerges out of the light. Feel her gaze penetrate you at every single level of your being and flood you with the essence of Divine mercy and compassion.

Take a moment to let this purest quality of compassion, mercy and forgiveness wash away any judgments or negativity that you have had toward self. Then let it spread outward to others in your personal life that are suffering due to lack of mercy, forgiveness and compassion. Let this same quality of compassion and mercy now flow outward to the entire planet, as you join with Quan Yin in her holy service, spreading Divine compassion, mercy, and forgiveness.

See now as Pallas Athena emerges from the light. Feel her qualities of Divine Love and Divine Strength enter into your being; recharging and reactivating these two aspects of the Divine Feminine as they commingle within her loving yet powerful essence. Take this in and know that that which is the most loving, tender, gentle, compassionate and nurturing feminine spirit, likewise holds within its aura power, strength, and command.

The "feminine" contains its own unique brand of power and strength, yet these Divine qualities are likewise part of that which is the all-embracing Divine Mother. Pallas Athena brings you the harmony of these energies in female form. Allow yourself to honor the Divine Feminine this moment by both honoring beloved Pallas Athena, and honoring your own feminine power, strength, and command!

Watch now as a golden glow alights your inner vision to unveil the face of Vesta, the feminine aspect of the Solar Logos! Let this golden glow stimulate the pure gold of your own true being as it pours forth and radiates out of Vesta herself. Allow yourself to connect with solar intent in a way that you have never done on a conscious level before. Feel the utter joy of knowing just how much a part of Vesta and this solar system of love/wisdom you truly are. Let this feeling now radiate outward into the Cosmos.

Now see Lakshmi emerge upon her lotus blossom as she awakens within you the full knowingness that the abundance of all things is there for each and every one of you. She asks you now to think upon that which for you is abundance and prosperity. Then hear her as she transmits to you the power to manifest your personal prosperity and abundance through the Law of Attraction. She wants you to know that you each have the power to do this by simply holding to the positive ideal of that which you seek, letting nothing whatsoever sway you from this focused intent.

Allow yourself a moment to do this.

Now think of a situation or place within the sphere of the planet that is in need of prosperity and abundance and hold your positive and focused attention there for a moment.

See now the Divine Mother of the Native Americans, who herself stands forth as representative of the soil, the grasslands, the rivers, oceans, mountains, trees, plants, animals and rocks. Allow all nurturing of earth to flow through her into yourselves. Feel yourselves anchor her Divine grace into the very core and heart center of our blessed planet.

Feel now the pervading presence of Isis. She breathes into each of you the "breath of antiquity," that you may awaken to the new and ancient glory of your own Goddess energies. She emits from her aura the ability to decode the "language of light," wherein the mysteries of your past, present, and future stand forth to be revealed.

Now behold Hera, Greek Goddess of Wisdom. She waves her wand upon you that you may have the wisdom to use the ever-awakening truths and mysteries for the benefit of all humanity.

See now each of the seven feminine Archangels, as one by one they come to bless you with the distinct quality of their ray. First comes Faith, then Christine, Charity, Hope, Mother Mary, Aurora and Amethyst.

Pause and receive their specialized blessings.

Now emerging are the feminine Elohim: Amazonia, Lumina, Amora, Astrea, Virginia, Aloha and Victoria.

Feel the enormity of their Divine Grace and blessing. Allow these most powerful co-creators within your field, and again drink deeply of the feminine strength and will to create!

See and feel the Goddess of Liberty, the Lady of Light, the Lady Nada, Parvati, Kali, Durga, Mary Magdalene, Portia, Mother Teresa, the Earth Mother, the Lady of the Lake, Lady Helena (formerly known as Madam Blavatsky), and the presence of all of the Lady Masters who have ever graced and touched this planet.

See the Gopis of Krishna dance before you. Allow yourself to become one of them and dance along with them as you yourself embrace the feminine aspect of self. At this moment it does not matter if you are in male or female embodiment, for that which is of the Goddess lives within all of you, and seeks to dance the great dance of Love Divine to the melodies of the flute of Krishna.

Once again be aware of the breath flowing in and out of your Heart Center. Be aware also that there is a heart center located in a hidden chamber within the Crown Chakra. This is known as the "Heart within the Head," and is one of the major access points where love and wisdom blend. The other major access point for the blending of these two energies is within the eye that is hidden in a secret chamber within the Heart Center. This point is known as the "Mind within the Heart."

Allow the breath now to flow evenly through your bodies while at the same time hold a point of focus in the "Heart within the Head" and the "Mind within the Heart."

Feel simultaneously as the solar plexus embraces the power of the feminine spirit. Know that this power is different from that which is contained with the masculine part of self and is different also from the power or will that is representative of the Divine Father, Divine Masculine or Yang energies. Each aspect, both feminine and masculine, has a point of balance within each other. So Divine Mother and Divine Father are complete within their own point of balance and are more "fully" complete when they merge their balanced essences within each other. Again, it is the place where these two energies fully merge that we call the GODHEAD.

Now take a moment to give thanks to Divine Mother Herself. Give thanks also to the essence of the Goddess energy as She manifests within yourself, upon the earth, and in all planes of existence. Likewise, give thanks to the many Lady Masters, Lady Archangels, and Lady Elohim who have given forth their unique blessings. Take a moment to give thanks to beloved Gaia, the Earth Mother. Now give thanks to the Feminine Spirit within each of your beloved brothers and sisters. Finally, give thanks to the feminine spirit within yourselves. Again, this applies equally to men and women alike.

To conclude this meditation, we call forth all the Lady Masters of the Planetary and Cosmic Hierarchy to now step forward once again and bring forth a Love and Light Shower to all who reside in the lotus blossom Merkabah in the Heart of the Divine Mother. Feel and experience now, my beloved brothers and sisters, the profundity of the Cosmic Feminine as Her infinite forms rain down their infinite blessings upon you. Completely soak in and bathe in this Love and Light.

(One minute of silence)

Now, beloveds of GOD, let us join our energies into this Love and Light Shower and let us rain our collective Love and Light upon all our beloved brothers and sisters on earth, as well as upon the Earth herself.

(One minute of silence)

Let us now bring this process to a close and as we do so the Divine Mother and Lady Masters gently and lovingly lift our Merkabah out of the Heart of the Divine Mother and gently and caressingly glides us down the

352 levels of Divinity back to earth and into our physical bodies. As we do so, feel the Earth Mother embrace us in gratitude and joy.

The Divine Mother wishes you all to know that a part of you still remains in Her Heart from this experience and She lovingly invites all to return in total consciousness any time you should feel the need or desire. She welcomes all Her prodigal daughters and sons home in support of their service missions on earth. She wants you to know that, in truth, anywhere you are, there She is also! There is no place in Heaven or Earth where you are out of the Divine Mother's embrace. Feel this, experience this, and know this in the very core of your being.

19

Ascension Activation Meditation and Treatment

Beloved GOD, Christ, Holy Spirit, beloved Mighty I Am Presence, my Monad, I Am That I Am, beloved Mahatma—the Avatar of Synthesis, Seven Mighty Elohim, Melchior—our Galactic Logos, Ashtar Command, Archangels Michael, Jophiel, Chamuel, Gabriel, Raphael, Uriel, Zadkiel, Metatron, Helios—our Solar Logos, Sanat Kumara—our Planetary Logos, Lord Maitreya—the Planetary Christ, Allah Gobi—the Manu, the Mahachohan, Sathya Sai Baba, beloved Chohans of the Seven Rays, El Morya, Kuthumi, Serapis Bey, Paul the Venetian, Hilarion, Master Jesus, St. Germain, the Lords of Karma, Djwhal Khul, Buddha, Vywamus, Virgin Mary, Quan Yin, Isis, Babaji, the Great Divine Director, Enoch, the Great White Brotherhood MAP Healing Team (Pan, Overlighting Angel of Healing, Ascended Masters and Monad), Order of Melchizedek, Spiritual Hierarchy, Great White Brotherhood, Masters of Shamballa!

Beloved GOD and beloved Mahatma, I choose now to accept and invoke a deep penetration of the Mahatma energy into my entire energy matrix, thereby allowing a full, open radiation of my Divine Self in service to All That Is, now.

I call forth from GOD and the GOD Force a series of golden balls of light. These large golden balls of light are coming down from GOD and my Mighty I Am Presence and moving down my chakra column, entering my seven chakras.

I let the golden ball of light enter my First Chakra. I now fully open and activate my First Chakra. I Am That I Am. Aum!

I let the golden ball enter my Second Chakra. I now fully open and activate my Second Chakra. I Am That I Am. Aum!

I now fully open and activate my Third Chakra. I Am That I Am. Aum!

I now fully open and activate my Fourth Chakra. I Am That I Am. Aum!

I now fully open and activate my Fifth Chakra. I Am That I Am. Aum!

I now fully open and activate my Sixth Chakra. I Am That I Am. Aum!

I now fully open and activate my Seventh Chakra. I Am That I Am. Aum!

Now call forth your Mighty I Am Presence and Archangel Michael and the Great White Brotherhood Medical Assistance Program (MAP) team (composed of Pan, Ascended Master healers, Angels of healing, and your own Monad) to enter each chakra and perfectly balance and attune it, removing any unwanted energies or cords of energy that are not for your highest GOD purpose and of your true Divine Monadic Blueprint. Take about fifteen seconds or more for each chakra to fully invoke cleansing, perfect healing, and balancing for each chakra. Once you have perfectly purified, cleansed, healed, and balanced each chakra with GOD's Healing Light, then request an activation for the perfect integration and balancing of your chakras so they function as one unified chakra.

Now call forth the Violet Flame of Saint Germain to bathe your entire being in his Violet Transmuting Flame. Let this beautiful violet energy flowing down from GOD transmute any and all negativity into the purity and perfection of GOD. After bathing in this energy for about fifteen to thirty seconds, call forth the golden Twelfth Ray and allow it to bathe your entire being in the energy of the Christ Consciousness. See your entire being and all seven bodies being filled with this luminous golden energy pouring down from GOD, your Mighty I Am Presence and the Ascended Masters. Bathe in this Twelfth Ray golden light for another fifteen to thirty seconds.

Now request GOD and the GOD Force to be placed within your living Light Merkabah vehicle. See the Merkabah vehicle as a double-terminated crystal that surrounds your entire body, with another horizontal double-terminated section coming out the front and back of the vertical part. The Merkabah vehicle will help to accelerate and quicken your overall vibrational frequencies. It is also a vehicle in which you can soul travel during meditation or while you sleep at night. Place yourself fully within the Merkabah vehicle now and allow it to spin clockwise. This spinning allows you to become even more attuned to the Cosmic pulse and frequencies of GOD and the GOD Force.

I am now ready for the ascension process to begin! (The *ascending* process is really the *descending* process of Spirit into matter.) Beloved GOD and GOD force, I now call forth my soul to fully descend into my consciousness and four-body system if it has not done so already. I Am That I Am. Aum!

I call forth my glorified Light Body to now descend into my consciousness and four-body system. I Am That I Am. Aum!

I call forth the Ascension Flame to descend and enter my consciousness and entire four-body system. I Am That I Am. Aum!

I call forth the full activation of my Alpha and Omega Chakras! I Am That I Am. Aum!

I call forth the Amrita, fire letters, sacred geometries, and key codes from the *Keys of Enoch* to now become fully activated. I Am That I Am. Aum!

I now call forth the full activation and creation of my full potential 12 strands of DNA within my physical vehicle. I Am That I Am. Aum!

I now call forth the full activation of my pituitary gland to create only the life hormone and to stop producing the death hormone! I Am That I Am. Aum!

I now call forth and fully activate my Monadic Divine Blueprints in my conscious, subconscious, and superconscious minds and four-body system. I Am That I Am. Aum!

I now call forth and fully activate my Kundalini energy as guided by my Monad and Mighty I Am Presence. I Am That I Am. Aum!

I now call forth a matchstick-sized spark of Cosmic Fire from the Presence of GOD Himself to illuminate and transform my entire being into the Light of GOD. I Am That I Am. Aum!

I now call forth a full axiatonal alignment as described in *The Keys of Enoch* to perfectly align all my meridian flows within my consciousness and four-body system! I Am That I Am. Aum!

I now call forth and fully claim my physical immortality and the complete cessation of the aging and death process. I am now youthing and becoming younger every day. I Am That I Am. Aum!

I now call forth the full opening of my Third Eye and all my psychic abilities and channeling abilities, that I may use them in the glory and service of the Most High GOD and my brothers and sisters in Christ on earth. I Am That I Am. Aum!

I now call forth perfect radiant health to manifest within my physical, emotional, mental, etheric, and spiritual bodies. I ask and command that these bodies now manifest the health and perfection of Christ. I Am That I Am. Aum!

I now call forth my Sixteenth Chakra to descend, moving all my chakras down my chakra column until my Sixteenth Chakra resides in my Seventh or Crown Chakra. I Am That I Am. Aum!

I now call forth my Fifteenth Chakra to descend and enter my Sixth, or Third Eye Chakra. I Am That I Am. Aum!

I now call forth my Fourteenth Chakra to descend and enter my Throat Chakra. I Am That I Am. Aum!

I now call forth my Thirteenth Chakra to descend and enter and reside in my Heart Chakra. I Am That I Am. Aum!

I now call forth my Twelfth Chakra to descend and enter and reside in my Solar Plexus Chakra. I Am That I Am. Aum!

I now call forth my Eleventh Chakra to descend and enter and reside in my Second Chakra. I Am That I Am. Aum!

I now call forth my Tenth Chakra to descend and enter and reside in my First Chakra. I Am That I Am. Aum!

I now see the rest of my chakras, nine through one, descend down my legs and into the earth in a corresponding fashion. I Am That I Am. Aum!

I now call forth the complete stabilization of my new fifth-dimensional chakra grid system within my consciousness and four-body system now. I Am That I Am. Aum!

I now call forth and see my chakra column lighting up like a Christmas tree with my First Chakra becoming a large ball of pearl-white light.

My Second Chakra now becomes a large ball of pink-orange light.

My Third Chakra now becomes a glowing ball of golden light.

My Heart Chakra now lights up with a pale violet-pink light.

My Fifth Chakra now lights up with a deep blue-violet light.

My Third Eye Chakra now lights up with a large ball of golden-white light.

My Crown Chakra now lights up with violet-white light.

My entire chakra column has now been ignited with the fifth-dimensional ascension frequency. I Am That I Am. Aum!

I now call forth with all my heart and soul and mind and might the collective help of my eleven other soul extensions in my ascension process. I Am That I Am. Aum!

I now call forth the combined collective help of the 143 other soul extensions of my monadic group in my ascension process, now. I Am That I Am. Aum!

I now call forth the complete descending and integration into my being of the "raincloud of knowable things"! I Am That I Am. Aum!

I now call forth the trinity of Isis, Osiris, and Horus, and all pyramid energies that are aligned with Source to now descend into my consciousness and four-body system and to become fully activated now.

I also call forth the Ascended Master Serapis Bey and his Ascension Temple energies from Luxor, to descend and become fully activated within my consciousness and four-body system now. I Am That I Am. Aum!

I now call forth an "ascension column of light" to surround my entire being. I Am That I Am. Aum!

I now call forth the complete balancing of all my karma from all my past and future lives. I Am That I Am. Aum!

I now call forth the raising of my vibrational frequencies within my physical, astral, mental, etheric, and spiritual bodies to the fifth-dimensional frequencies. I Am That I Am. Aum!

I now call forth the light of a thousand suns to descend into my being and raise my vibrational frequencies one-thousandfold. I Am That I Am. Aum!

I now call forth the sacred sound of "Aum" to descend and reverberate through my consciousness and four-body system. I Am That I Am. Aum!

I now call forth a complete and full baptism of the Holy Spirit. I Am That I Am. Aum! I Am That I Am. Aum!

I call forth the perfect attunement and completion of my dharma, purpose, and mission in this lifetime in service of GOD's plan. I Am That I Am. Aum!

I call forth my fifth-dimensional ascended self that is already ascended within the understanding of simultaneous time, to now meld its consciousness with my unified field and aura. I Am That I Am. Aum!

I call forth my spiritual teacher, *(insert name)*, to descend through my Crown Chakra and meld his or her ascended consciousness and light into my consciousness and four-body system. I Am That I Am. Aum!

I hereby call forth my Monad, my Mighty I Am Presence and Spirit to now fully descend into my consciousness and four-body system and transform me into Light and the Ascended Master that I truly am. I Am That I Am. Aum!

Take a few minutes of silence to allow the complete ascension to fully take place while remaining on earth. Upon complete merger with the Light in consciousness and in your four-body system, recite the following affirmations of truth:

> Be still and know I Am GOD! I Am That I Am. Aum!
> I Am the Resurrection and the Life! I Am That I Am. Aum!
> I Am the Mighty I Am Presence on earth forever more! I Am That I Am. Aum!
> I Am the Ascended Master (*insert your full name*)! I Am That I Am. Aum!
> The Mighty I Am Presence is now my real self. I Am That I Am. Aum!
> I Am the Ascension in the Light. I Am That I Am. Aum!
> I Am the Truth, the Way, and the Light! I Am That I Am. Aum!
> I Am the open door which no man can shut. I Am That I Am. Aum!
> I Am Divine Perfection made manifest now. I Am That I Am. Aum!
> I Am the Revelation of GOD. I Am That I Am. Aum!
> I Am the Light that lights every man that cometh into the world. I Am That I Am. Aum!
> I Am the Cosmic Flame of Cosmic Victory. I Am That I Am. Aum!
> I Am the Ascended Being I wish to be now. I Am That I Am. Aum!
> I Am the raised vibration of my full Christ and I Am Potential. I Am That I Am. Aum!
> I Am the "Aum" made manifest in the world. I Am That I Am. Aum!
> I Am a full member of the Great White Brotherhood and Spiritual Hierarchy. I Am That I Am. Aum!

I Am the realized manifestation of the Eternal Self. I Am That I Am. Aum!

I Am the embodiment of Divine Love in action. I Am That I Am. Aum!

I live within all beings and all beings live within me. I Am That I Am. Aum!

I Am now one with the Monadic Plane of consciousness on earth! I Am That I Am. Aum!

I Am now living in my glorified Body of Light on earth. I Am That I Am. Aum!

I now affirm my ability to transform my four bodies into Light and travel anywhere in GOD's infinite Universe. I Am That I Am. Aum!

I call forth to Helios, the Solar Logos, to now send forth into my consciousness through my Crown Chakra, the 64 Keys of Enoch in all five sacred languages so they are fully integrated into my being on earth. I Am That I Am. Aum!

I fully affirm my identity as the Eternal Self, the Christ, the Buddha, the Atma, the Monad, the I Am Presence on earth in service of humankind. I Am That I Am. Aum!

I fully affirm that I Am physically immortal and I can, if I choose, remain on earth indefinitely without aging! I Am That I Am. Aum!

I see every person, animal, and plant as the embodiment of the Eternal Self, whether they are aware of their true identity or not. I Am That I Am.

Aum!

I Am now the perfect integration of the Monad, soul, and personality on earth. I Am That I Am. Aum!

In this "holy instant" has salvation come. I Am That I Am. Aum!

I Am One Self, united with my Creator. I Am That I Am. Aum!

I Am the Light of the world. I Am That I Am. Aum!

I Am now a fully Ascended Being who has chosen to remain on earth to be of service to all sentient beings! I Am That I Am. Aum!

Kodoish, Kodoish, Kodoish, Adonai Tsebayoth! (Holy, Holy, Holy, is the Lord GOD of Hosts!) Kodoish, Kodoish, Kodoish, Adonai Tsebayoth! (Holy, Holy, Holy, is the Lord GOD of Hosts!) Kodoish, Kodoish, Kodoish, Adonai Tsebayoth! (Holy, Holy, Holy, is the Lord GOD of Hosts!) I Am That I Am.

Aum!

20

Specialized Ascension Activation from the Spiritual Hierarchy

Close eyes—let us begin by taking a deep breath—exhale.

We call forth all the Masters from the Planetary and Cosmic Hierarchy to help in this meditation.

We call forth a Planetary and Cosmic axiatonal alignment.

We call forth from Melchizedek, the Mahatma, and Metatron to now anchor the Platinum Net to clear away any and all unwanted energies.

We begin by calling forth Lord Buddha, our Planetary Logos, and requesting the permanent anchoring and activation of all GOD Crystals and Seed Packets from Shamballa.

We now move up one level to the Solar level, and call forth Helios and Vesta to now anchor and activate all the GOD Crystals and Seed Packets from the Solar Core.

We now move to the Galactic level and call forth Melchior, to anchor and activate all the GOD Crystals and Seed Packets from the Galactic Core.

We now move up to the Universal level and call forth Melchizedek, to anchor and activate all the GOD Crystals and Seed Packets from the Universal Core.

We move up again to the Multi-universal level and call forth the Multi-Universal Logos, to anchor and activate all the GOD Crystals and Seed Packets from the Multi-Universal Core.

We now move to the 352nd level of the GODHEAD, and call forth directly to GOD, the Cosmic Council of Twelve, and the "Twenty-Four Elders that surround the Throne of Grace," for the anchoring and activation of all the GOD Crystals and Seed Packets from the Heart of GOD.

As we continue to soak in and absorb the GOD Crystals, Seed Packets, and Cosmic energies from Source, the Mahatma has asked me to make a very special request to all of you that are gathered here physically and upon the inner plane—to take on a very specific and important spiritual assignment.

The assignment he has requested us all to take on as a group body is that of being a Planetary anchor and focus for his Cosmic energies.

So in this moment, I'm asking you all if you are willing to take on this spiritual assignment upon his request.

If so, inwardly give your consent and approval to the Mahatma within the core of your being.

For those who have now agreed, we will take 30 seconds of silence while he runs his Cosmic energy embodying all 352 levels of GOD through us.

We now also call forth from the Mahatma for the opening of the 352 levels of the Heart, in the sense of a holographic penetration of the Mahatma's entire being.

We call forth from Melchizedek, Metatron, the Mahatma, the Archangels and the Elohim Councils, for the anchoring and activation of all fire letters, key codes and sacred geometries, to anchor and activate the master Divine Blueprint for each person present.

We now call forth to our inner plane spiritual hosts, for the anchoring and activation of the Light Grid of Ascension, for all Monads of the 144,000 currently working on ascension.

We call forth the beloved Master Kuthumi, the Chohan of the Second Ray, who will now confer the status of "World Teacher" to all who are in attendance at this time, if you choose to receive this blessing.

Visualize yourself standing before Master Kuthumi, with your palms held open and turned upward, and see Master Kuthumi first touching your heart, then your Third Eye, and then your Crown Chakra.

Feel the spiritual current run through you as you take on this mantle of responsibility.

We now call forth the Divine Mother, Quan Yin, Vesta, Lakshmi, Lady of the Sun, Lady Liberty, Portia, Lady Nada, Pallas Athena, Lady of the Light, Lady Helena, Hilda, Alice Bailey, Isis, the Virgin Mary, and all the Lady Masters of the Planetary and Cosmic Hierarchy.

We call forth from this great Sisterhood of Light for the full anchoring and activation of the Divine Feminine within, in order that it resonates in perfect harmony to the Divine Masculine within.

We ask for a complete balancing of the male/female, yin/yang energies within each of our selves, so that these energies may flow and manifest in perfect harmony and ease as GOD would have it be.

Visualize now the Divine Mother placing a lotus blossom composed of the Love/Wisdom and Power of GOD, within the center of each person's heart.

We also request that the Divine Mother and Lady Masters become permanently anchored upon the inside of our hearts.

We now call forth Archangel Metatron and request a Divine dispensation for the full anchoring and activation of the Platinum Rod for each person in attendance who wishes to receive this grace and blessing.

We call forth the Ascended Master Djwhal Khul, from the Planetary Synthesis Ashram, to now officially anchor and activate, with the help of the Seven Chohans, each person's Divine puzzle piece so that each person may easily and effortlessly fulfill their Divine mission and life's purpose.

We call forth El Morya, Kuthumi, Djwhal Khul, Serapis Bey, Paul the Venetian, Hilarion, Sananda, St. Germain, Allah Gobi, Lord Maitreya,

Lord Buddha and Vywamus, for help in weaving each person's ascension fabric to take them to the next level of Planetary and Cosmic ascension realization.

We now call forth Melchizedek, the Mahatma, Metatron, Lord Michael, the Archangels, and the Elohim Councils for Light Quotient building at the highest potential available to each person individually, and to the entire group body.

We call forth the Divine Mother, Helios and Vesta, Quan Yin, Lord Maitreya and the Virgin Mary for Love Quotient building at the highest potential available to each person individually, and to the entire group body.

As the Love Quotient continues to flow in, we now conclude this specialized ascension activation.

21

Cosmic Ascension Activations from the Planetary and Cosmic Hierarchy

I call forth Mother Mary.

Mother Mary steps forth in radiant splendor and now showers each person individually and collectively with pink and magenta rose petals.

Feel these rose petals showering down upon us in Divine Gentleness and Unconditional Love of the most resplendent kind.

Sense the aroma and fragrance as these petals fall, surrounding each one of us in her eternal protection and love!

I call forth Quan Yin, Goddess of Mercy and Compassion, who now steps forward with the special Divine gift of stepping within each one of us for the sole purpose of filling us each completely and utterly with the essence of pure Compassion.

Allow her to fully enter, and feel this radiance of compassion well up within you for yourself first—now let it stream forth to every sentient being in all kingdoms and evolutions upon this earth...

Fully realize that this is a permanent and eternal anchoring and activation that beloved Quan Yin asks you to use every moment of your life and beyond. Beloved Quan Yin steps out of our vehicles, leaving the essence of her compassion eternally within you!

I call forth Pallas Athena, who serves as one of the members of the Karmic Board.

She comes forth now in energy essence as a Divine Receptacle to anchor the yin or feminine energy within all in attendance.

She comes aligned with the Divine Mother of the Universe, to stimulate and activate this most needed energy to bring balance and harmony.

Allow this activation to anchor fully within each cell and level of your beingness so that you may go forth and bring it into outer manifestation!

I now call forth His Holiness the Lord Sai Baba, who holds the mantle of the Cosmic Christ for planet earth.

He takes us all in our group Merkabah to his ascension seat, which is really more of a "love seat" or "love cushion" at the Universal level of Divinity.

Bathe in the Universal love and sweetness of this Cosmic Avatar.

Feel Sai Baba now sprinkling his sacred Virbutti ash upon our Crown Chakras and entire beingness to cleanse us of all impurity.

Sai Baba reaches his hand forward and places within each person's heart, as a sacred gift, an exquisite rose quartz filled with his eternal energy and love.

Anytime you need his help, and/or anytime you are giving or receiving love, this crystal will become activated and imbued with his everlasting love and blessing.

Let us now return to our group Merkabah and receive further blessings and gifts from the Masters.

I call forth Archangel Michael. He steps forward in a radiant aura of light, wielding his Blue-Flame Sword of Protection.

He asks you, beloved ones, to know that he has surrounded you and continues to surround you along with his Legions of Light, to serve as your personal and collective Divine Protector.

He also knows that it is time for each of us to share with him this mantle of Divine Protection.

In this vein and spirit, Archangel Michael, with a wave of his hand, has created an etheric replica of his Flaming Blue Sword so that you and he may work in co-partnership for the protection of self and others.

He asks that you continue to call on him at every opportunity, while at the same time lifting up your Sword of Protection that he has given in name and imbued with his power!

I now call forth Helios & Vesta who come forward as copper-gold flames of light from the Solar Core.

As each of us here already share part of their essence, they now magnify and ignite this Solar Essence within us ten-thousandfold as their gift and blessing for our participation in this most sacred event.

In so doing they further unite us to the Great Central Sun, which accelerates and advances us forward on our spiritual path, progression and ultimate destiny!

I now call forth Vywamus, the higher aspect of Sanat Kumara, who greets you and brings forth a most wonderful gift.

In celebration of the efforts of growth and initiation itself, he offers each one of us here a further unfolding of the inner senses.

This will manifest according to each person's unique tendencies, configurations and purpose; however, all are now being blessed with further activations to either see, hear, sense and attune to the inner realms in much greater ways than we have ever known before.

Let us sit in the silence for a moment to receive this blessing from beloved Vywamus!

I now call forth the Lord of Sirius, who steps forth from the home of the Great White Lodge on Sirius, which Shamballa is an outpost of.

The Lord of Sirius holds out his hand to each person in attendance and offers the gift of a "golden key."

This key holds the matrix which will unlock the inner sanctums and secret chambers residing within Shamballa that very few in the history of the earth have had access to.

This key will unlock secrets of the universe for the purposes of accelerated ascension and planetary world service.

This key is now given to you in great sanctity and reverence.

I call forth the Lord of Arcturus, who now steps forward from the great mother ship.

The Lord of Arcturus is known for helping to bring forward to humanity the spiritual attributes of Love, Unity, and Harmony that we are all familiar with.

Today, however, he brings forward a gift that is absolutely astounding in its effect.

The Lord of Arcturus offers us now the gift of his "Arcturian Joy Machine"!

Feel the pure joy welling up within you...

The element of joy rises on wings of delight and laughter and carries one effortlessly to the heights of Divinity.

It is one of the more vital elements all too often missing in our lives.

So let's take a minute to bathe in this joy...

The Lord of Arcturus invites you all to inwardly call upon this machine at anytime that you are in need of joy and want more lightness, fun and laughter in your lives!

The Lord of Arcturus is now turning it up full force!!!

I now call forth Lakshmi, the Goddess of Prosperity.

Lakshmi steps forward for all in attendance to make a cellular adjustment within each person to adjust their resonation and frequency on a conscious, subconscious and superconscious level, to attract and magnetize prosperity and abundance in all aspects of our lives.

Lakshmi, with outstretched hands, now places within each person's heart a "golden lotus blossom of prosperity."

Let us become receptive and allow this attunement and adjustment to take place on every level.

I now call forth the Planetary Christ, Lord Maitreya.

He steps forward in robes of white and welcomes you all into your own Self-Mastery. Lord Maitreya's gift is to offer a benediction to all assembled here.

I let him speak through me now the following words, "I, Lord Maitreya, grace you, beloved ones, with the abundant confidence in yourselves necessary to go forward into the multitudes and teach of the Oneness, Love and Light that radiates within your Soul and Spirit.

I join myself with you at this time, in a closer unity than we have ever known before; and our paths as teachers, leaders, and world servers blend and merge at the very core and heart of our beings.

Know, my beloved ones, as you go forth from this moment forward, you walk in my sandals and I in yours!

In gratitude for the planetary service work you have done and continue to do, I grace each of you with the knowledge that you never walk alone!

For I, Maitreya, share your footsteps. So let it be written, so let it be done!!!

I now call forth Allah Gobi, who serves in the spiritual government in the capacity of the Manu, which is a First Ray position overlighting El Morya.

He comes forth holding a great and vibrant staff of will and power in one hand and a giant holographic mandala of rotating wheels in the other hand.

With outstretched hands, he now offers each one of us a replica of this staff and mandala to help call forth the Will of GOD into action within the movement of each of our lives.

In so doing, he fully activates the "seed of will" within our beings, as well as the power to effectuate the appropriate transformation and movement both in our personal lives and in service to the planet.

Let us receive this gift and blessing now!

I now call forth Commander Ashtar of the Ashtar Command.

Commander Ashtar brings forth the gift of "spiritual discernment."

This quality of energy is now being beamed into the Third Eye of each person in attendance, from Commander Ashtar's mother ship.

This activation will make his job easier as a guardian and protector of this planet, along with his fleet, as each one of us integrates and uses this heightened sense of discernment and takes personal responsibility to close off from any energies that do not stem from Love, Unity and Light.

I now call forth Dr. Lorphan, who many of you don't know and who it is my great honor to introduce to you.

Dr. Lorphan is the director of the Healing Academy in the Great White Lodge on Sirius.

He is the inner plane Master/Physician who trains all teams and divisions of healers.

Dr. Lorphan steps forward with his Galactic Healing Team to offer all in attendance his personal assistance—24 hours a day, seven days a week—for all physical, etheric and electrical health lessons.

Dr. Lorphan and his team of Galactic Healers are the most advanced healers in the entire galaxy, and they await only your call to be of immediate service in this capacity.

Let us all now take a minute to inwardly ask specifically for help with any health lesson we are dealing with, or if you prefer, for helping someone you know.

Let us experience these healing forces now!

I now call forth the overlighting Guardian Angel of planet earth who oversees the work of each person's individual Guardian Angel.

This beloved Angelic Presence with the wave of her hands brings forward a gentle white mist which surrounds each person individually that serves to create a profound receptivity to each of our personal Guardian Angels.

Let us be quiet and receptive now and receive this gift and experience and feel this greater opening and attunement to our Guardian Angels that, in truth, never leave our side!

I now call forth Djwhal Khul, who holds leadership in the inner plane Synthesis Ashram, whose Second Ray work involves the spiritual training and education of all disciples and initiates on planet earth.

Another facet of his responsibilities is to bring forth vast amounts of pertinent mystical and occult information.

In this vein, Djwhal brings to you the gift and blessing of "brain illumination," which will serve to increase your capacity to integrate and assimilate ancient, present and future spiritual revelations.

This is being done personally for each person in attendance now through the use of Djwhal's holographic computer located in his personal office in his inner plane ashram.

Let us be still and quiet as we feel this stimulation and activation take place!!!

I now call forth the seven Chohans, who hold the position of Lords of the Rays. I call forth El Morya, Kuthumi, Serapis Bey, Paul the Venetian, Hilarion, Sananda, and St. Germain, who also holds the position of the Mahachohan.

Each of these beloved Ray Masters steps forward to offer a gift and ascension activation to each person in attendance.

El Morya steps forward with the gift and activation of greater "Personal Power" and the "Will to Good."

Receive this blessing now!

Kuthumi steps forward and offers the gift and activation of "Heart/Mind Integration."

Receive this blessing now!

Serapis Bey steps forward and offers the gift and activation of a "Quickening of the Ascension process."

Receive this blessing now!

Hilarion steps forward and offers the gift and activation of a greater understanding of the "science involved in the manifestation of the New Age on a personal and collective level."

Receive this blessing now!

Sananda steps forward and offers the gift and activation of "Greater Devotion and Commitment to the Higher Spiritual Principles and Ideals for which you stand."

Receive this blessing now!

St. Germain steps forward with the gift and activation of a "Greater Power and Strength in the utilization of the Violet Transmuting Flame."

In St. Germain's capacity as the Mahachohan in the Spiritual Government, he offers a second gift of "a greater understanding and inner sense of Spiritual Alchemy on all levels of our being in order to help us further advance and transform our civilization into that of the Golden Age, both on a personal and collective level."

Let us be still and quiet and receive these blessings now!

22

Planetary World Service Meditations

Planetary Axiatonal Alignment

As with all the following meditations, assume a comfortable position either sitting up or lying down, with your spine straight. Sitting up is preferable in these types of meditations, as you are generally more focused that way. Leaning against a wall if you are sitting on the floor, or upon the back of a chair is perfectly fine as long as the spine is held as straight as possible. Lying down is also all right, as long as you maintain your focus.

First request a personal axiatonal alignment so that you yourself are as balanced as possible. Then request a full axiatonal alignment for the Earth herself. Visualize the bodies of Earth on all the various levels, totally and completely aligned, with all energies of our planet as a whole fully aligned with Solar, Galactic, Universal, Multi-Universal and Cosmic Divine intent! Breathe slowly and relaxed, all the while holding the focus of a totally aligned, balanced and integrated Earth! Stay with this for as long as you feel comfortable, up to five minutes.

Platinum Net Sweep

Begin by asking for the Platinum Net to sweep over yourself and/or your group first, so that you can be cleared of your own misqualified energies. Then request that the same be done for the planet as a whole.

Request this for the physical, etheric, astral and mental atmosphere of Earth. In this way each of the four lower bodies of Earth herself will receive one of the most potent cleansing, purifying, and healing tools being currently offered by the Cosmic Masters. You need not remain in meditation too long, just long enough to fully visualize a gigantic Platinum Net sweeping over the four bodies of the planet and cleansing these bodies of as much debris as possible. The more this is done, the healthier the planet will become.

Meditation for the Earth Mother

When seated comfortably in your meditation position, call first for the overlighting presence of your own Monad. Then from that place, invoke within all of the Masters who work with the physical, etheric, astral, and mental bodies of Earth herself. Call specifically upon Lord Buddha, our Planetary Logos. Allow these wonderful healing energies to pour through you and fill your entire being. When you feel fully infused with these Divine energies, anchor your own grounding cord deep into the Earth. Turn your palms upward on your lap, or even extend the arms upward for a time if you like. Ask that the healing currents of all the blessed Masters whose presence you have invoked flow through you and outward into the Earth.

First visualize and direct these energies into the very Core Heart of Mother Earth. Ask that there be a balancing and harmonizing within the very foundation of the planet itself. Pour forth love that all that needs healing may be healed, balanced, and cleansed through grace rather than karma. Then put your attention upon the Earth's etheric body. Once again, ask all the Masters in attendance to help radiate through you their blessed healing energies. Do the same for the astral atmosphere and astral body of the Earth, that all negative emotions be brought to a quiet, peaceful, loving calm. Follow this with putting your attention upon the mental atmosphere or mental body of Earth. Send out only positive thought-forms. Ask the Masters to again bless and heal through you, and to infuse the mental world with their Divine and glorious vision of positivity. Ask them to fill the mental atmosphere with their own thought outpicturing of the wondrous expression of the next millennium. Let all these blessings come to harmony within yourself. Continue to meditate for as long as you feel comfortable, knowing that you are acting as a focal point for healing Mother Earth.

Political Hot Spots Meditation and Visualization

There are very definite political "hot spots" around the planet. The Middle East is certainly a very key one at this time, and has been for a very long time. Bosnia is, of course, another. Russia is undergoing enormous stress, change, and transformation. In fact, these political hot spots are so pervasive that I leave it up to your discretion and personal attunement to select the ones that you personally key into. Once you have done this, invoke the Masters who you are most connected with on a personal level, as well as calling upon beloved Masters St. Germain and El Morya.

Ask to be fully surrounded and protected by your semi-permeable bubble of golden-white light, as well as the pure white light of the Christ. Then connect your Third Eye with your Heart Chakra. Then align all of your chakras while at the same time keeping special attention and focus upon the Third Eye and Heart. Hold the particular political hot spot that you have chosen within your mind's eye, as well as within your heart. See all stresses and tensions melting away. Pray to the beloved Masters, Archangels, Angels and Elohim to help co-create and co-build a peaceful and harmonious situation. Prayer is most powerful in this specific world service meditation, as we are dealing with very delicate issues and really want to be sure to invoke and invite the help of the Masters. Call also upon the particular angel of the country that you are concentrating with. It is not necessary to know the name of the angel, just ask that the angel of that particular country and even geographical area come to offer their assistance by virtue of your invitation and prayer. Ask also for the assistance of the Arcturians and the Ashtar

Command, and they too will assist as far as their Law of Non-Interference permits.

Hold to your positive meditation for as long as you like. When you conclude, do remember to thank the Masters for their help and remember also to hold to your positive imagery as you go about your day!

Social Issues Meditation and Visualization

Each meditation that is done in regard for world service should first be applied to self. Before beginning your meditation for social issues, for example, ask that any disharmony within your personal social life be brought into a harmonious condition. A simple prayer such as this, beloved readers, helps to integrate you within the service work that you are doing for the world. You need not spend much time in this, just long enough to make the request. As each of us are part of the world for which we are praying, it makes perfect sense to ask for help in order to correct personal imbalances in ourselves that we are asking for the planet. Doing this both activates and demonstrates our own integration with the world. As I will not specifically stress this point again, please do remember to include this basic format in each of your world service meditations.

Once this is done and you are comfortably in meditation position, pick out one of the social issues to which you feel closely attuned. Examples of these might be the following: the integration of the races, children in need of greater protection, starving children, all starving people around the globe, elevating the consciousness of society's youths, the elimination of gang violence and the pervasive issue of homelessness. There are, of course, others that you might choose to focus upon, as there is no shortage in this department. Once again, call upon the Masters of your choosing. The Cosmic Avatar of Synthesis—the Mahatma, is an excellent being to call upon, as one of his prime functions is to integrate his high frequency energies into every level of existence. His power and presence is enormous, yet it filters down to the most basic level of life. Call him in, beloved readers, for he can serve through each of you who does so.

Fix your attention upon the particular social issue that you have selected as your world service meditation and begin to channel the Love, Light and Will-to-Good of GOD directly into the heart of that issue. See it transform within your inner vision from a situation of unfairness, disharmony, and discrimination, into a Love-infused Light-infused expression of GOD. Feel the healing Masters who work with these ideas pour their radiance through you. Feel the transformative and transmuting power of St. Germain as he graces the situation with the light/fire of his Violet Transmuting Flame. Feel the power of El Morya and Archangel Michael. Feel the immensity and enormity of the Mahatma, who through your willingness to serve, easily transmits his most glorious presence to the situation at hand, uplifting and transforming that all may come into the highest expression of GOD as possible, at any given time.

Stay within the healing and peace of your service meditation until you feel you are complete. Again, when you have concluded the meditation always give thanks to the Celestial Hierarchy who have helped you. Give thanks to your own Soul and Monad as well as to your self for entering into such a meditation. Remember to continue to hold a positive focus upon the issue you have prayed and meditated upon. If the news confronts you with negativity, if you even come face to face with the negativity that you are seeking to transmute, transform and heal, take note and then immediately shift gears to one of positive visualization, imagery and prayer. You are a healer in this regard, and just as does any good physician, you note the dis-ease but concentrate and devote all your energies upon the cure!

Child Abuse and Spousal Abuse Meditation and Visualization

Begin this meditation as you have been previously instructed. Ask for the proper protection and then ask that all abusive nature to self' be transmuted. Surround yourself with a field of unconditional self-love. Then invoke your Masters, including beloved Mother Mary, Quan Yin, and beloved Lord Maitreya.

This particular social issue has been singled out as it is also a personal issue that many suffer with in silence. It is often well-hidden from all except those that are most directly involved. By the power of this healing meditation, the required light and love will reach into those dark and hidden places. If there is a specific situation of this kind that you wish to focus on then do so. Otherwise, ask that your meditation go outward to anyone and everyone in need. This would include the abuser as well as the abused. Ask for the unconditional love of Mother Mary, the all-pervasive healing, compassion and mercy of Quan Yin, and the love/wisdom of the Christ to infuse all abusive situations. Also request of the Violet Flame of St. Germain that all misqualified energies contributing to the situation be transmuted. Visualize now this unconditional love, wisdom, mercy, compassion and Divine Alchemy transforming these particular energies of abuse into energies of love. See and feel that which you have invoked entering into the field and hearts of all involved in this type of situation, quieting all storms and allowing wisdom and love to rule rather than uncontrolled anger. Focus this mostly upon the perpetrator, yet do not forget to ask for the compassion and mercy of Quan Yin to enter the heart and minds of those who have themselves been abused. In order for a total healing to take place, all must ultimately be forgiven and brought to some form of harmony and peace. So, what we are trying to accomplish via the Masters' help is to help heal the entire situation in as complete a manner as possible. This is a most sensitive area that we have ventured into here, and we do our best work by means of prayer and requesting the Divine Intervention of the Masters as long as the Higher Selves of those involved agree. The most appropriate way to do this work is to allow the Masters to work through us.

These prayers are much needed, my beloved readers, and anyone who gives any service time by requesting to be conduits for this healing energy will surely be much blessed. At the conclusion of this meditation, be sure to ask to be cleared of any unwanted and extraneous emotional energies that you may have picked up.

Invocation to the Healing Angels

The Healing Angels are ever ready to be of service to anyone who is ill, in the hospital, or to come to the aid of any- and everybody involved in an accident, natural disaster, or harmed by any means. In truth, their Divine Presence can be seen and felt by those with inner vision in hospitals everywhere, and around the ill and wounded; however, their work and their numbers would exponentially increase by our simple prayers and invocations.

I again take a moment to remind you to request their presence within your own life and to help you with your own personal healing process. Then, focus your attention either on a particular individual who is ill, a specific hospital, hospitals in general, or upon any specific or generalized situation where their particular help is needed. Call upon the Mighty Archangels Raphael and Mother Mary to oversee this work. Then proceed to call upon the Angels of Healing in general and direct them to the area you have chosen. For the benefit of those of you leading meditations such as these, the following is an example of this particular type of meditation.

*   *   *

Close your eyes.

Assume a comfortable meditative posture, either sitting up or lying down. We now invoke the pure white light of the Christ and the semi-permeable bubble of golden-white light for protection. Only that which is good and of GOD can pass through this bubble. Only that which is of GOD can pass outward to our fellow human beings and to the planet. We are protected and act as conduits and servers for the highest purposes only.

We now invoke the blessed presence of Archangel Raphael and Mother Mary, his Divine Counterpart, to overlight this meditation.

We now invoke the presence of all of the Angels of the Healing Arts.

We ask that any and every aspect of disharmony or dis-ease within our own personal bodies be bathed and washed clean within your healing light.

We now direct our attention to all hospitals around the globe.

We ask for the overlighting presence of Archangels Raphael and Mother Mary to infuse these hospitals, that all may be bathed within your blessed healing love-light.

We now ask for as many Healing Angels that are needed in order to help effectuate healing on all levels of the four lower bodies to come and stand by the bedside of all that are suffering within the various hospitals everywhere.

We ask that you come in answer to our prayers and invocations, as long as the Higher Self of the individuals involved agree.

Please, oh blessed Angels, pour forth all the Divine and glorious healing force that you have into each and every one in need of you this moment.

Now let us be silent and allow the Angels to work.

(*Allow a few moments of silence*)

Now let us add our own love and healing energies to these places and the people in need, as we ourselves are healed by the force of the healing energies flowing through us.

(*Allow another few minutes of meditation*)

We give thanks to you Raphael and Mother Mary.

We give thanks to all the Angels of the Healing Arts who are answering our heartfelt prayers this very moment.

We ask that you stay as long as you are needed and that you continue to overlight any and all who are suffering.

When you feel ready, focus back into your bodies and open your eyes.

Carry this peace and healing radiance within you as you leave this meditation and resume your own work and go about your lives.

* * *

Invocation for the Highest Light
For Those Souls Making Their Transition

Close your eyes.

Find your meditative position.

We now call for a semi-permeable golden-white bubble of protection and for the pure white light of the Christ.

We ask that the little transitions that each one of us participating in this meditation is going though serves but to direct us to the highest light.

We call upon our Higher Self, Monad, the inner plane Hierarchy of Planetary and Cosmic Ascended Masters, all Archangels, Elohim and GOD.

We ask that anyone (*or give specific name if you are praying for someone you know*) who is now going through their transition called "death" seek only the highest light.

We pray to their particular Masters and Guardian Angels to help direct them to this light.

We pray also that they move quickly, gently and easily though any Bardo experiences that they may be having.

We ask that they know themselves to be the Light and Love of GOD, and that they joyfully merge with the highest possible Light of GOD Radiance that presents Itself to them.

We pray for their peace, joy, love, and glory as they merge with the Light of GOD and know themselves to be a flame of the ever-burning Fire of GOD.

May their lives on the inner plane be filled with the Love and Light that embraces them and calls them home.

Kodoish, Kodoish, Kodoish, Adonai Tsebayoth!

Invocation of Liberation for All Souls who are Earthbound and/or Are Trapped in the Astral Plane

Close your eyes.

Assume your meditation position.

We now call forth for a semi-permeable bubble of golden-white light for protection.

We invoke the Hierarchy of inner plane Planetary and Cosmic Ascended Masters, the Archangels and Elohim.

In whatever way we each are personally bound to the earth or trapped within the lower caverns of our astral nature, we now ask for the Divine Assistance of the Masters to help to set us free!

On behalf of any of our brothers and sisters (*specific trapped souls that you may have either encountered or know of can be named here in place of a more generalized prayer*) that are trapped within the lower astral realms and are tied or held to the earth in any unhealthy manner, may they immediately be assisted to make their full transition to the inner planes in order to continue their evolution.

We ask and invoke the Masters' and Angels' aid to help awaken these earthbound souls to their situation that they may willingly and joyfully let go of all attachments that no longer serve and seek their rightful place within the Father's Mansions.

We pray that they accept the help being offered them this moment, and joyfully find their higher purpose within the Light.

We ask that any negativity or emotionalism that we may have unknowingly taken in be immediately removed by the Masters.

We give thanks.

(*Sound three Oms*)

Come back into the room, into the body, open your eyes.

Integration and Harmony Between the Human, Elemental and Angelic Kingdoms

Close eyes.

Assume comfortable meditative position.

We call forth our semi-permeable bubble of golden-white light for protection and ask to be surrounded by the pure white light of the Christ.

The Light of Lord Buddha, His Holiness Sai Baba, Krishna, Babaji, and so forth can also be used. Again, this depends upon your particular connection and the tone of the particular group you are dealing with. Invoking the pure white light of the Christ has been used for a long period of time and is found to be quite effective, so I am choosing to write the meditations in this format. Feel free to invoke or include any of the Masters that you wish.

We invoke the entire Hierarchy of inner plane Planetary and Cosmic Ascended Masters, all the Archangels and Elohim.

We each individually set our intention to work in harmony with the Nature Spirits, Devas, Elementals and all of the Angels and lesser builders, as well as the Archangels and Elohim.

Within our inner vision and imagination we can see the elementals and nature spirits at work within the grasslands, meadows, gardens, forests, oceans, lakes, rivers, and within the currents and streams of air, wind and the movement of the seasons. We see these beings dancing within the flames that heat our food and warm our bodies, and within the great fire of the sun.

We breathe in unconditional love from our own Mighty I Am Presence.

We now breathe this love outward to the other streams of evolution that share the work and the glory of establishing the Seventh Golden Age upon our world.

We seek them to know us as beings of Light and Love and we likewise acknowledge them as such beings.

We call upon the Masters to help guide us that we may walk gently upon the soil and that our actions are in harmony with the purpose of the whole, which includes the Divine purpose of the nature spirits and elementals.

We ask to be guided and shown how to properly respect and honor them, and request the same from them that we may work in closer and closer cooperation.

We especially invoke the guidance and direction of the great Archangels and Elohim.

We now meditate upon the love, joy, and peace of this Divine cooperation and integration.

(*Allow some time for silent meditation*)

We come back into our bodies, infusing each cell with the joy, love, peace, and harmony that we have meditated upon.

We give thanks for the work of the Nature Spirits and Elementals, for the lesser builders, the Angels, the grace of the Archangels, and the Elohim.

We establish our grounding cord within the earth and in so doing make a deeper connection from Spirit to Earth.

We now open our eyes.

Core Fear Matrix Removal Program for the Earth Mother and for All of Humanity

Close eyes.

Assume meditation position.

We invoke our bubble of protection.

We call forth the Hierarchy of inner plane Ascended Planetary and Cosmic Masters, all Archangels and Elohim.

We call forth the Presence of Divine Mother and the Lady Masters.

We call forth Lord Buddha, Sanat Kumara, and Vywamus.

We ask that the Core Fear Matrix Removal Program be brought into effect for the collective body of humanity including ourselves, and for the Earth Mother herself.

We request that any and all fear within the four lower bodies of the Earth Mother and the collective body of humanity be lifted, plucked out, and completely removed.

We watch with our inner eye as these black weeds are taken from the field of the Earth Mother and lifted directly into the center of the Violet Fire of Transmutation.

All that is of a fearful and negative nature within the bodies of the Earth Mother and the collective body of humanity are transmuted into energy that shall be used only for positive purposes.

In place of the fear that has been removed, we now ask the Divine Mother and Lady Masters to fill it with Unconditional Divine Love.

As part of the Earth Mother and the collective of humanity, we feel this love filling our physical, etheric, emotional/astral and mental bodies.

We give thanks to the glorious beings that have assisted us in this work.

Extend grounding cord deep within the earth's core.

Send or channel love through that cord and feel the nectar of this Divine Love bathe you in Its sanctified Light.

Come back fully into the body.

Open eyes.

Bridging the Extraterrestrials with the Consciousness of Lightworkers to Prepare for more Open Dialogue *Meditation*

Close eyes.

Assume meditation position.

Invoke the bubble of protection and the pure white light of the Christ.

Call forth the Hierarchy of inner plane Cosmic and Planetary Ascended Masters, the Archangels and Elohim.

We now open ourselves up to the Confederation of Planets that have come from other worlds in order to assist the earth in its evolution.

We now visualize the most spiritually attuned political leaders being elected into office.

We ask the Hierarchy to intercede in whatever manner that they are able in order to place lightworkers in these key political positions. We specifically request the help of El Morya and St. Germain.

We now ask for the mass mind of humanity itself to begin to open to greater and greater awareness and acceptance of these benevolent beings that have come to aid us in our evolution

We also visualize all the lightworkers of the world becoming clearer in their attunement to the work of our Extraterrestrial brothers and sisters.

We now see, with our inner vision, the governments of the planet openly communicating with our space brethren for the purpose of the betterment of earth and the cooperation of our planet with Divine Intent.

We visualize clearly that the masses of humanity are now aware and educated through the intervention of governmental leaders taking a stand for "truth," as to the reality and purpose of our space brothers and sisters.

We also see, with our inner vision, how the lightworkers of the planet are able to work openly and collectively upon their particular mission in mutual cooperation with the Confederation of Planets.

We can feel the joy of all of humanity, as well as that of our space brethren, as together we participate in manifesting the Plan of GOD, and bringing the earth forward into ever higher frequencies of Light, Love, Power and the Will-to-Good.

We take a few moments to now connect ourselves with any incoming transmissions from this aspect of the Celestial Command. We know that if we are not consciously hearing their intent, we are nevertheless receiving it through the universal "language of light."

We bathe in this wonderful outpouring of grace and connectedness.

(*Allow some time for silence*)

We now thank the Celestial Hierarchy from other worlds that are here on humanity's behalf.

As we prepare to leave this meditation we know that we will hold to the vision of lightworkers entering and being elected into the foreground of politics both in the United States and in all the countries of the world.

We feel the joy of transformation through the mutual cooperation of humanity and the civilizations and beings who form the Confederation of Planets.

We establish our grounding cords, come back into our bodies, and open our eyes.

The Golden Cylinder over the Whole Planet *Meditation*

Close eyes.

Assume meditation posture.

Invoke the golden-white semi-permeable bubble of light for protection and the pure white light of the Christ.

Call forth the Hierarchy of inner plane Ascended Planetary and Cosmic Masters, as well as the Archangels and the Elohim.

We now call forth the "Golden Cylinder of Light," to envelope ourselves within its cleansing and purifying radiance, that it may lift from within our personal auric fields any negative debris, negative elementals, thoughtforms, emotional currents or misqualified energy of any kind and remove it from our four lower bodies.

Now visualize within your mind's eye this Golden Cylinder growing larger and larger, merging with all the Golden Cylinders that each one of you have invoked.

The Golden Cylinder keeps growing in size until it encompasses the entire planet, enveloping within its radiant sphere the collective bodies of humanity as they exist on the physical, etheric, astral and mental levels.

Now watch with the inner eye of visualization as the Golden Cylinder begins to draw all misqualified energy that has lodged within the dense physical vehicle of Earth herself upward, until it reaches unfathomable heights where it is broken apart into so many little fragments of dust.

See this dust, bathed within the golden light itself, transformed into light patterns of energy.

Know within your minds and hearts that this once misqualified and negative energy has now been transformed into pure light.

Watch as it gently falls back upon the physical earth as pure light substance which acts as a stimulant for healing.

Rejoice as you feel and see how that which was once toxic and misqualified energies has been changed by the Golden Cylinder into that which is a generator of light and healing.

Now see this process repeat itself as all etheric debris rises upward within the Golden Cylinder of Light to likewise be transformed into sparkles of light.

Watch and feel the transformation, as this new transmuted energy falls from the mysterious heights to which the Golden Cylinder has carried it, back into the planet's etheric body, to heal and regenerate.

Now see and deeply feel the impact of the same process as it repeats itself upon the astral plane. Watch as all negative emotional elementals that have been created from humanity's uncontrolled feeling vehicle rise upward within the Golden Light Cylinder.

Feel the joy of unconditional love as these negative elementals return in a transmuted form, falling gently and sweetly back into the astral body of the planet as pink, white and golden hearts, tinged with the Violet Flame of Transmutation.

Take one of these hearts and place it within your own. Feel the impact of this most pure love.

Taste the sweetness of transmutation as you fully realize that it is within the co-creative power of you and the GOD-Force to transform all negative and misqualified energies into pure Love and Light.

Watch as this process repeats one final time. The Golden Cylinder sweeps upward the mass of negative thoughtforms and lifts them beyond harm's way, out of earth's atmosphere entirely.

These thoughtforms are then transmuted into minute particles of light and gently rain down upon the Earth's mental body, cleansing, clearing, purifying and helping to uplift and stimulate the minds of all.

Now the Golden Cylinder itself lifts up, getting smaller and smaller as it fades from sight.

Sit for a few moments and bathe in the Divinely rarefied air that now pervades the collective consciousness of Earth and all humanity.

Meditate upon the joy, love, and lightness that at once pervades you and fills you.

(*Allow for a few minutes of silence*)

Ground yourself now fully into the physical body, extending your grounding cord within the earth.

When you are ready, open your eyes, feeling refreshed and renewed!

Preservation of the Rain Forests Meditation

Close eyes.

Assume meditation posture.

Invoke the golden-white semi-permeable bubble of protection and the pure white light of the Christ.

Call forth the inner plane Hierarchy of Ascended Planetary and Cosmic Masters, the Archangels and the Elohim.

Silently and within yourself bless the rain forests and ask that the Masters and overlighting Devas of the rain forests carry your personal prayer into the collective consciousness of those who execute their power to render decisions upon the fate of the rain forests.

Now join with each other to form a group conscious prayer that links you with the group body of those who share the same concern over the preservation of the rain forests.

Call upon the Earth Mother to support you in this prayer. Call once again upon the overlighting Deva of the rain forests.

Ask them to assist you in building a group thoughtform that is strong enough to affect the thoughtforms of those who wish to destroy these sacred woodlands.

Ask that truth be revealed, and that all alike may see and intuit the preciousness of the hallowed ground and know that it is in Divine order that the rain forests be left to thrive.

Visualize these forests thriving healthily and functioning in wonderful harmony with humanity and all the various kingdoms of evolution upon this planet.

Feel the blessings of Lady Gaia and that of the overlighting Deva as they support this visualization and do all within their power to help you manifest your Divine intention.

Allow yourself to smell the forest and to feel the gentle breezes of the woodland as they caress you in love.

Meditate for a few moments upon the harmony of all nature.

(*Allow time for silence*)

Give thanks to all the various beings that help to maintain the growth of the rain forests, and to the forests themselves.

When you feel ready, anchor your grounding cord fully into the Earth and send love and blessing through that cord into the very core structure of the Earth.

When you feel ready, open your eyes.

Endangered Species and the Tender Handling of the Animal Kingdom *Meditation*

Close eyes.

Assume meditation posture.

Invoke the golden-white semi-permeable bubble of light and the pure white light of the Christ for personal protection.

Call forth the inner plane Hierarchy of Ascended Planetary and Cosmic Masters, all of the Angels and the Elohim.

Send a personal message of love and tenderness to yourself.

Ask to be cleared of all blockages that are a potential danger for you to freely and lovingly express who you are within the Divine Plan of GOD.

Now call upon beloved Master Kuthumi, who as you know in a past incarnation blessed this earth as St. Francis.

Call also upon gentle Jesus/Sananda, who holds within his beingness the quality of pure "devotion." Call also upon Quan Yin, Goddess of Mercy and Compassion.

Ask these wonderful beings to assist you in your meditation to protect the endangered species of our world, to help put a stop to animal abuse in any and every kind, and to help in its place promote the tender handling of the Animal Kingdom.

Visualize the animals of the wild roving freely about, following their natural instincts without interference by humanity.

See the forests and jungles free and clear of any traps that could potentially harm these animals.

Watch as they run wild and free.

Allow your visualization to expand and include tenderness to all animals.

See alternatives being imprinted upon the mind of humanity that will allow the knowledge that is currently sought through animal experimentation to utterly cease, being replaced instead by benign forms of study.

Hear within the joy, as all animals know that they are free to follow their own destiny without any harmful interference by man.

Now let your thoughts and feelings drift to Divine harmony between humanity and our animal brothers and sisters.

See the loved and cared for animals living, learning, loving and evolving along with its human family.

Go deep within to that place where love alone abides and that time where the lion shall indeed lie down with the lamb.

Feel the utter joy that exists between the Kingdom of Humanity and the Kingdom of Animals.

Meditate upon this harmony.

(Allow time for silence)

Place your hands over your hearts that you may carry this love with you.

Anchor in your grounding cord, and when you are ready, open your eyes.

Mass Implant and Negative Elemental Removal for the Entire Planet *Meditation*

Close eyes.

Assume meditation posture.

Invoke the golden-white bubble of light and the pure white light of the Christ for personal protection.

Call forth the inner plane Hierarchy of Planetary and Cosmic Ascended Masters, the Archangels and the Elohim.

Call upon Vywamus, Lenduce, Djwhal Khul, and St. Germain to assist you in neutralizing and eliminating all negative implants within your four lower bodies.

Thank these beloved Masters and ask them to remain in order to help to remove and deactivate all negative implants within all of humanity around the entire globe, as well as from within the fields of our pets.

Call upon Archangels Michael and Faith for extra protection.

Call also upon the Lord of Arcturus for any assistance he and his fellow Arcturians can provide with their advanced technology.

Call also upon beloved Lord Buddha, our Planetary Logos, and upon Sanat Kumara.

See within your inner sense pure golden light flowing into the mental, emotional, etheric and even physical bodies of every single person around the globe.

Watch as this light neutralizes any and every implant within the four lower bodies.

See this light become the hands of Vywamus, Sanat Kumara, Lenduce and St. Germain as they lift these implants and elementals out of every aspect and area in which they have been lodged.

The ones that are lifted by Vywamus, Lenduce and Sanat Kumara are transmuted by the touch of their golden light. The ones being lifted out by the hands of St. Germain are transmuted by his Violet Transmuting Flame that glows from within his hands. Djwhal Khul does this process through the use of his holographic computer.

Feel a lightness come over your entire being and let this lightness flow across the globe as you visualize all implants and elementals of a negative nature being either removed altogether or turned totally inactive.

Ask beloved Archangels Michael and Faith for extra protection against any further negative implants being installed. Request this also from the Lord of Arcturus, so that he and the Arcturians may intervene.

Ask to be filled with the essence of pure love and radiant light and the infusion of the First Ray of Will. Specifically request El Morya to assist you in strengthening your own willpower and that of all humanity as the will of all merges with the Will of GOD.

Know within the core of your being that unconditional pure Love, pure Light, and the Will-to-Good act as barriers against any outside interference.

Once again invoke the added protection of Archangels Michael and Faith. Invoke them each and every night before you go to sleep, both for your further protection and for the protection of all humanity and the animals that reside within our dwelling.

Return into your newly cleansed bodies. Remind yourself to stay ever centered within Light, Love, and Power, and build up an impenetrable force field of protection. Pray that all of humanity comes to the understanding and application of Divine Law.

Thank all the beloved beings of the Celestial Realms who have been of assistance during this meditation.

Anchor your grounding cord and open your eyes.

Mass Clearing of All Unwanted Astral Entities Interfering With Humanity's Free Will *Meditation*

Close eyes.

Prepare for meditation.

Put on your semi-permeable bubble of golden-white light and invoke the pure white light of the Christ for protection.

Call upon the entire inner plane Hierarchy of Ascended Planetary and Cosmic Masters, all Archangels and Elohim.

Attune to your specific lineage of Masters and to the Master that you are working most closely with.

Ask them to help remove all unwanted astral entities, elementals or thoughtforms that are clouding your own vision, intuition, judgment, or who may be directly trying to interfere with your own free will by clouding your perception.

Now ask the appropriate Masters to help in the clearing of the unwanted astral entities, elementals or thoughtforms that are clouding the feeling and perception of humanity as a whole.

Ask that any astral entities engaged in direct interference with anyone's free thinking, clarity of vision or free will be immediately escorted to the astral sphere which best matches their vibratory rate.

Ask that a ring-pass-not be placed around them to hold them there in order that they may learn their appropriate lessons while at the same time being kept at a safe distance from meddling with humanity and our Divine gift of free will.

See them being removed from both your personal sphere and the sphere of all of humanity while being held in unconditional love.

It is not our place to judge them, but it is certainly our place, our right, and even our obligation to ask them to be removed from our personal and collective worlds.

Feel a new clarity of feeling, thought, vision and intuition fill both you and the world of incarnated souls.

Sit and meditate upon this feeling of freedom, clarity, and light.

(*Allow time for silence*)

Give thanks to your personal lineage of Masters and the Master or Masters who you have worked most closely with.

Thank all in the Celestial Hierarchy who have aided in this process for every single person upon earth.

Anchor your grounding cord and open your eyes.

Healing any Auric Holes, Spots, Irritations and Leakages in the Physical, Etheric, Astral and Mental Body of Planet Earth *Meditation*

Close eyes.

Assume meditation posture.

Invoke the golden-white bubble of protection and pure white light of Christ.

Call upon the entire inner plane Hierarchy of Ascended Planetary and Cosmic Masters, all Archangels and all Elohim.

Call upon Helios & Vesta, Lord Buddha, Sanat Kumara and the Chohans of each of the rays, as well as the Manu, the Christ, and the Mahachohan.

Ask them to send their healing radiance in order that any personal auric holes, leakages, spots, and irritations within your four lower bodies be healed.

Now call upon the Divine Mother, Lord Melchizedek, the Mahatma, and Archangel Metatron.

Request that they radiate their Cosmic healing energies, along with the other Masters who have been invoked, in order to plug up any leakages, auric holes, and to clear up all spots and irritations in the physical, etheric, astral and mental bodies of the planet as a whole.

Feel the Divine aura surrounding and penetrating the entire planet as you make this invocation.

Feel health and vitality returning to the Earth and all that dwell therein.

Sit and bathe in this most Divine radiance and benediction as you feel this enormous healing and cleansing taking place.

Drink in the aura of Divinity within all of your four lower bodies and all your spiritual bodies as well.

Let us sit and meditate upon the Divine healing that is now occurring for the Earth and each one of us who have prayed on her behalf.

(Allow time for silence)

Anchor your grounding cord into the core of the Earth and radiate your own love and light into her.

Accept back her all-encompassing love as it is radiated to you through the stream of light moving through your grounding cord.

Silently and deeply thank all of the Planetary and Cosmic Masters who have aided the Earth in this healing.

Fully anchor back into the body and open your eyes.

Cosmic Vacuum for Clearing Up All Planetary Glamour, Maya and Illusion *Meditation*

Close eyes.

Assume meditation posture.

Put up your golden-white bubble for personal protection and call also to be clothed and protected in the pure white light of the Christ.

Call upon the entire inner plane Hierarchy of Planetary and Cosmic Ascended Masters, the Archangels and Elohim.

First call upon your own personal Ascended Master lineage and request that all personal glamour, illusion, and maya be vacuumed up from the aura of your four lower bodies.

Now call forth the Mahatma, Melchizedek, and Metatron.

Request that they use their Divine powers to vacuum up the mass consciousness of glamour, maya, and illusion that is affecting the planet as a whole.

Watch as glamour, illusion, and maya are lifted from the veil of delusion of the entire planet.

See the earth stand crystal clean and pure, radiating only that which is true, holy, sanctified and of GOD.

As this process continues, bask in the glow of the radiance of these Cosmic Masters.

Feel the incredible blessing of love, light and synthesis as the entire planetary aura grows cleaner, clearer and ever more reflective of Source Itself.

Mediate in silence and stillness upon the pure Light and Love of GOD.

(*Allow time for silence*)

Feel yourself become a greater and greater reflection of pure Divine Essence, even as this is happening for the planet as a whole.

Give thanks to His Holiness Lord Melchizedek, the Mahatma, and Metatron and to the group of Ascended Masters that you have called upon. Also give thanks to all of the Masters who have participated in this clearing on behalf of each and every individual upon planet earth.

Anchor your grounding cord, feel yourself back in the body, and open eyes.

Ashtar Command and Lord of Arcturus—To Help Vacuum Up Physical Pollution in the Atmosphere and Help Repair the Ozone Layer *Meditation*

Close eyes.

Assume meditation posture.

Put up your golden-white semi-permeable bubble for protection and call upon the pure white light of the Christ.

Call upon the entire inner plane Hierarchy of Ascended Planetary and Cosmic Masters, all Archangels and Elohim.

Invoke the presence of beloved Commander Ashtar and the entire Ashtar Command, as well as the beloved Lord of Arcturus and the Arcturians who serve with him.

Ask first that they use their advanced technology to vacuum up all negative energies that form the personal pollutants in your own physical and etheric bodies. In this manner your own bodies will be in a state of much increased purity in order that you can serve as a better vessel for the service work that you are now engaging in.

Allow for a moment of silence as you visualize all negative energies within your aura being vacuumed up by these wonderful beings.

See these energies lift from your four-body system upon a stream of light that serves as a highly developed etheric vacuum, to be taken from you and transmuted and neutralized into harmless energy upon their great ships.

Trust in their advanced technology to do this work, and enjoy the feeling of lightness coming into your physical and etheric vehicles.

Now ask that they use their combined energies to sweep across the entire planet and to vacuum up all physical pollution that has lodged itself within earth's atmosphere on both a physical and etheric level.

Visualize their combined technologies creating a vacuum that spans the globe, and watch as all the pollutants that we have let loose within the physical/etheric atmosphere of our world are lifted up upon this energy stream, to be rendered neutral and harmless aboard their ships.

Feel a wonderful sense of purity and cleanliness pervade the entire planet.

While still holding to this visualization, also ask them to use their advanced technologies to help repair the ozone layer all around the globe.

Know in your heart that by making this request they will give all the help that they are able to.

They cannot, however, act without being asked, so feel the joy within the making of these requests, for you are helping to create the world as GOD would have it be.

Sit in meditation for a while, feeling a lightness, purity and healing taking place both within your own physical vehicle and within the physical/etheric body of the Earth herself.

Visualize all the pollutants being vacuumed out of the earth's atmosphere and feel also the incredible love and compassion of these wonderful beings who are helping us according to our request.

Enjoy the feeling of increasing lightness, purity, and love which fills you and radiates around the globe at this time.

(*Allow a few moments for silence*)

Give thanks to the Lord of Arcturus and Commander Ashtar and all those who work beside them.

When you have done this, anchor your grounding cord, feel yourself fully in the body and upon the earth, and open your eyes; feeling cleansed and refreshed.

Anchoring the Monadic Blueprint Body for the Earth *Meditation*

Close eyes.

Assume meditation posture.

Put up your golden-white semi-permeable bubble of light and call upon the pure white light of the Christ.

Call upon the entire inner plane Hierarchy of Ascended Planetary and Cosmic Masters, all Archangels and all Elohim.

Invoke the presence of beloved Melchior, Helios & Vesta, Sanat Kumara and Lord Buddha.

Now call upon the particular Master or Masters with whom you work. Ask for a full and complete anchoring of your own personal Monadic Blueprint Body.

Feel the activation, joy, love, and light as this is deeply installed within you.

Meditate for a moment upon this feeling.

Feel also the tingling sensation as the "language of light" is activated within you through this process, and all key codes, sacred geometries and fire letters are fully installed and stimulated at this time.

Now tune in once again to Melchior, Helios and Vesta, Sanat Kumara and Lord Buddha. Ask that the Monadic Blueprint Body be anchored into and around the entire globe.

Call upon the help of beloved St. Germain to help in this process, as you again make this prayer request for the Divine Monadic Blueprint Body to be anchored within Earth herself.

Ask that all who are ready gain access to the "language of light" and that the highest activation possible of all key codes, sacred geometries and fire letters be given to those upon the planet who are able to receive them.

Sit now for a few minutes in silent mediation as you visualize this great downpouring of light, the anchoring of the Planetary Monadic Blueprint Body, and the installation and activation of the key codes, fire letters and sacred geometries around the globe.

(Allow a few short moments of silence)

Know that the Divine Celestial Masters will give the highest blessing or activation that each may personally receive, and that your prayers and invocations are helping to safely accelerate the evolution of the globe.

Meditate and enjoy this feeling
(*Allow time for silence*)
Give thanks to all the Masters who have helped in this sacred process.

Feel yourself align with your own Monadic Blueprint Body while at the same time fully integrate within your 12-Body System.

Establish and anchor yourself back into your mental, emotional, etheric and physical vehicles.

Anchor in your grounding cord.

Open your eyes.

23

The Cosmic and Planetary Hierarchy Protection Meditation

Close your eyes.

We begin this meditation by calling forth Archangels Michael and Faith and their legions of First Ray Angels.

We also call forth Melchizedek, the Mahatma and Archangel Metatron as well as each person's Higher Self and Mighty I Am Presence.

We begin by calling forth from Melchizedek, the Mahatma and Metatron for a Platinum Net to anchor and to remove all negative and imbalanced energies.

We also request at this time that all negative implants and elementals be immediately cleared from the field.

We call forth to all the Cosmic and Planetary Masters gathered, for a permanent "pillar of Cosmic and Planetary light, love and power" to be placed around all who are participating in this meditation.

We call forth from Melchizedek, for an additional permanent golden dome of protection to be placed around each person.

We call forth to Melchizedek, the Mahatma, and Metatron to place around each individual a permanent wall of "light protection."

We call to Archangel Michael to place around each individual his permanent Blue Shield Armor of Protection.

We call to Archangel Faith to place around each individual a permanent, ever-rejuvenating ring of red roses that will absorb all negative energy before it enters the field.

We call to the Mahatma to place a permanent "rainbow bubble of light" around each person's auric field as an additional protection.

We call to Archangel Metatron to place a permanent Platinum Tube of Light around each person as still an added protection.

We call forth His Holiness the Lord Sai Baba to place around each individual his permanent protective "robe of love, wisdom and power" to prevent any unwanted energies from entering your auric field without your permission.

We call forward Lord Buddha and the Karmic Board for a "ban of non-interference" against all energies of psychic attack from within and without!

We call forth to Helios and Vesta to place around each individual a "copper-golden sun of protection" that is so bright and so filled with GOD's Love that all misqualified or negative energy is immediately burned up and transmuted into the pure, radiant Light of GOD.

We now call forth Melchior to bring forth a "matchstick's worth" of the Cosmic Fire from the Great Central Sun to burn away in a completely safe manner any negative energy that remains in the field.

We call forth the Lord of Arcturus to anchor the Arcturian Liquid Crystals to deactivate and rebalance all negative energy in the field.

We call forth Dr. Lorphan and the Galactic Healers to tighten the grids and strengthen the spiritual, psychological and physical immune system of all listening to this meditation.

We call forth the Healing Angels to now balance the chakras and four-body system.

We call forth the Lord of Arcturus and Djwhal Khul to now anchor and activate the Prana Wind Clearing Device, to blow pranic energy through all the meridians and nadis, to clear them and strengthen them and completely clear the 12-body system.

We call forth to the Divine Mother and the Lady Masters to bring forward a Platinum Net through each person's house to clear it of all etheric, astral and mental energies that are not completely of the Christ/Buddha energy.

We call forward to beloved Saint Germain and Lady Portia for the anchoring and activation of a permanent pillar of the Violet Flame that will transmute any and all misqualified energy from entering the auric field from within and without.

We call forth the legions of First Ray Angels and each person's Guardian Angels to stand as sentries around each individual doing this meditation, to protect them on all sides—24 hours a day, 7 days a week, 365 days a year—during waking and sleeping hours.

We call forward the 14 Mighty male and female Elohim to anchor and activate a special Elohim Shield of Protection against all negative thought-forms from, within and without.

We call forth Melchizedek, the Mahatma and Metatron to bring down a Platinum Net around each individual every morning, afternoon and night before bed for one year's time as a special dispensation of protection.

We call forth the Divine Mother to place a permanent Platinum Net of Protection around each person's house, and in every doorway, window and opening of their home or apartment.

We call forth the Divine Mother and Lady Masters to place around each individual a protective field of pink "love light," that is so filled with Divine Love that no misqualified energy can penetrate its radiance.

We call forward the Holy Spirit to undo all negative energy and conflict that has been set in motion in the past, so as to erase the need for any karmic return of as much negative energy as possible. We ask that this transmuted energy be used to increase unconditional love and service of the planet.

We call forward the Lord of Arcturus and the Arcturians to bring forward their advanced Arcturian technology to protect the energy fields of this Son or Daughter of GOD.

We call forward Commander Ashtar and the Ashtar Command to overlight this individual with one of your lightships and/or lightcrafts from your motherships, to protect this individual at night while they sleep and during the day while they demonstrate GOD on earth.

We call forward Lord Maitreya and Lord Buddha to place around each person a "pillar of wisdom and light," which causes all negative energy from within and without, to bounce off this pillar as though it's a rubber pillow.

We call forth to the Seven Chohans to create a "ring pass not" around each individual that serves to create an invulnerable protective shield of protection that is invincible to negative energy from within and without.

We call forward Quan Yin to place each person in a lotus blossom of pink-blue light of protection.

We call forth Vywamus and Djwhal Khul to tighten the etheric, emotional, mental and spiritual webbing of the four-body system, to provide greater protection as would be GOD's Will.

We call forward Mother Mary to now place around each individual an etheric rosary filled with the full protective powers of Mother Mary herself in all her glory.

We call forward the 14 male and female Archangels to place around this individual a special Archangelic Light of Protection that we request be reinforced every morning and every night as a Divine dispensation of protection for this individual.

We call forward the Lord of Sirius and the Lady Master of Sirius to now fully anchor and activate within each individual their Anointed Christ Overself Body and their Zohar Body of Light for the purpose of spiritual advancement and greater protective light.

We call forth Lenduce and Sanat Kumara to place around each individual an "ascension column of light" for greater spiritual advancement and protection.

We call forward Isis and Serapis Bey to place around each individual a permanent "pyramid of golden-white light" that will serve as a mystical shield of protection the rest of this incarnation.

We ask that this enormous protective field that has been established be completely cleansed from within, so that only energies of GOD and Christ/Buddha Consciousness live now within this protective forcefield.

We call forth the entire Planetary and Cosmic Hierarchy from the Three-Fold Flame of GOD and the Twelve Cosmic Rays of GOD and request for a Divine dispensation of merging your Light Bodies with all who are doing this meditation. This will serve as an invulnerable shield of love, wisdom and power the rest of this incarnation so that this individual may be free to dedicate their life to serve GOD and their brothers and sisters.

We call forward the beloved Presence of the Godhead to now permanently anchor and fully activate the Lord's Mystical Body for the supreme purpose of protection by your Divine Grace.

I ask each person doing this meditation to now fully claim and own their personal power, which will be visualized as holding in their right hand the Blue Flaming Sword of Archangel Michael.

I now ask each person doing this meditation to place around themselves a golden bubble of light to keep out others people's negative energy and any negative energy from your subconscious mind in the form of negative thoughts or negative feelings.

I ask now for each person to fully claim their unconditional love and self-worth, which appears as a golden-platinum-pink rose in your heart.

I ask each person now to fully claim their attunement to GOD, their own Mighty I Am Presence and their own Higher Self, which can be visualized as a tube of platinum-gold light coming down directly from GOD through each person's Mighty I Am Presence and Higher Self, and into each person's Crown Chakra and entire chakra column.

See this platinum-golden light filling your entire 12-body system on a permanent basis.

See this bubble of protection keeping out all negative energy, but allowing in all thoughts and feelings of love, positivity and kindness.

All negative ego fear-based energy and/or separative energy is denied entrance.

I ask each person doing this meditation to now make a commitment to GOD and to yourself, to every moment of your day and night to never allow a negative thought or negative feeling to enter your consciousness.

Every time a negative thought tries to enter, make a solemn oath to GOD and yourself that you will remain vigilant to push those negative thoughts and feelings out of your mind and you will replace them with only Christ/Buddha positive thoughts and feelings.

Make a firm commitment to GOD and yourself to never allow yourself to lose your personal power again.

Make a firm commitment to GOD and self in this moment to never give your power to any person, to your mind, your emotions, your physical body, to fatigue, to your subconscious mind, to your inner child, to lower-self desire, and most of all to the negative ego thought system.

Make a firm commitment in this moment to GOD and to self to be decisive at all times and to never allow yourself to be indecisive and sit on the fence.

Make a firm commitment in this moment to be vigilant at all times to deny any thought that is not of GOD to enter your mind.

Make a firm commitment in this moment to never allow yourself to have any attachments to any thing, only preferences, which hence allows you to be happy if something is taken away.

Make a firm commitment in this moment to look at everything that happens in life as a teaching, lesson, challenge, and most of all a spiritual test.

In this moment, make a firm commitment that you will pass every test to the best of your abilities and if you don't, you will forgive yourself, learn the lesson, gain the "golden nugget of wisdom" and do better the next time.

Make up your mind in this moment that you will fully claim your personal power in an unconditionally loving manner even in relationship to the inner plane Ascended Masters and in relationship to GOD, who wants you to own your power and your true identity as the Eternal Self.

Make a 100% commitment now to GOD and self that you will be a spiritual warrior on earth for GOD and unconditional love, and no matter what happens in life and no matter how you are tested, you will not give up even for an instant.

As you make this commitment, Archangels Michael and Faith, Melchizedek, the Mahatma, Archangel Metatron, His Holiness the Lord Sai Baba, your Guardian Angels, and the Legions of Angels of Archangel Michael and Faith, and all the Masters helping in this meditation, all step forward in front of you and bow to you in respect as the Spiritual Master you are, in truth.

Lord Melchizedek, the Mahatma, Metatron and Archangel Michael now anoint you with their "light rods" on the top of your head.

They also wave their collective light rods around your auric field to permanently seal all the work that has been done in this meditation.

They bid you now to go forward, handing you one last gift that they place in your left hand which is the "Rod of Love, Wisdom and Power."

They bid you to go forth in absolute knowingness that you are now completely protected, for the Ascended Hosts are protecting you, and even more importantly, you are protecting yourself as well.

The inner plane Ascended Hosts make one final request of you which is to every morning when first arising re-attune to this meditation for at least 30 seconds.

They say that it will be there 100% even if you don't; however, it is important for the conscious mind to re-attune each morning, even if just for a second, to resolidify it for the conscious mind to keep the GOD Flame of Self Mastery ever present in your conscious mind.

They also request in extreme situations when testing may be occurring that this meditation be done every day and even twice a day if necessary until 100% self-mastery and protection is fully established again which is your natural God-state!

So let it be written! So let it be done!

To reactivate this meditation any time you need a boost of protection, call to GOD and the GOD Force and say, "I now request to reactivate the full Love, Wisdom and Power of Protection of my Protection Meditation!"

24

The Lord of Arcturus and Arcturian Ascension Activation Meditation

Please close your eyes.

We now call forth the Cosmic and Planetary Hierarchy and most specifically the Lord of Arcturus and the Arcturians!

We call to Archangels Michael and Faith to place a golden dome of protection around all involved in this meditation!

We call forth Melchizedek, the Mahatma and Metatron to bring forth a Platinum Net to remove any and all imbalanced energies.

We call forth to the Lord of Arcturus and the Arcturians to now take us in our etheric bodies to your ascension seat on the Arcturian mothership…

We call forth to the Lord of Arcturus to bring down the Prana Wind Clearing Device to cleanse and clear all our nadis and acupuncture meridians…

We call forth to the Lord of Arcturus to now install the Arcturian Plating System to each person's highest potential…

We now call forth the Lord of Arcturus and the Arcturians for a Light and Love Quotient building, to each person's highest potential.

We now call forth to the Arcturians for the tightening of each person's grids to each person's perfect balance as GOD would have it be…

We now call forth the Lord of Arcturus to anchor the Arcturian Liquid Crystals into each person's four-body system to deactivate any and all negative energies

We call forth to the Lord of Arcturus for the anchoring and activation of the "golden cylinder," to remove any and all negative energies 100% completely, including all negative implants and negative elementals.

We call forth to the Lord of Arcturus to now be taken to the Arcturian Light Chamber.

We now call forth to be taken on the Arcturian mothership to the Arcturian Healing Chamber, for the specific healing of any and all etheric and/or physical health lessons.

We now call forth from the Lord of Arcturus and the Arcturian Temple workers, for the "Arcturian revitalization program".

Lastly, we call forth the Arcturian "Joy Machine." I tell you now, my friends, there is not a person on planet earth who I have found who could not stop smiling or laughing once this Arcturian Joy Machine was turned on…

We now call to the Lord of Arcturus to connect each person officially up to your computers on your mothership, so if they ever want to call on you again they are "on-line"!

Take one last moment to thank the Lord of Arcturus and the Arcturians for their most gracious and generous help!

We ask the Lord of Arcturus now to help gently guide us in our etheric bodies back to earth and safely back into our physical bodies, bringing with us in total recall all the Light and Love we have just experienced!

25

GOD and the Cosmic and Planetary Hierarchy "Higher Light Body" Ascension Activation Meditation

Please close your eyes.

We call forth to GOD and the Cosmic and Planetary Hierarchy to help in this meditation.

We call forth from GOD, Melchizedek, the Mahatma, and Metatron for the anchoring and activation of a gigantic "pillar of light and ascension column" from Source.

We call forth Archangels Michael and Faith for a gigantic platinum "dome of protection" for this entire meditation.

We call forth from the 14 Mighty Archangels for the anchoring of a Platinum Net to remove any unwanted energies.

We begin by calling forth Quan Yin and Mother Mary for the permanent anchoring of each person's Oversoul and Monad.

We call forth Lord Buddha to fully anchor and activate each person's Buddhic Body.

We call forth to St. Germain to anchor and activate each person's Atmic Body.

We call forth Allah Gobi and El Morya to anchor and activate each person's Monadic Body.

We call forth Sanat Kumara to anchor and activate each person's Logoic Body.

We call forth Helios and Vesta, our Solar Logos, to anchor and activate each person's Solar Body.

We call forth Melchior, our Galactic Logos, to fully anchor and activate each person's Galactic Body.

We call forth Melchizedek, our Universal Logos, to fully anchor and activate each person's Universal Body.

We call forth the Multi-Universal Logos to fully anchor and activate each person's Multi-Universal Body.

We call forth Master Kuthumi to fully anchor and activate each person's Causal Body.

We call forth Djwhal Khul to fully anchor, activate, and illuminate each person's Higher Mental Body.

We call forth Serapis Bey to fully anchor and activate our Mayavarupa Body.

We call forth Master Hilarion to fully anchor and activate our Monadic Blueprint Body to replace or enhance our Etheric Body, as GOD would have it be.

We call forth Melchior to fully anchor and activate our Anointed Christ Overself Body.

We call forth to Sananda to fully anchor and activate our Zohar Body of Light.

We call forth to Vywamus to fully anchor and activate our Light Body Merkabah for each person at their highest potential.

We call forth Lord Maitreya to fully anchor and activate our Higher Adam Kadmon Body.

We call forth Paul the Venetian to fully anchor and activate our Gematrian Body for realization of full Planetary ascension.

We call forth the Lord of Sirius to fully anchor and activate our Epikinetic Body to help us learn teleportation.

We call forth the Lord of Arcturus to help us to fully anchor and activate our Eka Body.

We call forth Isis and Osirus to help us fully anchor and activate our Electromagnetic Body.

We call forth Lenduce to help us fully anchor and activate our Overself Body.

We call forth the Paradise Sons to fully anchor and activate our Paradise Son's Body.

We call forth the 14 Mighty Elohim and ask them now to fully anchor and activate our Elohistic Lord's Body.

We call forth Commander Ashtar and the Ashtar Command to fully anchor and activate each person's 50 chakras.

We call forth Babaji to fully anchor and activate each person's first 100 chakras.

We call forth His Holiness the Lord Sai Baba to fully anchor and activate each person's first 150 chakras.

We call forth Archangels Gabriel and Hope to fully anchor and activate each person's first 200 chakras.

We call forth the 14 Mighty Archangels to fully anchor and activate each person's first 250 chakras.

We call forth the Mighty Elohim to fully anchor and activate each person's first 330 chakras.

We call forth Archangel Metatron to fully anchor and activate the Garment of Shaddai, also known as the Light Body of Metatron.

We call forth Archangels Jophiel and Christine to fully anchor and activate each person's Cosmic Astral Body.

We call forth Archangels Chamuel and Charity to fully anchor and activate each person's Cosmic Mental Body.

We call forth Archangels Raphael and Mother Mary to fully anchor and activate each person's Cosmic Buddhic Body.

We call forth Archangels Uriel and Aurora to fully anchor and activate each person's Cosmic Atmic Body.

We call forth Archangels Zadkiel and Amethyst to fully anchor and activate each person's Cosmic Monadic Body.

We call forth the Council of Twelve to fully anchor and activate each person's Cosmic Logoic Body.

We call forth the Mahatma to fully anchor and activate his "Light Body of Synthesis" with our own.

We call forth the Cosmic Christ Spirit, which is the second aspect of the Trinity of GOD, to fully merge all His Light Bodies on all levels back to Source, if this prayer be in harmony with GOD's Will.

We call forth the 14 Mighty Archangels to fully anchor, activate, and merge on a permanent basis their Light Bodies with our own.

We call forth the 14 Mighty Elohim to fully anchor and activate on a permanent basis their Light Bodies with our own.

We call forth the Holy Spirit to now fully anchor and activate on a permanent basis the Lord's Mystical Body with our own.

We call forth the entire Cosmic and Planetary Hierarchy and the power of over one million inner plane Masters, to fully anchor and activate on a permanent basis your "Collective Light Body" with each of us individually and as a group.

For our final "Higher Light Body" activation, the beloved Presence of GOD steps forth for a final anointing and blessing of all blessings.

The beloved Presence of GOD brings forth His "Rod of Light," and now fully anchors and activates what can only be esoterically described as the "Light Body of GOD"!

If you choose to receive this gift of all gifts, be still, and receive this blessing now…

We now call forth Archangel Sandalphon, the Earth Mother, and Pan to help us fully ground into our physical bodies and the earth all the Higher Light Bodies we have received.

Be still and receive this blessing now…

Take a moment to fully thank GOD and the Cosmic and Planetary Hierarchy for their generous and most gracious gifts and blessings this evening.

When you are ready you can open your eyes; fully holding within yourself all the "Higher Light Bodies" as well as the Love and Light that have been fully anchored and activated.

26

Revelation of GOD Ascension Activation Meditation

Let us begin by closing our eyes.

We now call forth GOD, Christ, and the Holy Spirit as well as the entire Cosmic and Planetary Hierarchy to help with this meditation.

We begin by calling forth a Cosmic "pillar of light" from the beloved Presence of GOD.

We call forth the Divine Mother and the Divine Father to balance the energies in the room and of all in attendance.

We call forth Melchizedek, the Mahatma, and Archangel Metatron to bring forth the Platinum Net through all in attendance.

We call forth Archangels Michael and Faith to place around this room and all in attendance a "golden dome of light of protection."

We formally begin this meditation by grounding ourselves into the Physical Body of GOD.

We do this by calling forth the Cosmic Mother of GOD's infinite Physical Universe and our Planetary Earth Mother.

We also call forth Archangel Sandalphon, Pan, and the mountain of Mt. Shasta, to help us now collectively establish a grounding cord down through our spine into the center of the earth.

Feel this grounding cord of GOD moving down into the very granite core of the earth and establish itself there unshakably like the Sword of Excalibur.

Feel now, with the help of these beloved Masters, roots growing out of your feet into the earth.

Feel these roots, with the help of the Cosmic and Planetary Earth Mother, grow at a rapid rate like a gigantic Cosmic Tree of Life that is firmly and unshakably planted into the earth.

Breathe now your love through your grounding cord and roots, into your feet and into the very center of Mother Earth.

Now feel Mother Earth breathe her love back through your grounding cord and roots into your feet, up through your physical body, igniting the Three-Fold Flame in your Heart Chakra.

Firmly now connected and attuned to GOD's Physical Body, we now begin our ascension and climb up through the "Seven Chakras of GOD."

This process begins with the beloved Presence of GOD, Christ, and the Holy Spirit sending down through GOD's Pillar of Light what can only be described as "The Merkabah of GOD."

This Merkabah is made of such a fine and sublime sacred geometry that words do not suffice to describe it.

Feel GOD's Merkabah, also known as the "Merkabah of the Trinity of GOD," descend now collectively upon this esteemed group gathered here.

Feel the Merkabah begin to rise and lift us into the First Chakra of GOD, while simultaneously still keeping our connection to the Physical Body of GOD.

GOD's First Chakra is like an enormous "Cathedral of Light, Love and Power" stretching through infinity.

In GOD's First Chakra there is a faint reddish-pink color and light pervading this entire infinite cathedral.

In the background can be seen and heard choirs of Angels singing the glory of GOD to the "Music of the Spheres."

Here we are met by all the Archangels, Angels, Elohim, Elementals, Devas, Plant Spirits, Nature Spirits, Earth Spirits, Gnomes, Sylphs, Salamanders, and Undines connected with the Material Universe of GOD.

This cathedral is so magnificent it defies description. It is filled with the crystals of the Twelve Rays of GOD and of the Ten Lost Cosmic Rays of GOD.

Every color can be seen, ordaining the actual cathedral which is infinite in size.

It is here that GOD, Christ, and the Holy Spirit now merge their First Chakra with our First Chakra on a permanent basis, so they are forever more one in consciousness.

If you would like to receive this blessing, be still and receive this blessing now!

As this occurs, GOD's Merkabah now lifts us into His Second Chakra and cathedral.

This cathedral is even more beautiful and spectacular than the previous one, and is pervaded by an orange glow that spreads out infinitely.

Again, the cathedral is made of crystals and gemstones of all the colors of GOD.

Here the Divine Mother, all the Lady Archangels, Lady Elohim and Lady Masters step forward led by Mother Mary, Quan Yin and Isis, to name a few.

The Divine Mother and these beloved Masters step forward as representatives of GOD to help now in the process of merging and integrating GOD's Second Chakra perfectly into our own on a permanent basis.

If you would like to receive this blessing, be still and receive this blessing now!

As this great blessing occurs, GOD's Merkabah lifts us into His Third Chakra and cathedral of Light, Love and Power.

This great crystal cathedral, spanning infinitely through time and space, is colored with a tinge of beautiful yellow, like the sun.

Here we are met by Lord Buddha, Lord Maitreya, Saint Germain, Allah Gobi, the Seven Chohans, Djwhal Khul, Helios and Vesta, and all the Planetary and Solar Masters of the Planetary and Cosmic Hierarchy.

With all the Archangels, Angels, and Elohim Masters looking on, these beloved Masters help this group, and each person individually, merge your Third Chakra with the Third Chakra of GOD.

If you would like to receive this blessing, be still and receive this blessing now!

As this great blessing occurs, we now move in GOD's Merkabah into GOD's Fourth Chakra also known as GOD's Heart Chakra.

In this incredibly magnificent crystal cathedral, there is a tinge of emerald-green light pervading this infinite holy sanctuary.

The Light and Love here is so sublime and beautiful, it is almost intoxicating.

The Holy Spirit asks us now to be completely silent and still so we may listen and attune to the "Heartbeat of GOD…"

By doing this in this moment, we are attuning to the actual heartbeat of the infinite, multi-dimensional Omniverse of GOD.

Stepping forward now as representatives for GOD's Heart Chakra are the Divine Mother, His Holiness the Lord Sai Baba, Lord Maitreya, Sananda, Paul the Venetian, Mother Mary, Quan Yin and Isis.

These beloved Masters step forward to help us now merge, blend and integrate our Heart Chakra and heartbeat with GOD's Heart Chakra and heartbeat.

If you would like to receive this blessing, be still and receive this blessing now!

As we receive this blessing, GOD, Christ, and the Holy Spirit's Merkabah lifts us even higher into GOD's Fifth Chakra and cathedral.

This infinite crystal cathedral is pervaded by the color light blue; like the sky on a beautiful, clear summer day.

This magnificent crystal cathedral with all the colors of the rainbow, shimmers with this beautiful blue color in its reflection.

In this wondrous cathedral and Fifth Chakra of GOD, we are met by Melchior, Vywamus, the Lord of Sirius, the Lord and Lady of Arcturus and the Arcturians, Sanat Kumara, Lenduce, Commander Ashtar and the Ashtar Command, and all the Galactic Masters of the Cosmic Hierarchy.

These beloved Masters as representatives of GOD, now step forward to help us completely merge and integrate our Fifth Chakra with the Fifth Chakra of GOD.

If you would like to receive this blessing, be still and receive this blessing now!

As this great blessing takes place, we are now lifted by GOD's Merkabah into GOD's Sixth Chakra and crystal cathedral of Light, Love, and Power.

This crystal cathedral of Light, Love, and Power, and Sixth Chakra of GOD, also known as the Third Eye of GOD, is tinged with the color indigo.

The most exquisitely colored indigo crystals and clouds color the infinite panorama of this cathedral.

Stepping forward as representatives of GOD in this cathedral are His Holiness Lord Melchizedek, all the Archangels connected with Earth's evolution, and all the Elohim Councils connected with Earth's evolution.

These beloved Masters offer their assistance in helping us to now merge our Sixth Chakra with the Sixth Chakra of GOD.

If you would like to receive this blessing, be still and receive this blessing now!

GOD's Merkabah now lifts us even higher still into GOD's Crown Chakra and crystal cathedral of Light, Love, and Power.

Here we are bathed in the most beautiful violet light you have ever seen or experienced.

The cathedral is made of beautiful amethyst crystal, interspersed with gemstones of all the colors of the Rays.

In the violet clouds and sun can be seen the Angels, Seraphim, and Cherubim, dancing and singing to the "Music of the Spheres."

Stepping forward here are the Twenty-Four Elders of Light, and the Twelve Cosmic Logoi and/or Cosmic Ray Masters, the Mahatma, Archangel Metatron, Archangels Michael and Faith, all the Archangels, Elohim Councils and the entire Cosmic and Planetary Hierarchy.

They collectively offer their assistance now in helping us to merge our Seventh or Crown Chakra, with the Seventh or Crown Chakra of GOD.

If you would like to receive this blessing, be still and receive this blessing now!

Beloved brothers and sisters, we have now, by the Grace of GOD, Christ, and the Holy Spirit, and the Cosmic and Planetary Hierarchy, merged, integrated and perfectly aligned on a permanent basis our seven basic chakras with the seven Cosmic Chakras of GOD, Christ, and the Holy Spirit!

Praise be to GOD, Christ, the Holy Spirit, the Cosmic and Planetary Hierarchy and ourselves, for All is One!

By the Grace of GOD, Christ, and the Holy Spirit, we are now being taken in GOD's Merkabah up through the "Ain," the "Ain Soph," and the "Ain Soph Or"; also known as the "Limitless Love and Light" to "GOD's Secret Crystal Chamber," where the Three-Fold Flame of GOD's own Heart resides.

We find ourselves now in the "Cathedral of all Cathedrals"!

This cathedral is filled with the most exquisite clear light you could possibly imagine.

The Angels in the background are singing hymns of praise to the "Most High GOD."

The beautiful smell of roses of all colors pervades this magnificent cathedral.

Standing before us on the "Altar of GOD" is the "Three-Fold Flame of GOD's own Heart," burning eternally as it has from the beginning of time.

It is in this sanctified and holy cathedral that GOD, Christ, and the Holy Spirit give to us, His beloved Sons and Daughters of GOD, the gifts and activations of all Creation!

If you would like to receive these "72 GOD Activations of all GOD Activations," be still and receive these gifts of all gifts now!

GOD, Christ, and the Holy Spirit now fully anchor and activate into each person's chakra system and 12-body system, the following activations:

GOD, Christ and the Holy Spirit now request that we all be like a sponge and sit back now in "GOD's Ascension Seat," which He is now placing around us, and soak in this first GOD Activation He is now giving us.

For our second GOD Activation, we now call forth from GOD, Christ, and the Holy Spirit, the "Light Rod of GOD," to ignite our entire chakra system and 12-body system.

We now call forth the "Love Rod of GOD," to completely ignite the anchoring and activation of our Zohar Body of Light, Anointed Christ Overself Body, Higher Adam Kadmon Body, and the Lord's Mystical Body.

We now call forth the "Power Rod of GOD," to fully anchor and activate the 330 Chakras of GOD and the 48 Dimensional Bodies of GOD.

We now call forth the "Cosmic Fire of GOD," and the perfect amount for each person to completely cleanse and purify each person's auric fields.

We now call forth the complete anchoring and activation of the "Cosmic Tree of Life of GOD."

We now call forth an anchoring and activation of the "Twelve Sephiroth of GOD," and the "Hidden Sephiroth of Daath."

We now call forth the complete anchoring and activation of the "Sacred Ember of GOD" from "The Sacred Fire of GOD"!

We now call forth an anchoring and activation of the the "Divine Scriptures of GOD."

We now call forth an anchoring, activation, and Divine merger with the "Divine Blueprint of GOD."

We call forth an anchoring and activation of the "Divine Seed of GOD."

We call forth an anchoring and activation of the "Holy Scrolls of the Living Light of GOD."

We call forth an anchoring, activation and opening of the "Seven Seals of GOD."

We call forth an anchoring and activation of the "Tetragrammaton of GOD" as described in *The Keys of Enoch*.

We call forth a reawakening on a conscious and subconscious level of each person's "Original Covenant of GOD."

We call forth a total downpouring of the "Language of Light of GOD," to activate full God Realization on all levels to each person's highest potential in this moment.

We call forth from GOD, Christ, and the Holy Spirit for the complete anchoring, activation and opening of the "Gifts of the Holy Spirit," to each person's highest potential in attendance!

We call forth the anchoring, activation and merger into each person in attendance to their highest potential of the 72 Sacred Universes of GOD as described in *The Keys of Enoch*.

We call forth in this "Holy Instant," for a "Divine Revelation of GOD," to each person's highest potential and in the way best suited for each person in attendance.

We now call forth the complete anchoring and activation of "GOD's Transmitting System" into our chakras and 12-body system!

We now call forth the complete anchoring and activation of "GOD's Divine Plan, Mission, and Puzzle Piece" for your life on earth.

We now call forth "GOD's Complete Cleansing all the way back to Source."

We now call forth the complete anchoring and activation of "GOD's 72 Names" to eternally run through our chakra system and 12-body system.

We now call forth the complete anchoring and activation of "GOD's Fire Letters, Key Codes and Sacred Geometries."

We now call forth a "Baptism of GOD, Christ, and the Holy Spirit."

We now call forth an anchoring and activation of the "Cosmic Antakarana of GOD."

We now call forth a complete merger with the "Clear Light of GOD."

We now call forth a permanent anchoring of the "72 Virtues and Attributes of GOD."

We now call forth a complete anchoring, activation and brain illumination of the "72 Areas of the Mind of GOD" into our brain and mind now.

We now call forth an anchoring and activation of the "Electron of GOD."

We now call forth a complete anchoring and activation of all levels of the "Cosmic Christ of GOD."

We now call forth and ask to completely merge with the "Cosmic Pulse of GOD."

We now call forth and ask to fully merge with the "Cosmic Aum of GOD."

We now call forth and ask to merge and integrate with the "Cosmic Monad of GOD."

We now call forth and ask to merge and integrate with all "352 Levels of GOD."

We now call forth and ask to completely merge and integrate with the "Ten Lost Cosmic Rays of GOD" and the "Yod Spectrum of GOD."

We now call forth and ask to merge and completely integrate with the "Divine Template of GOD."

We now call forth and ask to merge and fully integrate with the "Ray of GOD."

We now call forth an anointing given through the vehicle of the direct "Shaktipat of GOD."

We now call forth an anchoring and activation of the "Light Packets from the Treasury of Light of GOD."

We now call forth an anchoring and activation of the "Love Packets from the Treasury of Love of GOD."

We now call forth an anchoring and activation of the Power Packets from the Treasury of Power of GOD."

We now call forth an anchoring and activation of the "Crystals and Diamonds of GOD."

We now call forth an anchoring and activation from the "Gemstones of GOD."

We now call forth an anchoring and activation of the "Book of Life of GOD."

We now call forth an anchoring and activation of the "Seed Atom of GOD."

We now call forth a complete integration and merger with the "Burning Bush of GOD," that purifies but does not consume.

We now call forth from GOD, Christ, and the Holy Spirit, an anchoring and activation of the "Holy Breath of GOD."

We now call forth from GOD the "Keys to the Kingdom of GOD"; to be given to each person's highest potential.

We now call forth an anchoring and activation of "GOD's Cosmic Book of Knowledge."

We now call forth the "Full Spectrum Seeing and Vision of GOD" to merge and integrate with our vision.

We now call forth a complete merger and integration with "GOD Consciousness."

We now call forth to merge and fully integrate with the "Joy and Bliss of GOD."

We now call forth to merge and fully integrate with the "Heart of GOD."

We now call forth a complete merger and integration with all the "Infinite Universes of GOD."

We call forth an anchoring and activation of the "Cosmic Pyramid of GOD."

We now call forth a complete anchoring and activation of the "Waterfall of GOD."

We now call forth a complete merger and integration with the "Light Body of GOD."

We now call forth a complete merger and integration with the "Love Body of GOD."

We now call forth a complete merger and integration with the "Power Body of GOD."

We now call forth a complete integration with the combined "Love, Light and Power Bodies of GOD."

We now call forth an anchoring and activation of the "Love Shower of GOD, and the entire Cosmic and Planetary Hierarchy."

We now call forth an anchoring and activation of the "Light Shower of GOD and the entire Cosmic and Planetary Hierarchy."

We now call forth an anchoring and activation of the "Power Shower of GOD and the entire Cosmic and Planetary Hierarchy."

We now call forth an anchoring and activation of the combined "Love, Light and Power Shower of GOD and the entire Cosmic and Planetary Hierarchy."

We now call forth a complete merger and integration on all levels with GOD, Christ, and the Holy Spirit.

We now call forth a complete merger and integration with the "Consciousness of GOD on All Levels Known and Unknown."

We now call forth a Divine anchoring of a "Revelation of GOD" for each person in the way that is the best for each person to receive.

We now call forth a complete merger and integration with the "Unfathomableness of GOD."

We call forth an "Ordination by GOD, Christ, and the Holy Spirit" for each person in attendance to be a "Messenger of Light and Love, with the Authority to Teach and Demonstrate as a Basic Pillar and Witness to the Kingdom of GOD."

We now call forth to GOD, Christ, and the Holy Spirit in this Holy Instant for all who choose to receive this, for a Divine Marriage with the God/Goddess within.

Now, my beloved brothers and sisters, GOD, Christ, and the Holy Spirit's final activation and gift for this meditation is to now receive from GOD a complete merger and integration with His Three-Fold Flame into your personal three-fold flame, which is now burning eternally on the Altar of GOD before you.

If you choose to receive this blessing, be still and receive this blessing of all blessings now!

In the sanctuary of your own heart, take a moment now to thank GOD, Christ, and the Holy Spirit for their most sublime and sanctified gifts you have just received.

Also take a moment to thank the entire Cosmic and Planetary Hierarchy for their bountiful gifts and blessings as well.

GOD, Christ, and the Holy Spirit have now one final request that they would like to make to us all.

They collectively request in "One Voice" that we take the bountiful blessings given forth to us during this meditation and dedicate our lives from this moment forward to our highest potential, and share these blessings in unconditional love with our brothers and sisters on earth and with all sentient beings.

Our brothers and sisters and all sentient beings on earth, regardless of their level of consciousness, are all incarnations of GOD. For there is only one Being in the infinite universe, and that is GOD, and we all share in that one identity.

Let us all dedicate our lives to sharing GOD's Love and Blessings, as GOD, Christ, and the Holy Spirit have so freely and generously shared their love, blessings and gifts with us!

Let us all make this dedication now, in the "silent sanctuary of our own heart," in the way and manner that is comfortable and right for each of us.

As we conclude this process, GOD's Merkabah now appears and we begin to be lifted out of the Secret Cathedral and Chamber of GOD.

We begin moving down through the Ain Soph, the Ain Soph Or, the Ain and/or Limitless Love and Light.

We begin descending now into GOD's Crown Chakra and cathedral, being bathed in violet light, sound, and color.

We continue descending, into GOD's Sixth Chakra and cathedral, being bathed in indigo light, sound, and color.

We continue descending, into GOD's Fifth Chakra and cathedral, being bathed in light-blue light, sound, and color.

We continue descending, into GOD's Fourth Chakra and cathedral, being bathed in emerald-green light, sound, and color.

We continue descending, into GOD's Third Chakra and cathedral, being bathed in yellow light, sound, and color.

We continue descending, into GOD's Second Chakra and cathedral, being bathed in orange light, sound, and color.

We continue descending, into GOD's First Chakra and cathedral, being bathed in pinkish-red light, sound, and color.

Now feel GOD's Merkabah fully anchored back into your physical body, onto GOD's Physical Body, the Material Universe, and Mother Earth.

Here we are greeted again by the Earth Mother, the mountain of Mt. Shasta, Pan, and Archangel Sandalphon.

Feel yourself now back in the room, and feel yourself now fully grounded back onto the earth and into the earth.

Feel your grounding cord still fully established into the center of the earth.

Feel your feet again growing roots, filling the entire earth with these roots.

Breathe now again all the Love, Light and Power you have received from GOD, Christ, the Holy Spirit, and the Cosmic and Planetary

Hierarchy, into the Earth Mother, through your grounding cord and your feet like the Cosmic Tree of Life!

Feel yourself as fully connected to your physical body and the Earth Mother as you feel to GOD, Christ, the Holy Spirit, and the Cosmic and Planetary Hierarchy.

Fully now realizing that ascension is not leaving the world, but rather it is fully anchoring the Presence of GOD into your physical body on earth and manifesting Heaven on Earth!

Feel how good it feels to feel so connected to GOD, Christ, the Holy Spirit, and the Godforce, as well as your physical body and the Earth Mother, simultaneously!

In final conclusion, take one last moment to share the Love and Light that you have received from Heaven and Earth, and now inwardly, fully open your heart as wide as it has ever been before, and inwardly share this unconditional love that you feel with your brothers and sisters in this room.

When you are ready you may open your eyes.

27

My Spiritual Mission and Purpose by Dr. Joshua David Stone

My Spiritual mission and purpose is a multifaceted process. Spirit and the inner plane Ascended Masters have asked myself and Wistancia (married since 1998), to anchor onto the Earth an inner plane Ashram and Spiritual/Psychological/Physical/Earthly Teaching and Healing Academy! This Academy is called the Melchizedek Synthesis Light Academy! We are overlighted in this mission by Melchizedek, the Mahatma, Archangel Metatron, the Inner Plane Ascended Master Djwhal Khul, and a large group of Ascended Masters and Angels such as the Divine Mother, Archangel Michael, Archangel Gabriel, Sai Baba, Vywamus, the Lord of Arcturus, Lord Buddha, Lord Maitreya, Mother Mary, Quan Yin, El Morya, Kuthumi, Serapis Bey, Paul the Venetian, Master Hilarion, Sananda, Lady Portia and Saint Germain, and a great many others who we like to call the "Core Group"!

I have also been asked by the inner plane Ascended Master Djwhal Khul, who again wrote the Alice Bailey books, and was also involved in the Theosophical Movement, to take over his inner plane Ashram when he moves on to his next Cosmic Position, in the not too distant future.

Djwhal holds Spiritual Leadership over what is called the inner plane Second Ray Synthesis Ashram. On the inner plane the Second Ray Department is a gigantic three story building complex with vast gardens.

The Ascended Master Djwhal Khul runs the first floor of the Second Ray Department in the Spiritual Hierarchy. Master Kuthumi, the Chohan of the Second Ray, runs the second floor. Lord Maitreya the Planetary Christ runs the third floor! When Djwhal Khul leaves for his next Cosmic Position, I will be taking over this first floor Department. The Second Ray Department is focused on the "Spiritual Education" of all lightworkers on Earth and is the Planetary Ray of the Love/Wisdom of God. What is unique, however, about the Synthesis Ashram is that it has a unique mission and purpose which is to help light-workers perfectly master and integrate all 12 Planetary Rays which is one of the reasons I love this particular Spiritual leadership position and assignment so much! For this has been a great mission and focus of all my work!

Wistancia's and my mission has been to anchor the Synthesis Ashram and Teaching Academy onto the physical Earth, which we have done and are continuing to do in an ever increasing manner on a global level. Currently there are over 15 branches of the Academy that have been set up around the world! The Academy actually first came into existence in 1996! This we have been guided to call the Melchizedek Synthesis Light Academy for the following reasons. It is called this because of the Overlighting Presence of Melchizedek (Our Universal Logos), the Mahatma (Avatar of Synthesis), and the Light which is the embodiment of Archangel Metatron, who created all outer light in our Universe and is the creator of the electron! These three beings, Djwhal Khul, and a very large Core Group of inner plane Planetary and Cosmic Masters help us in all this work.

I have also been asked by the inner plane Ascended Masters to be one of the main "High Priest Spokespersons for the Planetary Ascension Movement on Earth." I have been asked to do this because of the cutting-edge, yet easy to understand nature of all my books and work, as well as certain Spiritual Leader-ship qualities I humbly possess. In this regard, I represent all the Masters, which works out perfectly given the Synthesis nature of my work. I function as kind of a "Point Man" for the Ascended Masters on Earth, as they have described it to me.

The Masters, under the guidance of Lord Buddha our Planetary Logos, have also guided us as part of our mission to bring Wesak to the West! So, for the last six years we have held a Global Festival and Conference at Mt. Shasta, California for 2000 people. This, of course, honors the Wesak Festival, which is the holiest day of the year to the inner plane Ascended Masters, and the high point of incoming Spiritual energies to the Earth on the Taurus full moon each year! We invite all lightworkers to join us each year from all over the world for this momentous celebration, which is considered to be one of the premiere Spiritual Events in the New Age Movement!

The fourth part of my mission and purpose is the 30 volume "Easy to Read Encyclopedia of the Spiritual Path" that I have written. So far, I have completed 27 volumes in this Ascension Book Series. The Ascended Master Djwhal Khul prophesized in the 1940's that there would be a third dispensation of Ascended Master teachings what would appear at the turn of the century. The first dispensation of Ascended Master teachings was the Theosophical Movement, channeled by Madam Blavatsky. The second dispensation of Ascended Master teachings was the Alice Bailey books, channeled by Djwhal Khul, and the *I AM Discourses*, channeled by Saint Germain. My 30 volume series of books is by the grace of GOD and the Masters, the third dispensation of Ascended Master teachings as prophesized by Djwhal Khul. These books are co-creative channeled writings of myself and the inner plane Ascended Masters. What is unique about my work is how easy to read and understand it is, how practical, comprehensive, cutting-edge, as well as integrated and synthesized. Wistancia has added to this work with her wonderful book *Invocations to the Light*.

The fifth aspect of our work and mission, which is extremely unique, is the emphasis of "Synthesis." My books and all my work integrate in a very beautiful way all religions, all Spiritual paths, all mystery schools, all Spiritual teachings, and all forms of psychology! Everyone feels at home in this work because of its incredible inclusive nature! This synthesis ideal is also seen at the Wesak Celebrations, for people come from all religions, Spiritual paths, mystery schools, and teachings. The event is overlighted by over one million inner plane Ascended Masters, Archangels and Angels, Elohim Masters, and Christed Extraterrestrials. Wesak, the books, the Academy, and all our work embody this synthesis principle. This is part of why I and we have been given Spiritual Leadership of the Synthesis Ashram on Earth, and soon on the Inner Plane as well. This also explains our unique relationship to Melchizedek who holds responsibility for the "synthesis development" of all beings in our universe. Our connection to the Mahatma is explained by the fact that the Mahatma is the Cosmic embodiment of "synthesis" in the infinite Universe. This is also why the Mahatma also goes by the name, "The Avatar of Synthesis." Archangel Metatron who holds the position in the Cosmic Tree of Life of Kether, or the Crown, hence has a "Synthesis Overview" of all of the Sephiroth or Centers of the Cosmic Tree of Life! Djwhal Khul holds Spiritual leadership of the "Synthesis Ashram" on the Planetary, Solar, and Galactic levels for the Earth! The Core Group of Masters that overlight our mission are, again, the embodiment of the synthesis understanding!

The unique thing about our work is that it teaches some of the most cutting-edge co-created channeled work on the planet, in the realm of Ascension and Ascended Master Teachings. This can be seen in my books *The Complete Ascension Manual, Beyond Ascension, Cosmic Ascension, Revelations of a Melchizedek Initiate,* and *How To Teach Ascension Classes.* Because of my background as a Psychologist and licensed Marriage, Family and Child Counselor, I also specialize in some of the most advanced cutting-edge work on the planet in the field of Spiritual psychology. In this regard, I would guide you to my books, *Soul Psychology, Integrated Ascension, How To Clear the Negative Ego,* and *Ascension and Romantic Relationships*! Thirdly, I also have humbly brought forth some extremely cutting-edge work on the physical/earthly level in the field of healing, Spirituality and society, politics, social issues, Extraterrestrials, Spiritual leadership, Spirituality and business, Goddess work with Wistancia, and of course the annual Wesak Celebrations. This can be found in my books: *The Golden Keys to Ascension and Healing, Hidden Mysteries, Manual for Planetary Leadership, Your Ascension Mission: Embracing Your Puzzle Piece, How to be Successful in your Business from a Spiritual and Financial Perspective*, and *Empowerment and Integration Through The Goddess*—written by Wistancia and myself.

Adding to this, the 11 new books I have just completed and am completing. *The Golden Book of Melchizedek: How to Become an Integrated Christ/Buddha in this Lifetime, How to Release Fear-Based Thinking and Feeling: An In-depth Study of Spiritual Psychology, The Little Flame and Big Flame* (my first children's book), *Letters of Guidance to Students and Friends, Ascension Names and Terms Glossary, Ascension Activation Meditations of the Spiritual Hierarchy, The Divine Blueprint for the Seventh Golden Age, How to do Psychological and Spiritual Counseling for Self and Others, God and His Team of Super Heroes* (my second children's book) and *How to Achieve Perfect Radiant Health from the Soul's Perspective*!

Currently I have completed 27 volumes in my Ascension Book Series. Fourteen of these books are published by Light Technology Publishers. A newer version of *Soul Psychology* is published by Ballantine Publishers, owned by Random House, which I am quite excited about as well! The other books are in manuscript form and I am currently negotiating with various publishers for publishing rights! My books have also been translated and published in Germany, Brazil, Japan, Holland, Israel and this process continues to expand.

Spirit and the inner plane Ascended Masters have told me that because of this unique focus, that what I have actually done in a co-creative way and manner with them, is open a new Portal to God. This new portal opening stems out of all the cutting-edge Ascension Activations and Ascended Master Teachings, the totally cutting-edge Spiritual Psychology work because of my background as a Psychologist and licensed Marriage, Family and Child Counselor, and the unique ability to ground all the work into the physical/earthly world in a balanced and integrated manner. Spirit and the Masters have told me that this new Portal to God is on an inner and outer plane level, and continues to be built in a co-creative way with Spirit, the Masters, myself, and certain other Masters and High Level Initiates who are helping me on the inner and outer planes! I have Spiritual leadership, however, in spearheading this project, and it is one of the most exciting projects I am involved in.

In terms of my Spiritual initiation process as I have spoken of in my books, I have currently now taken my 14th major initiation. These are not the minor initiations that some groups work with, but are the major initiations that embody all the minor initiations within them. The Seventh Initiation is the achieving of Liberation and Ascension. The 10th Initiation is the completion of Planetary Ascension and the beginning of Solar Initiation. The 11th Initiation, being the first Galactic Initiation. The 12th Initiation, being the first Universal Initiation from an Earthly perspective. Having taken my 14th initiation, what is most important to me is that these initiations have been taken in an "integrated manner," for, in truth, the Masters told me that they are not really into Ascension, which may surprise a great many lightworkers. The Masters are into "*Integrated* Ascension"! There are many lightworkers taking initiations, but many are not doing so in an integrated and balanced manner! They are taking them on a Spiritual level, but they are not being properly integrated into the mental and emotional bodies or psychological level properly. They are also not transcending negative ego fear-based thinking and feeling and properly balancing their four-body system. They are also not integrating their initiations fully into the Physical/Earthly level, addressing such things as: Healing, Grounding their Missions, Finding their Puzzle Piece Mission and Purpose, Prosperity Consciousness and Financial and Earthly Success, Integrating the God/Goddess, Embracing the Earth Mother and the Nature

Kingdom, Properly Integrating into Third-Dimensional Society and Civilization in terms of the focus of their Service Mission. This is just mentioned as a very loving reminder of the importance of an integrated and balanced approach to one's Spiritual Path. The grace to have been able to take these 14 major initiations and be able to have completed my Planetary Ascension process and to have moved deeply into my Cosmic Ascension process, I give to GOD, Christ, the Holy Spirit, Melchizedek, the Mahatma, Archangel Metatron, and the Core Group of Masters I work with. I have dedicated myself and my life to GOD and the Masters' service, and I have humbly attempted to share everything I know, have used, and have done in my Spiritual path and Ascension process with all of you, my Beloved Readers!

Melchizedek, the Universal Logos, has also inwardly told me, that because of the Cosmic work I am involved with, that I have taken on the Spiritual assignment of being one of the "12 Prophets of Melchizedek on Earth." I am very humbled to serve in this capacity. For Melchizedek is the Universal Logos, who is like the President of our entire Universe. In truth, all Religions and Spiritual teachings have their source in Melchizedek and in the Great Ancient Order of Melchizedek. It is my great honor and privilege to serve GOD and Melchizedek in this capacity. This is something I have never spoken of before, although I have known of this for many, many years. I have been guided after all this time to share a little more deeply about my Spiritual mission on Earth at this time.

The Academy Website is one of the most profound Spiritual Websites you will ever explore because it embodies this "synthesis nature" and is an ever-expanding, living, easy-to-read Spiritual "encyclopedia" that fully integrates all 12 Rays in design and creation! This is also embodied in the free 140 page information packet that we send out to all who ask who wish to get involved and know more about our work! The information in the information packet is also available by just exploring the Academy Website!

We have also set up a wonderful Ministers Ordination and Training Program, which we invite all interested to read about. I am also very excited about a relatively recent book I have written called *How to Teach Ascension Classes*. Because I have become so busy with my Spiritual leadership and global world service work, I really do not have the time to teach weekly classes, as I have in the past. I firmly believe in the motto "Why *give* a person a fish, when you can *teach* them to fish!" In this vein, the Masters guided me to write a book on how to teach people to teach Ascension classes based on my work. I humbly suggest it is a most wonderful channeled book that can teach you in the easiest way and manner on every level to teach Ascension classes in your home or on a larger level if you choose. These classes are springing up now all over the globe and have been successful beyond my wildest dreams and expectations. When I wrote the book I was so involved with the process of writing it, I never fully envisioned the tremendous success it would have on a planetary and global level. Using this book and my other books, I have really done the initial homework for you, which can and will allow you to immediately begin teaching Ascension classes yourself. I humbly suggest that you look into the possibility of doing this yourself if you are so guided!

One other very interesting aspect of our Spiritual mission is something the Masters have been speaking to us about for over 10 years which is what they described as being "Ambassadors for the Christed Extraterrestrials"! We have always known this to be true! This was part of the reason I wrote the book *Hidden Mysteries*, which I humbly suggest is one of the best overviews in an easy to read and understand manner, of the entire Extraterrestrial Movement as it has affected our planet. If you have not read this book, I highly recommend that you do so. It is truly fascinating reading! My strongest personal connection to the Extraterrestrials is with the Arcturians! The Arcturians are the most advanced Christed Extraterrestrial race in our galaxy. They hold the future blueprint for the unfoldment of this planet. The Arcturians are like our future planet and future selves on a collective level. Part of my work, along with the

Ascended Master Teachings I have been asked to bring through, has been to bring through a more conscious and personal connection to the Arcturians, the Ashtar Command, and other such Christed Extraterrestrial races. This year's Platinum Wesak, because of being the year 2001, will have a special connection to these Christed Extraterrestrials, and we invite you all to attend for this reason and for many others! I also encourage you to read my book *Beyond Ascension* where I explore some of my personal experiences with the Arcturians, and how you may do so as well!

Currently, behind the scenes, we are working on some further expansions of this aspect of our mission, which we will share at a later time! Wistancia has also been involved with "White Time Healing," which is another most wonderful Extraterrestrial healing modality that she offers to the public!

One other aspect of our mission deals with having developed, with help from the inner plane Ascended Masters, some of the most advanced Ascension activation processes to accelerate Spiritual evolution that has ever been brought forth to this planet. In this co-creative process with the Masters, we have discovered the "keys" to how to accelerate Spiritual evolution at a rate of speed that in past years and centuries would have been unimaginable! This is why I call working with the Ascended Masters "The Rocketship to GOD Method of Spiritual Growth." There is no faster path to God Realization than working with the Ascended Masters, Archangels and Angels, Elohim Masters and Christed Extraterrestrials! What is wonderful about this process is that you do not have to leave your current Spiritual practice, religion, or Spiritual path. Stay on the path you are and just integrate this work into what you are currently doing! All paths as you know, lead to GOD, my friends! This is the profundity of following an eclectic path, and path of synthesis! I humbly suggest I have found some shortcuts! I share this with all lightworkers on earth, for I love GOD with all my heart and soul and mind and might, and I recognize that we are all incarnations of GOD, and Sons and Daughters of this same GOD, regardless of what religion, Spiritual path, or mystery school we are on. We are all, in truth, the Eternal Self and are all God! There is, in truth, only GOD, so what I share with you, I share with you, GOD, and myself for in the highest sense we are all one! What we each hold back from each other, we hold back from ourselves and from GOD. This is why I give freely all that I am, have learned and have, to you, my Beloved Readers, giving everything and holding back nothing! In my books and audiotapes, I have literally shared every single one of these ideas, tools, and Ascension activation methods for accelerating evolution that I have used and come to understand. My Beloved Readers, these tools and methods found in my books and on the audiotapes will "blow your mind as to their effectiveness," in terms of how profound, and easy to use they are! I would highly recommend that all lightworkers obtain the 13 Ascension Activation Meditation tapes I have put together for this purpose. Most of them were taped at the Wesak Celebrations with 1500 to 2000 people in attendance, with over one million inner plane Ascended Masters, Archangels and Angels, Elohim Masters, and Christed Extraterrestrials in attendance, under the Wesak full moon and the mountain of Mt Shasta. You can only imagine the power, love, and effectiveness of these Ascension activation audiotapes. I recommend getting all 13 tapes and working with one tape every day or every other day! I personally guarantee you that these tapes will accelerate your Spiritual evolution a thousandfold! You can find them in the information packets and on our Website. They are only available from the Academy! Trust me on this, the combination of reading my books, Wistancia's book, and working with these audio ascension activation tapes, will accelerate your Spiritual evolution beyond your wildest dreams and imagination!

One other extremely important part of my mission, which is a tremendous Spiritual passion of mine, is the training of lightworkers on earth in the area of Spiritual/Christ/Buddha thinking and negative ego/separative/fear-based thinking! These are the only two ways of thinking in the world, and each person thinks with one, the other, or a combination of both. If a person does not learn how to transcend negative ego thinking and feeling, it will end up, over time, corrupting every aspect of their lives including all channeling work, Spiritual teaching, and even healing work! One cannot be wrong with self and right with GOD. This is because our thoughts create our reality, as we all know! I cannot recommend more highly that every person reading this book, read my other books: *Soul Psychology*, *The Golden Book of Melchizedek: How to Become an Integrated Christ/Buddha in this Lifetime*, and *How to Release Fear-Based Thinking and Feeling: An In-depth Study of Spiritual Psychology*! I humbly suggest that these three books will be three of the most extraordinary self-help books in the area of mastering this psychological area of life. They are extremely easy to read, very practical and filled with tools that will help you in untold ways. Being a channel for the Ascended Masters and being uniquely trained as a Spiritual Psychologist and Marriage, Family and Child Counselor, as well as being raised in a family of psychologists, has given me an extraordinary ability to teach this material through my books in a most effective manner. The combination of my books on Ascension, and these books on Spiritual Psychology, along with Wistancia's book on the art of invocation, will literally revolutionize your consciousness in the comfort of your own home! The most extraordinary thing about all this work is how incredibly easy to read, and easy to understand it is. It is also incredibly comprehensive, completely cutting-edge, and totally integrated, balanced, and synthesized. It contains the best of all schools of thought in the past, present, and channeled cutting edge future understanding that is available now! I humbly ask you to trust me in this regard and just read one of these books and you will immediately want to buy the others!

One other aspect of our work and mission is our involvement with the "Water of Life" and the Perfect Science products for the healing of our own physical bodies and the physical body of Mother Earth of all pollution in the air, water and earth. This is the miracle Mother Earth has been waiting for to bring her back to her "original edenic state" after so much abuse. This is not the time or the place to get into this subject in detail; however, I invite you to check out the "Water of Life" and the Perfect Science information in the Information Packet and on the Academy Website! It is truly the miracle we have all been waiting for to help heal the Earth!

One other aspect of our work and mission is a project that the Ascended Masters have asked us to put together on behalf of lightworkers and people around the globe. It is called the "Interdimensional Prayer Altar Program"! that the Masters have guided us to set up in the Academy in Agoura Hills, California on the property we live on. We have set up a "Physical Interdimensional Prayer Altar" where people can send in their prayers on any subject and we will place them on this Altar. In consultation with the Masters, Archangels and Angels, Elohim Masters, and Christed Extraterrestrials, we have set up an arrangement with them that all physical letters placed upon this Altar will be immediately worked upon by these Masters. We have been guided by the inner plane Ascended Masters to create 15 Prayer Altar Programs in different areas of life that people can sign up for. For example, there is one for health and one for financial help in your Spiritual mission. Two-thirds of these programs are totally free. There are five or six that are more advanced Spiritual acceleration programs where written material is sent to you to work with in conjunction with these programs so as to accelerate your Spiritual growth. All letters we receive by e-mail, fax, or letter are placed on the Altar by myself or my personal assistant. It is kept 100% confidential and is an extremely special service provided by the inner plane Ascended Masters and Angels to help all lightworkers and people on Earth with immediate help for whatever they need, should they desire assistance. Other examples of Prayer Altars are: Building your Higher Light Body, Extra Protection, Relationship Help, World Service Prayers, Help for your Animals, Prayer Altar for the Children, Integrating the Goddess, Integrating your Archetypes, Integrating the Seven Rays and working with the Seven Inner Plane Ashrams of the Christ, Integrating the Mantle of the Christ, Ascension

Seat Integration, and Light, Love, and Power Body Building Program! These Prayer Altar Programs have been co-created with the inner plane Ascended Masters as another tool for not only helping all lightworkers with whatever they need help with, but also as another cutting-edge tool to accelerate Spiritual evolution!

In a similar regard, the Masters have guided us to set up a Melchizedek Synthesis Light Academy Membership Program which is based on three levels of involvement. Stage One, Stage Two, and Stage Three! Stage One and Stage Three are totally free. Stage Two costs only $20 for a Lifetime Membership with no other fees required. You also receive free large colored pictures of Melchizedek, the Mahatma, Archangel Metatron, and Djwhal Khul for joining. It is not necessary to join to get involved in the work; however, it has been set up by the inner plane Ascended Masters as another service and tool of the Academy to help lightworkers accelerate their Spiritual evolution! When joining the different Stages, the Masters take you under their wing, so to speak, and accelerate your evolution by working with you much more closely on the inner plane while you sleep at night and during your conscious waking hours. The joining is nothing more than a process that gives them the permission to work with you in this more intensive fashion! Again, it is not necessary to join to get involved in the work, and is really just another one of the many fantastic tools and services the Academy has made available to you to accelerate your Spiritual, psychological, and earthly/physical evolution in an integrated and balanced manner!

I had a dream shortly after completing my two new books, *The Golden Book of Melchizedek: How To Become an Integrated Christ/Buddha in This Lifetime*, and my book *How To Release Fear-Based Thinking and Feeling: An In-depth Study of Spiritual Psychology*. In the dream, I was being shown the different Spiritual missions people had. My Spiritual mission was the embodiment of the Holy Spirit. I clearly was shown how other people within GOD, Christ, and the Holy Spirit had missions of being more detached off-shoots of the Holy Spirit, and continuing outward from there, had all kinds of different Spiritual missions. However, mine was the embodiment of the Holy Spirit on Earth.

My Beloved Readers, I want to be very clear here that in sharing this I am in no way, shape, or form claiming to be the Holy Spirit. There is enough glamour in the New Age Movement and I am not interested in adding any more to it. What I am sharing here, which is being given to more clearly and precisely share my Spiritual mission and purpose, is that which I am here to strive to embody and demonstrate. The Holy Spirit is the third aspect of the Trinity of GOD. I have always greatly loved the Holy Spirit, for the Holy Spirit is like the "Voice of GOD"! It is the "Still, Small Voice Within"! When one prays to GOD, it is the Holy Spirit who answers for GOD. The Holy Spirit is the answer to all questions, challenges, and problems. The Holy Spirit speaks for the Atonement or the At-one-ment! It teaches the Sons and Daughters of GOD how to recognize their true identity as God, Christ, the Buddha, and the Eternal Self! In truth, there are only two voices in life! There is the voice of the negative ego and the "Voice of the Holy Spirit"! There is the voice of negative ego/fear-based/separative thinking and feeling, and there is the Voice of God/Spiritual/Christ/Buddha thinking and feeling! There is the "Voice of Love" and the voice of fear! There is the "Voice of Oneness" and the voice of separation!

I was given this dream after completing these two books because, I humbly suggest, this is the energy I was embodying in writing them and that I am striving to embody at all times in my Spiritual mission and purpose on Earth. This is not surprising in the sense that this has always been my Spiritual ideal and the dream was just an inward confirmation in that moment that I was embodying and demonstrating that Spiritual Ideal in the energy flow I was in. This is what I strive to do in all my work, be it my Ascension Book Series, Wesak Celebrations, Teaching, Counseling, Videotapes, Audiotapes, and all my work, which is to strive to be the embodiment of a "Voice for God"! By the grace of GOD, Christ, the Holy Spirit, and the Masters, I provide a lot of the "answers" people and lightworkers are seeking! I teach people how to "undo" negative ego/fear-based/separative thinking and feeling, and show then how to fully realize God/Christ/Buddha thinking and feeling! I show them how to release and undo glamour, illusion, and maya, and instead seek "Truth, as GOD, Christ, the Holy Spirit, and the Masters would have you seek it!"

My real purpose, however, is not to just be the embodiment of the Holy Spirit on Earth, for I would not be embodying the Voice and Vision of the Holy Spirit if I just focused on this. The Voice and Vision of GOD, Christ, the Holy Spirit, and Melchizedek is that of synthesis! This is the other thing I feel in the deepest part of my heart and soul that I am here to embody! So my "truest and highest Spiritual ideal" that I am here to strive to embody, is GOD, Christ, the Holy Spirit, the inner plane Ascended Masters, the Archangels and Angels of the Light of GOD, the Elohim Councils of the Light of GOD, and the Christed Extraterrestrials of the Light of GOD. I feel in the deepest part of my heart and soul, and what I try to embody every moment of my life is "All that is of GOD and the Godforce on Earth!" In this regard, it is my Spiritual mission and purpose to strive to be the embodiment of the "synthesis nature of God on Earth"! This is why I have been given Spiritual leadership of the Synthesis Ashram and Academy on Earth and future leadership of the inner plane Synthesis Ashram that governs our planet.

The other thing I strive to do in my Spiritual mission is to embody Spiritual mastery on a Spiritual, psychological, and physical/earthly level. What most people and lightworkers do not realize is that there are three distinct levels to God Realization. There is a Spiritual level, a psychological level, and a physical/earthly level! To achieve true God Realization, all three levels must be equally mastered! Another way of saying this is that there are "Four Faces of GOD"! There is a Spiritual Face, a Mental Face, an Emotional Face, and a Material Face! To truly realize God, all four must be equally mastered, loved, honored, sanctified, integrated, and balanced! The "Mental and Emotional Faces of

GOD" make up the psychological level of GOD. So, my Spiritual mission and purpose is to fully embody Spiritual mastery and unconditional love on all three of these levels and in all Four Faces of GOD! In a similar vein, my Spiritual mission and purpose is to embody self-mastery and proper integration of all "Seven Rays of GOD," not just one or a few. For the "Seven Rays of GOD" are, in truth, the true "Personality of GOD"! My Spiritual mission and purpose is to not only strive to embody all levels of GOD, but to also try and develop all my God-given abilities and Spiritual gifts, on a Spiritual, Psychological, and Physical/Earthly level, and in all Four Faces of GOD!

My Beloved Readers, all these things that I have written about in this chapter are what I strive to fully embody and demonstrate on the Earth every moment of my life, and is what I strive with all my heart and soul and mind and might to teach others to do as well!

As the Founder and Director of the Melchizedek Synthesis Light Academy along with Wistancia, with great humbleness and humility, it has been my great honor and privilege to share "my Spiritual mission and purpose" in a deeper and more profound manner at this time. I do so in the hopes that all who feel a resonance and attunement with this work will get involved with the Academy's "Teachings" and all that it has to offer. I also share this so that all who choose to get involved might join this vast group of lightworkers around the globe, to help spread the teachings and work of the inner plane Ascended Masters. The inner plane Ascended Masters and I, along with the Archangels and Angels, Elohim Councils, and Christed Extraterrestrials, put forth the Clarion Call to lightworkers around the world to first explore this work, then integrate this work, and then become Ambassadors of the Ascended Masters so we may at this time in Beloved Earth's history bring in fully now the Seventh Golden Age in all its Glory!

About the Author

Dr. Joshua David Stone has a Ph.D. in Transpersonal Psychology and is a licensed Marriage, Family and Child Counselor in Agoura Hills, California. On a Spiritual level he anchors **The Melchizedek Synthesis Light Academy and Ashram**, which is an integrated inner and outer plane ashram that seeks to represent all paths to God! He serves as one of the leading spokespersons for the Planetary Ascension Movement. Through his books, tapes, workshops, lectures, and annual Wesak Celebrations, Dr. Stone is known as one of the leading Spiritual Teachers and Channels in the world on the teachings of the Ascended Masters, Spiritual Psychology, and Ascension! He has currently written over 27 volumes in his Ascension Book Series, which he also likes to call "The Easy to Read Encyclopedia of the Spiritual Path"!

For a free information packet of all Dr. Stone's workshops, books, audiotapes, Academy membership program, and global outreach program, please call or write to the following address:

Dr. Joshua David Stone
Melchizedek Synthesis Light Academy
28951 Malibu Rancho Rd.
Agoura Hills, CA 91301

Phone: 818-706-8458
Fax: 818-706-8540
e-mail: drstone@best.com

Please come visit my Website at:
http://www.drjoshuadavidstone.com

Printed in the United States
98197LV00003B/69/A